This book is extraordinarily helpful in presenting a picture of children and adolescents with bipolar disorder. The case illustrations present a very clear picture of the symptoms that define the disorder. The information on psychopharmacological treatment and psychological treatment are valuable resources for parents and professionals alike.

> —Ira Glovinsky, Ph.D., director of the Childhood Mood Disorder Program at the Interdisciplinary Center for the Family in West Bloomfield, MI, and adjunct professor of psychology at Madonna University in Livonia, MI

Drs. Faedda and Austin have done a remarkable job of describing bipolar disorder in children. Their combined clinical experience lends richness to the practical suggestions they have for families in managing this difficult illness. Reading Parenting a Bipolar Child *will bring relief to stressed and confused parents struggling for answers as they navigate the complex diagnostic and treatment pathway for youth with bipolar disorder.*

> — Mary A. Fristad, PhD, ABPP, professor of psychiatry and psychology at Ohio State University and author of *Raising a Moody Child*

Parenting a Bipolar Child

What to Do & Why

GIANNI L. FAEDDA, MD

NANCY B. AUSTIN, PSY.D.

New Harbinger Publications, Inc.

Distributed in Canada by Raincoast Books

Copyright © 2006 by Gianni Faedda and Nancy Austin
New Harbinger Publications, Inc.
5674 Shattuck Avenue
Oakland, CA 94609

Cover design by Amy Shoup; Acquired by Catharine Sutker;
Text design by Tracy Marie Carlson; Edited by Kayla Sussell

New Harbinger Publications' Web site address: www.newharbinger.com

---

Library of Congress Cataloging-in-Publication Data

Faedda, Gianni L.
   Parenting a bipolar child : what to do and why / Gianni L. Faedda and Nancy B. Austin.
        p. cm.
   Includes bibliographical references (p. 275).
   ISBN-13: 978-1-57224-423-8
   ISBN-10: 1-57224-423-2
   1. Manic-depressive illness in children. 2. Parenting. I. Austin, Nancy B. II. Title.
RJ506.D4F34 2006
618.92'895—dc22

                                                    2006024434

08   07   06

10   9   8   7   6   5   4   3   2   1

First printing

To my parents, and to all the parents
To Elio, and to all the children

—G. F.

We dedicate this book to every parent and child who has been touched by bipolar disorder. Over the years, many courageous children and parents battling bipolar disorder have taught us a great deal about compassion and resilience. Their determination has been a source of inspiration in our work.

—N.A. & G. F.

Contents

Acknowledgments

First and foremost, I am grateful to my family, for their unreserved love and support throughout my life.

I am especially thankful to my coauthor, Dr. Nancy Austin, for inviting me to contribute my ideas and writings to help the families struggling with bipolar disorder, and especially for all her insights and patience.

I am eternally indebted to Gilbert Barretto for his guidance, teaching, and compassion. His encouragement made this project possible.

My deepest appreciation goes to my mentors, Athanasios Koukopoulos and Ross Baldessarini. Their intuitions, persistence, and scientific curiosity at the service of relieving human suffering have been an inspiration and a standard to strive for.

Among many other colleagues and dear friends that have inspired my work, I would like to gratefully thank the following: Robert Akeret, Hagop Akiskal, Ngaere Baxter, Bruce Cohen, Paolo Decina, Janice Egeland, Gianfranco Floris, Harris Gelbard, Jeffrey Gilbert, Ira Glovinsky, John Gunderson, Joseph Hirsch, James Hudson, Paul Keck, Gopinath Mallya, Susan McElroy, GianPaolo Minnai, Demitri and

Janice Papolos were most generous with their help, support, and especially, their loving friendship. Harrison Pope, Robert Post, Daniela Reginaldi, Zoltán Rihmer, Jonah Schrag, Andrew Stoll, Stephen Strakowski, Harris Stratyner, Trisha Suppes, Alan Swann, Elaine Swenson, Martin Teicher, Mauricio Tohen, Leonardo Tondo, and Herman vanPraag.

Special thanks to Deborah Schoeberlein for her advice, dedication, encouragement, and insightful editing; to Ellen Aspland for her tireless assistance in the preparation of the manuscript; to Cinthya McGreenery for her precious help in our research efforts; and to Kayla Sussell for superb editing.

I am profoundly indebted to Catharine Sutker, Matt McKay, and New Harbinger Publications for making this book possible, and for their great support, guidance, and help in every step of this process.
—G.F.

Many thanks to all of the people who have supported me throughout the process of writing this book. First and foremost is my coauthor and colleague, Gianni Faedda, MD, for his constant encouragement throughout the collaboration. Thanks to Matt McKay at New Harbinger Publications who first encouraged me to write, along with Catharine Sutker, whose vision smoothed the inevitable bumps in the road. Kayla Sussell's editing helped the vision become a reality.

There are numerous professional colleagues to thank, including Demitri Papolos, MD, who sat at lunch with me in 1997 discussing a young patient, explaining the basics of bipolar disorder, and ultimately, together with Janice Papolos, showing confidence in my work. I am indebted to Ira Glovinsky, Ed.D., whom I think of as a professional brother, and who has been generous with his ideas, especially regarding sensitivities in young bipolar children. In 2001, together we wrote about how to deal with rages, in order to help the parents, and he has kindly allowed ideas in that original draft to be included in chapter 11.

Other important professional influences include Mary Fristad, Ph.D., and David Miklowitz, Ph.D., who have introduced groundbreaking clinical work with families of bipolar children, Steve Mattis, Ph.D., and Dana Luck, Ph.D., leaders in neuropsychological assessment of children with bipolar disorder, Sheri Baron and Neal

Rosenberg. I could not have completed this book without the graceful help of Helen Golden, Ph.D.

My family and friends have never wavered in their belief in me. Roberta Small Risch, my best friend since sixth grade, has been a shining light of support. My talented daughter, Elana Frankel, who is a professional editor in her own right, taught me much about writing and editing, while her husband, Dan Tashman, used his graphic skills to make the Upset Scale and figure 1 in chapter 2 a reality. My loving daughter Erica and her husband Jeff Christ, along with their daughter Julia, a grandmother's dream, have given me hours of joy and respite throughout this process. No one who has met my mother-in-law, a retired librarian, Ethelind Elbert Austin, will be surprised that, at age ninety-five, she read every word of the first draft of this book. And finally, my deepest love and appreciation go to my husband, John H. M. Austin, MD, who is never too tired to read and comment helpfully on my work and never too busy to bring an espresso.

—N.A.

Introduction

Parents tell us extraordinary stories about their children with bipolar disorder (BD). To many people, these stories might sound like exaggerations or even fantasies, but these are real life experiences. Children with BD are different from other children and the differences are often apparent early, some even from birth. They can show precocious and unusual talents mixed with developmental delays, or deficits, and an overall uneven functioning.

Most of the children described in this book are unable to modulate their emotions. They are more sensitive than most kids are, and more reactive. From an early age, children with BD can be very easily upset, difficult to soothe, and inconsolable. They do not follow rules, or daily routines, and they're irritable, demanding, and have severe tantrums. As a parent seeking help for your child, you may feel you've failed, or haven't been a "good enough" parent. Meanwhile, relatives, teachers, and/or doctors may think that your reports are exaggerated, or they may blame you for your child's behavior. For many of you, life at home is a secret, solitary, and painful struggle, until effective treatment brings hope.

A WORD ABOUT THE AUTHORS

Drs. Gianni Faedda and Nancy Austin have researched, evaluated, and helped children with BD and their families for many years. Drs. Austin and Faedda's approaches stem from very different backgrounds but integrate well together. Their ongoing collaboration at the Mood Disorders Center in New York City has been a source of hypotheses and novel approaches to the challenges presented by childhood mood disorders. They share a unique focus on the child's developmental needs, the role of parental guidance and support, and the importance of lifestyle changes complementary with pharmacological treatment and psychotherapy. They have refined and tested this approach over many years.

Dr. Faedda, psychiatrist and founding director of the Mood Disorders Center, has more than twenty years of experience in research and clinical management of patients with BD. He has published numerous research articles on the effects of environmental and pharmacological factors on the course of BD, mixed states, and their occurrence in young patients. An extensive review of the world literature and the features of mania in children remains an important resource for professionals and parents (Faedda et al. 1995). His recent work has focused on the clinical characteristics and early course of BD in children and adolescents and the destabilizing effect of certain medications on BD.

Over the years, Dr. Faedda has developed a unique approach to the diagnosis and treatment of children, adolescents, and adults with bipolar disorder. Dr. Faedda's approach helps patients and families to better understand BD and to become actively involved in its treatment, including necessary lifestyle changes and ongoing self-monitoring, with an emphasis on the child's and parents' cooperation.

After receiving her doctorate in child psychology in 1988, Dr. Austin worked as a staff psychologist at a center for young children and as a special education school psychologist. While she established a private practice in New York City and Westchester County, she spent an additional four years in intensive training to become a psychoanalyst. During this training and practice, the concept of bipolar disorder intrigued her, and her practice grew to develop a special focus on the most difficult cases.

As associate director of the Mood Disorders Center, Dr. Austin works in a simple and focused way with families who face the complex disorder of BD in childhood and adolescence. She concentrates on the three most salient aspects of regulatory functioning: that is, medication, sleep, and school. Helping the family learn how to focus and how to apply positive reinforcement can help the child to regulate his or her life in these three basic areas. Good habits replace bad habits.

The work that is at the heart of this book brings hope and the opportunity to foster a healthier family life.

HOW THIS BOOK WORKS

The first half of this book addresses issues related to diagnosis. Chapter 1 provides information about the basics of BD. Chapter 2 defines BD and discusses how it presents at different ages, how symptoms appear or group together in syndromes like mania, depression, and mixed states, and the reasons why misdiagnosis remains an all too common occurrence. Chapter 3 describes how BD "looks" in children at different stages of their development and maturation. The clinical features of BD in adolescents are discussed in chapter 4. In chapter 5 we outline some of the tools helpful in the diagnostic assessment, and describe how they can be used in planning treatment interventions. Co-occurring, or comorbid, diagnoses, learning disabilities, and sensory dysregulation in children with BD are all discussed in chapter 6.

The second half of the book is devoted to treatment. In chapter 7 we review available treatment options including medications and psychotherapy, so you can see how the different treatment components fit and work together. The use of medication in children and adolescents with BD, including efficacy, side effects, and long-term use, is reviewed in chapter 8. Chapter 9 is devoted to understanding sleep disorders and will inform you about how to intervene to improve your child's sleep. The emphasis of chapter 10 is on regulating and improving home life. Chapter 11 discusses specific techniques to help you manage rages, anger, and irritability, which are always present or just below the surface. Chapter 12 focuses on psychotherapy and its many benefits for children with BD. School decisions and strategies to get your child needed accommodations are reviewed in chapter 13. And lastly, in chapter 14, special topics including self-harm, violence, suicide, and hospitalization will allow you to prepare in advance for necessary crisis intervention.

Appendix I shows current diagnostic criteria for bipolar disorder with manic, hypomanic, mixed, and depressed episodes, and cyclothymia. In appendix II we present the MoodLog, discussed in chapter 5, and appendix III has helpful Web site addresses and other resources for parents.

1

Growing Up with Bipolar Disorder

Laura walked into the office beaming with confidence. A pretty seven-year-old, Laura loves being the center of attention and is completely at ease with adults she's never met before. She seems more mature than her age and talks to her parents as if they were her peers. When her parents began to describe how she gets "out-of-control angry" almost every day, Laura started cartwheeling through the office. Her mother asked her to stop, and she sat down for a few seconds, but then got up and started pacing. Her mother described Laura as irritable, rude, argumentative, angry, and sometimes full of rage. When asked about her rage, Laura spoke quickly, emphatically, and was very articulate. She said that most of the time she feels mad and can't calm down; she doesn't know why.

Laura has problems falling asleep at night and getting up in the morning; she also has difficulty making it to school regularly because she often feels sick and nervous. Her mood changes quickly, going from normal to irritable and angry, from being okay to feeling sad and teary. Or she becomes happy, excited, giggly, and euphoric for no apparent reason. In spite of being very bright, creative, and talented, Laura is socially awkward and doesn't have many friends.

BIPOLAR DISORDERS: THE BASICS

Bipolar disorder, previously known as "manic-depressive illness," is a biological brain disorder that causes severe disruption of emotional balance. Different forms of this illness affect 1 to 5 percent of the population depending on the definition used. Bipolar disorder (BD) causes episodes of mania, depression, mixed states or psychosis, sometimes alternating with symptom-free intervals. A genetic predisposition to develop the illness, combined with environmental factors, can lead to the onset of BD at different ages. Although the majority of cases manifest in late adolescence and early adulthood, childhood onset is not rare. The distinguishing features of BD in childhood are atypical when compared to adult forms of the disorder.

Children's Symptoms of BD

Compared to adults with BD, children show chronic moodiness and irritability rather than clear episodes of mania and depression. Common symptoms (see chapter 2) include hyperactivity, sleep disorders, anxiety, distractibility, *pressured speech* (fast and/or loud), racing thoughts, impulsivity, and aggressive behavior.

Many people have described BD as a roller coaster going up and down, or as a pendulum swinging back and forth. These metaphors refer to the different, changeable moods that a child with BD experiences several times in the course of one day.

If you parent a child with BD, you know that mood is just one of many variables that are constantly changing. You may see daily changes in your child's energy, appetite, or sleep; anxiety or aggression levels may fluctuate; and your child's ability to function in school, at home, or in social situations may shift from one extreme to the other, for no apparent reason. One day your child can be attentive and compliant in class; another day the teacher might phone you at home to complain about your child's hyperactivity, calling out in class, or not following directions.

This unevenness and inconsistency of behavior and functioning is one of the defining features of BD. However, because people are used to *fixed deficits*, that is, they are used to consistently abnormal behaviors, transient, fluctuating symptoms may be considered proof that the behaviors are manipulative or willful. This is often not the case with BD.

GROWING UP WITH BIPOLAR DISORDER

Over the years, parents and children have taught us what it is like for a child to grow up with BD. It is a struggle, a painful and confusing experience for most children, their parents, and other family members. As a parent, understanding your child's experience can help you to become part of the solution. To help you understand what it's like for your child to go through life with BD, we often describe the child as "lacking emotional shock absorbers."

Emotional Shock Absorbers

Emotional shock absorbers are coping mechanisms that soften the impact of various events on the child's emotional balance. For instance, in a very young child who has not yet developed language skills to make his or her needs understood, frustration will be more frequent and intense compared to children who can express what is upsetting them. Children with BD may become overwhelmed by extreme emotions in response to daily events. In these cases, soothing or reassurance from parents or caretakers will not help. A small disappointment or a parental "no" might throw your child off balance into a state of emotional upset or out-of-control rage. The effect of a small disappointment on mood and behavior can last anywhere from hours to days.

When confronted with a disappointment or a change of plans, rather than experiencing normal, manageable emotions, your child may become extremely sad and anxious or angry and explosive. Also, he or she might withdraw or become aggressive in response to what you may see as a minor event. These out-of-control emotional reactions are like "emotional seizures" that leave you and your child confused, frustrated, and hopeless.

The inconsistency of these responses is even more confusing and irritating. Sometimes your child will be able to manage well in a situation that only a few days earlier caused a major meltdown. However, the child might "lose it" minutes later over another seemingly insignificant issue. The unpredictable emotional outcomes of daily stressful events can keep you and your child in a state of tension, as if you were constantly "walking on eggshells."

The most common types of emotional shock absorbers are as follows:

- Ability to respond to parental soothing or reassurance

- Degree of language development

- Ability to inhibit emotional responses

- Ability to self-soothe

- Cognitive maturation of the child and the fear of consequences (social or legal)

A child with BD will need more help in navigating daily experiences, and more support and comforting when unable to maintain emotional balance. As a parent, you may instinctively shelter your child from becoming overstimulated, frightened, injured, or hurt. Functioning as a buffer, you provide a filter to all that your child is exposed to. When your child becomes upset or overwhelmed by extreme emotions, you help the child recover emotional balance by acting in a soothing and comforting manner. For these reasons, a child with BD needs parental help in managing throughout the day more than other children do.

Is Treatment Necessary?

Many parents are concerned that if their child is diagnosed with BD, the child will have to take medications (and deal with side effects) for the rest of his or her life. Before making any decision about treatment, you should be aware of the potential consequences of doing nothing. As you will realize while reading through the first few chapters of this book, BD is like a spiral: on this spiral your child moves up (and improves), or down (and worsens), but never stands still.

Treatment helps your child move up the spiral, compensating for the various obstacles that BD puts on his or her developmental path, providing him or her with more of an even playing field. When BD is allowed to run its course unchecked, it will progressively interfere with family, school, and psychological functioning; and the consequences can be very serious.

To keep your child moving up the spiral, toward his/her full potential, you will need the help provided by this book. The best way to get help for your child is to put together an effective treatment team (see chapter 7). Some of you will find a ready-made treatment team; others will have to find the individual members and bring them together as a treatment team.

Treatment Offers Hope

Based on our clinical experience, we are convinced that most problems caused by BD can be helped with accurate diagnosis and proper treatment. Since Demitri and Janice Papolos published their groundbreaking book *The Bipolar Child: The Definitive and Reassuring Guide to Childhood's Most Misunderstood Disorder* (1999), many publications have appeared to assist parents in diagnosing early-onset BD. Information about diagnosis, pharmacological and psychological treatment, and the education and caretaking of children with BD is now widely available in print and on the Internet.

Nevertheless, many parents are overwhelmed by the task of having to make difficult and urgent decisions without a clear understanding of what should be done and why. If you are reading this book, you may suspect or even know that your child suffers with BD. We hope to help you make decisions on how to obtain a diagnosis, formulate a treatment plan, and how to implement that plan with the help of qualified professionals. This book offers you a comprehensive and practical guide that outlines a therapeutic approach for children with BD that can be used throughout your child's treatment, growth, and development.

A THERAPEUTIC APPROACH

A child with BD presents many challenges to parents, families, and schools. Nothing goes smoothly. Everything is either a battle, a negotiation, or a compromise that parents feel bad about. Many parents become more flexible to avoid problems, but they are then accused of not providing adequate limit-setting. The first step toward securing a diagnosis, pursuing a treatment plan, and obtaining results is to have a better understanding of what your child is going through. Treatment can transform a hopeless situation into a more manageable one, providing hope and improving family life. Five main concepts are essential to our approach:

1. *Observation* of symptoms is essential to diagnosing, treating, and maintaining BD in remission.

2. *Mania* (the excitatory phase of BD; see chapter 2) is the key to *cycling* (the alternating of different mood states; see chapter 2), and the main target of treatment.

3. *Normal sleep* is necessary to stabilize BD.

4. *Parents* must be well-informed about BD, and actively involved in its management.

5. *Collaboration and communication* between child and parents are essential. For a positive outcome, it is also essential that your child's treatment team collaborates and communicates both with you and your child.

Observing the Symptoms

In our treatment approach, careful observation of symptoms is helpful in the diagnostic evaluation, the initial treatment (stabilizing symptoms), and maintenance treatment (see chapter 7). Initially, parents learn to observe their child's behaviors and emotions as events, without judging or criticizing them. Gradually, the parents develop a language to communicate their observations to their child and the treatment team. Later on, the parents become able to teach this skill to their child, thus giving their child a way of self-monitoring.

As the child starts observing his/her own behavior, he/she develops insight, learns better coping mechanisms, and gains more self-control. During this long and uneven process, your child should not feel criticized or experience a loss of self-esteem, but rather should feel supported and empowered.

As you and your child observe these behaviors and moods, and intervene accordingly, this process will bring you closer. Parent and child are helped and supported through crises, and they gradually gain a better understanding of what happens in BD, and why. With this foundation, a team is formed that includes a psychiatrist, a therapist, and school staff. The team can then use these observations both as a target for intervention and to monitor progress.

Preventing Mania Stops the Cycling

The overall approach suggested in this book can be best understood with the metaphor of the pendulum. If we think of BD as a pendulum that swings out of balance toward extremes of mania or depression, our goal is to bring the pendulum into the range of balance and stability. Once the pendulum has been set in motion, it gains momentum and usually does not slow down or stop without intervention. *Rebalancing the pendulum* means reducing stimulation and removing every known cause of instability.

In our approach, the main treatment target is mania, hypomania, or any excitatory state. Depression is viewed as the result of an excitatory phase (a manic or mixed state). Our focus is on treating, or better yet, preventing mania as a way to avoid the whole cycle. Too much stimulation usually leads to manic excitement and mood instability; therefore, we make an effort to identify all possible sources of stimulation, and we discuss how to reduce their negative effects. The most common causes of instability are drugs, certain medications, lack of sleep, and environmental overstimulation. Some of these negative factors can be prevented, while others are beyond anybody's control (i.e., life events).

Sleep Stabilizes Mood

Sleep loss or deprivation has a destabilizing effect on BD, while normal, restful sleep is essential in the effort to stabilize BD. Any intervention will be more effective if sleep is adequate; conversely, any intervention will be undermined by the failure to address sleep disturbances. Chapter 9 is devoted to sleep hygiene, which is one of the pillars of our treatment approach. The importance of sleep in the process of putting BD in remission requires the active cooperation of the child, his or her parents, and occasionally other family members and school personnel.

The Parent as a Balancing Force

As parents, you are an anchoring point for your child, but you cannot overcome a biological disorder. Throughout your child's life, you've been a source of help and understanding and, very often, you've been a calming influence and a balancing force. Many of you do this instinctively, without realizing how important your role is. For the first four or five years of your child's life, you may have been the main, sometimes the only, source of emotional support and balance. For some, kindergarten and school may have added additional support and guidance, for others, school is a stressor and a destabilizing force. Thus, parents are their child's lifeline for providing a source of stability and balance throughout adolescence and sometimes even later. Learning how to make the best use of this role and strengthening the skills involved can be a challenge.

The parents of children with BD are an integral part of the child's treatment. As a parent you need to be knowledgeable about BD. You must learn the signs and symptoms of BD in general, and how certain symptoms manifest in your child. A knowledgeable parent can observe his or her child's symptoms, and then report them to a trained mental health professional, which is an essential step in diagnosing BD and in monitoring the child's response to treatment.

A deep understanding of symptoms, triggers, and the course of BD over time is helpful in adjusting your response to the situation. For the most part, as parents you are asked to defuse your child's emotional responses when their intensity is too much for them to handle. By *defuse* we mean preventing the escalation from a minor disappointment or disagreement to a full-fledged loss of emotional and/or behavioral control. This can sometimes be accomplished by soothing, reassuring, calming down, or distracting your child.

This need might change over time. You might not be able to defuse a very young child's explosive response, but it will be easy to contain the child's behavior and keep him or her safe. This might require isolating the child by giving a time-out in his/her room, having the child avoid contact with siblings or peers, eliminating objects (knives, sharp or pointy objects) that could be used as weapons, and, if absolutely necessary, physically restraining the child. This should be done with guidance from the physician or other experienced mental health professional, and only as a last resort to maintain safety. In an older adolescent, physical restraints usually lead to escalation of anger and aggression.

As a parent, you need to meet your child where he or she "is at." To do this you need to understand the psychological and social consequences of having an illness for months or years, the developmental delays that this may have caused (if any), and the best ways to help your child cope, by maximizing his/her strengths and minimizing his/her weaknesses.

Understanding your child's condition helps you fulfill your stabilizing role, deflect tension, and restore safety and rational behavior. Rather than getting upset at your child's demands at bedtime, you learn to see this as part of a pattern of activation in the evenings. If you are able to keep matters in perspective, rather than becoming upset and rigid, you can remain calm. You will no longer be paralyzed by fear, nor will you blindly react to your child's demands. You will be able to choose to stay calm based on what you know about BD, and how it affects your child. Hopelessness will give way to optimism.

Teamwork

During the diagnostic evaluation, you and your child have an opportunity to reflect on the past, recognize symptoms, and know how they change over time. Often this is the first opportunity for parents, children, and the whole family to acknowledge how hard things have been. With a new understanding of the problem, you can become more active in your child's treatment, and you will find new hope.

You will need the support of the treatment team in many different situations. When setbacks occur during your child's treatment, always return to the basic coping skills you will have learned. Remember, complete stability is not possible, and balance has to be found on a daily basis; you do that by adjusting to specific symptoms and specific circumstances. Constant monitoring and adjustments are necessary as your child grows, matures, and his or her needs change. With medical stabilization and improved home and school life, parents can begin to feel more competent and their child can begin to thrive.

2

Diagnosing Bipolar Disorder

During our first meeting, David, a seventeen-year-old high school senior, twirled his umbrella, interrupted us as we introduced ourselves, and asked with a beaming smile and a resounding voice, "Can I tell you why I'm not bipolar?" We didn't have a chance to reply, as David's uninterrupted and rapid speech continued: "I was told bipolar disorder is having ups and downs, highs and lows, being too happy and being too depressed. I have the ups, but I'm never depressed, so I'm not bipolar." He smiled broadly, proud of his logic and of having scored his first point.

After sitting down for a few seconds, David jumped to his feet and, amused by his own performance, announced: "I'm feeling great. What's wrong with that? My mother has problems, but she keeps on saying there is something wrong with me!" And winking at us, he said, "I am fine." David also said that he is always very happy and that he would be fine if he could just get what he wants.

David has been prescribed several stimulants and antidepressants, all of which have caused a worsening of his symptoms, once putting him in the hospital for ten days. He knows he often feels "high" and euphoric but he is emphatic about never feeling depressed. His mood, however, is not always so pleasant.

*His mother reported he is usually irritable, short-tempered, agitated,
explosive, and hostile. She said, "He reminds me of my father.
He was wonderful with everybody outside of the family, but at
home we were scared of him. You never knew what he would do.
I don't want David to be like him."*

In just a few seconds, David exhibited some of the most typical symptoms of mania. He was euphoric and grandiose, his speech was pressured (very fast), intrusive, and loud, his behavior was restless and impulsive, and his judgment and insight seemed impaired.

In this chapter we will discuss emotional regulation, mood disorders and their classifications, basic mood states and their symptoms, as well as the differences between bipolar disorder (BD) and manic depressive illness (MDI).

EMOTIONAL REGULATION

Normal, healthy emotions, like sadness, elation, irritation, and anxiety, can manifest with different degrees of intensity. Healthy emotions do not interfere with daily living. In fact, changes of mood are adaptive and help us to function in the world. For instance, anxiety can be useful when we are in danger, redirecting our attention and effort to restore safety.

For most people, changes of mood (the emotion you feel) and *affect* (the emotional state you show to others) are part of everyday life. We all experience a normal range of emotions elicited by a variety of stimuli, both internal (thoughts and memories) and external (events). Sometimes, a negative occurrence such as being fired or losing a loved one will cause an episode of depression. However, this is only a temporary loss of emotional balance under extremely stressful circumstances. After a few months, the sadness resolves and the person feels normal again.

EMOTIONAL DYSREGULATION

Any persistent disruption of emotional balance that is disproportionate to the *trigger* (the event causing the emotion) indicates a dysregulation of the neurophysiological systems controlling emotions. Normal emotional reactions are commensurate with the stimulus: for example, when a sudden, loud noise induces fear, a normal person needs to verify that there is no imminent threat. Once reassured, the fear subsides within seconds. In this case, fear doesn't produce impairment since the person realizes that, in fact, there is no danger and rapidly returns to feeling safe and calm.

In the case of an abnormal reaction like a panic attack, things are quite different. The intensity of the emotion (fear) can be severe (a panic attack) and cause impairment that can last for hours, even after the person has realized there is no danger.

Emotional dysregulation extends the range of emotions to abnormal extremes. For example, rather than experiencing normal joy, someone with BD might experience intense euphoria and elation that lasts for hours or days. Instead of sadness over a disappointment lasting several minutes or hours, one might feel despondent or even grief-stricken for days or weeks. Extreme feelings of happiness, irritability, anger, sadness, and despair can be difficult to manage, especially in childhood.

Normal Versus Abnormal Moodiness

The first two questions that most parents ask us are "How can you tell what is normal moodiness and what is not?" and "What are the signs that my child might be suffering from depression or bipolar disorder?" There is no simple answer to these questions, but most clinicians assess symptoms, triggers (such as life events), family history, and disability. For example, how frequent, severe, and long-lasting are the child's moods or mood swings? Are there other symptoms (sleep disturbances, hyperactivity, aggression) occurring with the moodiness? Are there known precipitants or triggers (drugs, stressors)? What are the consequences of these mood swings? What is the course of the symptoms over time (duration, severity)? Is there a family history of BD, depression, or substance abuse?

"Normal" moodiness is usually transient, mostly short-lived, and of mild intensity. It is sometimes brought on by fatigue, lack of sleep, disappointments, hormonal changes, physical pain, or illnesses. Normal mood swings improve spontaneously and usually do not cause severe consequences or disability.

Pathological mood swings, as you will see, are very intense and can last a long time. In BD, the loss of emotional balance is recurrent, severe, and usually disabling. Temper tantrums, meltdowns, and fits are only a few of the names used to describe episodes of emotional dyscontrol. One minute of listening to your child raging can seem like a lifetime. The precipitant, usually minor, can be something as simple as a parent telling a child to turn off the TV, saying no, or canceling or changing plans.

The child's reaction can be violent, with a rapid escalation to rage, sometimes including verbal or physical abuse. Some of these rages can last for hours (even days) and can paralyze the entire household, causing great discomfort to everyone, or even causing family members to live in fear. If you are parenting a child with BD, almost certainly you have been traumatized. There have been frequent arguments, chronic irritability, and aggressive behavior. The child's responses are excessive, inappropriate, or defiant. Insults and violent outbursts are frequent.

Mood swings are not always so intense or severe, and symptoms can be more subtle. In these less intense cases, BD can go undetected for a long time, sometimes causing chronic problems at home, school, and socially. If symptoms are present only at home, and school behavior and grades remain satisfactory, parents, teachers, and some professionals may attribute the symptoms to parent/child conflict. In these cases, even though therapy may ameliorate the situation temporarily, lack of adequate treatment will likely produce little or no lasting improvement.

Symptoms of aggression that are highly destructive, regardless of severity or setting, are readily recognized and reported. Acts of aggression can lead to suspensions or even expulsions from one or more schools. This indicates greater severity of the illness and a greater need for treatment to prevent these symptoms from interfering with education and socialization.

MOOD DISORDERS

Mood disorders, including BD, are medical illnesses that cause profound and often recurrent emotional dysregulation. Most of the time, emotional dysregulation is associated with other symptoms, like disturbances of activity, sleep, and cognitive or behavioral changes.

One of the central features of a mood disorder is that the *intensity* of emotions is too great; it is way outside the normal range. Most people with mood disorders are unable to modulate their responses. It is as if the volume of their emotions is turned up to the maximum. If they loose their emotional balance, it is difficult to recover it.

This difficulty modulating emotional responses or recovering from intense emotions causes great mood instability. These changes or shifts of mood (often called *labile mood*) can occur so quickly that the individual might not even be aware of the change, or might recognize the change only after it has taken place. The type and duration of such emotional disturbances depend on individual characteristics as well as the trigger (precipitant). For instance, if a playdate is cancelled, a child with BD who is also very sensitive to rejection might be upset or angry for several hours or days, while a normal child would find another activity and not be so profoundly affected by the change of plans.

Classification of Mood Disorders

In modern psychiatry, clinicians and researchers use classification systems as guidelines for diagnosing different disorders. The need for criteria that can be used in different countries and cultures prompted the development of guidelines in the United States and in Europe. The *Diagnostic and Statistical Manual of Mental Disorders* (DSM; American Psychiatric Association 2000), now in its fourth edition, text-revision (DSM-IV-TR), is the current classification system used to diagnose psychiatric disorders in all age groups.

BASIC MOOD STATES

There are three basic mood states: depressive, manic, and mixed (see appendix I for the diagnostic criteria). These states differ from *euthymia* (normal mood) not only because of changes in mood, but also due to changes in energy, sleep, judgment, and impulse control.

Table 1 summarizes some of the most common changes from the normal range.

Table 1: Symptoms of Basic Mood States

Depression	Well (Euthymia)	Mania
Down, sad, blue	**Normal mood**	Euphoric, irritable
Low self-esteem	**Normal self-esteem**	High self-esteem
Slow thoughts	**Normal thoughts**	Racing, crowded thoughts
Lacks interest	**Normal interest**	Many interests
Needs more sleep	**Normal sleep**	Needs less sleep
Low energy	**Normal energy**	High energy
Low activity	**Normal activity**	Hyperactivity
Procrastinates	**Normal impulse control**	Impulsive
Fair to poor judgment	**Good judgment**	Poor judgment

Figure 1: Range of Severity in Mood Disorders

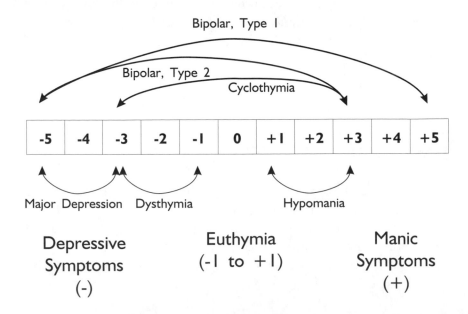

In figure 1, mood is charted on a scale that ranges from -5 (most depressed) to +5 (most manic) and from -1 to +1 (the "normal" range known as euthymia).

Subtypes of Bipolar Disorder

The DSM defines bipolar disorder by an episode of spontaneous mania or hypomania. In BD type-I (BP-I), the criteria for mania are met at least once. These same patients also experience depression in various degrees of severity (see table 2).

Table 2: Classification of Mood Disorders				
Type of Illness	**Depression**	**Mania**	**Hypomania**	**Recurrence**
Major depressive disorder				
Single episode	Mild - Severe	No	No	No
Recurrent	Mild - Severe	No	No	Yes
Bipolar disorder				
BP-I	Mild - Severe	Yes	Yes	Yes
BP-II	Severe	No	Yes	Yes
Unipolar mania or hypomania	None - Mild	Yes/No	Yes/No	Yes
Chronic mania	None - Mild	Yes	Yes	No
Cyclothymia	Mild	No	Yes	Yes
Dysthymia	Mild	No	No	No

Those with BD type-II (BP-II) meet the criteria for hypomania but not for mania. In BP-II disorder, depressive symptoms are the most prominent clinical manifestation. It is not surprising that these depressions are often confused with major depressive disorder (MDD). Depressive episodes draw attention from patients and their families, as well as doctors, because depressive symptoms tend to be more disabling and more disturbing. Hypomanic episodes, on the other hand, tend to be considered as a form of healthy exuberance by many patients (and their families and friends), at least for some time.

Cyclothymia has both hypomanic and depressive symptoms but not as severe as in BP-I or BP-II.

According to the DSM, manic episodes triggered by medications or drugs are not to be diagnosed as BD: that is, if your child has developed manic symptoms during the course of antidepressant treatment for depression, or stimulants for Attention-Deficit Disorder, he or she cannot technically be diagnosed with BD (see Treatment-Emergent Mania in chapter 8).

Common Symptoms of Depression in Adults

Symptoms of depression usually include low energy and depressed mood, or sadness. As depression sets in, a person gradually (or suddenly) loses interest in most activities and hobbies, family, friends, food and sex. The ability to take pleasure in usually enjoyable activities diminishes (called *anhedonia*), and mental functions are slowed down, sometimes causing poor concentration and impaired memory. Many people may experience sleep difficulties, appetite disturbances, crying spells, low self-esteem, a sense of hopelessness and, at times, thoughts of suicide. Social or emotional withdrawal, difficulty making decisions, and a negative, pessimistic outlook on life are often the first symptoms of depression.

The symptoms of depression vary: Although some people do not feel sad, they may cry easily, and look and act depressed or worried and slowed down. Almost always, the symptoms are worse in the morning and less severe or improved in the late evening, a phenomenon called *diurnal mood variations.*

Depressive symptoms can occur as an isolated episode of major depression (MD, single episode) or as a recurrent illness (recurrences of major depression, or the depressive phases of BD). Some clinicians and researchers believe that many forms of depression are manifestations of BD, and require specific treatment for BD.

Dysthymia, a milder but prolonged form of depression, shares many features with major depression, except for the severity of its symptoms.

Common Symptoms of Mania in Adults

Mania and hypomania are characterized by increased energy or hyperactivity; sleep disturbances; and an elated, euphoric, jovial mood (that can sometimes turn into irritability or hostility). Pressured speech, racing or crowded thoughts, impulsive behavior, and impaired judgment are also very common.

Hypomania

Although mania exhibits hard-to-miss prominent symptoms and thus is relatively easy to recognize, *hypomania* can be subtle and is probably one of the most challenging conditions to diagnose. The sense of well-being, short duration of symptoms, increased productivity, lack of insight, and impaired judgment that characterize this disorder are also some of the reasons for difficulty in identifying hypomania.

During *euphoric hypomania*, the patient feels well and is able to function well (or even better than usual). Often, the patient's mood is jovial or euphoric. Energy and self-esteem are increased; mental acuity and creative abilities are heightened and are accompanied by a feeling of well-being. There may be increased talking (chatty) and, sometimes, a decreased need for sleep. At the same time, impaired judgment, impulsivity, and risk-taking behaviors can be present. Many patients do not see hypomania as a problem and actually resist being treated for it. For the most part, they want to extend, or increase, their hypomania, and seek help only when it comes to an end and depression sets in.

In other words, they don't see hypomania and depression as part of the same cycle, the two sides of one coin. In general, unless it is chronic (see below), hypomania cannot be sustained; when it subsides, depression often sets in, as if the system was compensating for the enormous expenditure of energy with a general slowdown, or even a complete shutdown (depression). Most patients with hypomania are not aware of it, and might not report it to their doctor. During periods of depression, they might not remember ever being hypomanic, and they confuse hypomania with "well-being." For this reason, only the patient's relatives or close friends may be able to report the symptoms of hypomania or answer questions about impulsive behaviors, increased energy and self-esteem, or impaired judgment.

During *dysphoric hypomania*, the mood is not euphoric; rather it is irritable, anxious, unpleasant, or depressed. In these cases, the patient will be disturbed by irregular or interrupted sleep, inability to focus or relax, angry outbursts, constant worrying, and endless complaints.

For some, hypomania is a chronic state. *Chronic hypomania* can be viewed as a set of "personality features," inasmuch as these traits have been present for a lifetime. Their occurrence in families leads to a commonly held belief that these are typical "family features." With this belief comes a reluctance to see these behaviors as symptoms, and a great resistance to treatment. Additionally, the reluctance of many adult patients to involve their relatives or significant others in the assessment process can deprive the clinician of valuable information, and contributes to misdiagnosis.

Finally, the use of arbitrary criteria regarding the duration of hypomania in most classification systems, including the DSM, permits a diagnosis of hypomania in a surprisingly small minority of those suffering with it. Particularly among children, adolescents, and young adults, hypomanic symptoms are often of extremely short duration. When duration or severity criteria are not met (see below), professionals can diagnose BD-Not Otherwise Specified (NOS), a category that includes forms of BD that do not fit in the DSM system. In spite of this, many professionals are reluctant to give a diagnosis of BD-NOS.

Cyclothymia

Cyclothymia manifests as an attenuated form of BD, and appears with milder and short-lived hypomanic and/or depressive symptoms. Cyclothymia can cause chronic mood fluctuation with different degrees of impairment, usually less severe than those of major depression or BD.

Mixed States

When symptoms of mania/hypomania and depression occur at the same time, the resulting episode is called a *mixed state*. Originally believed to be uncommon, mixed states are being recognized more and more often in adults, and they are the most frequent type of episode in young patients with BD. Mixed states cause great suffering and increase the risk of abusing alcohol and other substances, as well as the risk of aggression, self-harm, and suicide. If hypomania is associated with depression, it can seem like an agitated depression and worsens, rather than improve, when it is treated with antidepressants.

DURATION OF SYMPTOMS

In adults, symptoms of mania and depression, including their co-occurrence in mixed states, tend to last for weeks, months, and sometimes years. In younger patients, during the early course of the illness and in some forms with rapid cycles, the symptoms may last only for minutes, hours, or days. Often the symptoms do not meet the duration criteria required by the DSM, and many clinicians doubt the validity of the diagnosis of BD in children because their clinical features are not fully consistent with the adult presentation.

Rapid cycling (RC) is the term used to describe four or more discrete episodes of illness in a twelve-month period. Terms like rapid cycling or ultra-rapid cycling BD are now used to describe the fluctuating course and rapid resolution of some symptoms in children. Dr. Barbara Geller, professor of psychiatry at Washington University Medical School in St. Louis, suggested the use of the term "ultra-rapid cycling" (URC) to describe patients with more than 4, but fewer than 365, episodes per year, and the term "ultra-ultra-rapid cycling" (UURC) to identify cases with more than one episode per day (Geller et al. 1995). Although these definitions allow researchers to describe an important clinical feature of early-onset BD, these symptomatic periods are not really episodes, and do not give way to discrete periods of illness symptom-free intervals. Therefore, these terms are used descriptively until better terms can be agreed upon.

Manic Depressive Illness and Bipolar Disorder

Manic depressive illness (MDI) is often confused with BD, and the two terms are frequently used interchangeably. However, the two are quite different. MDI, an older and broader category, is a clinical diagnosis that is not defined by inclusions, exclusions, or duration criteria. The diagnosis of MDI is based on:

1. Characteristic symptoms

2. Patterns of recurrence

3. A family history of mood disorders

4. Improvement when the patient is on mood-stabilizing agents and/or precipitation or worsening of manic symptoms with some medications (antidepressants, stimulants, steroids)

Manic depressive illness includes both *bipolar* forms (mood disorders with both depressive and manic symptoms) and *unipolar* forms (mood disorders that have either depressive or manic symptoms, but not both).

The relationship between BD and MDI is like that of a yolk to the whole egg: MDI includes both unipolar and bipolar forms of depression and mania that would not meet the DSM criteria, or would fall into the BD-NOS category. BD (the yolk) includes only conditions where both depression and mania are present.

Although the term "manic depressive illness" is more accurate and inclusive, the term BD has become customary in recent scientific and popular literature. For this reason, this book uses BD to describe all the forms of recurrent mood disturbance with a family history of BD, whether the individual meets DSM criteria or not (see The Bipolar Spectrum below).

The distinction between MDI and BD is important, even though it might seem to be a technical issue of little practical relevance. Consider the case of an adolescent with a history of several episodes of depression, some with psychotic symptoms; a positive family history of BD; and past experiences of becoming extremely agitated, sleepless, and anxious on antidepressant medications. The DSM-IV criteria (see appendix I) would not allow a diagnosis of BD, and most psychiatrists would diagnose recurrent major depression and treat this youth with antidepressants. Another clinician might suspect MDI or "latent" bipolar disorder and predict, based on current research findings, that hypomanic or manic symptoms will develop later and recommend treatment with a mood stabilizer.

In an attempt to broaden research criteria that are widely seen as too restrictive when it comes to diagnosing BD in its early manifestations, or when the symptoms are too "soft," the concept of a bipolar spectrum has gained many supporters.

The Bipolar Spectrum

The concept of a bipolar spectrum broadens the boundaries of the DSM's narrowly defined description of BD. Dr. Hagop Akiskal, professor of psychiatry at the University of California in San Diego, proposed the term "bipolar spectrum" to include a host of conditions such as schizoaffective mania, bipolar disorder type I, bipolar disorder type-II, bipolar disorder type-III (type III is a pharmacologically induced mania or hypomania that was not present before it was induced by medication), bipolar disorder type-IV (recurrent depression with a family history of bipolar disorder), cyclothymia, and dysthymia (Akiskal and Mallya 1987).

This expanded concept of bipolar disorder includes some forms of recurrent depression and borderline personality disorder. There is significant overlap between major depressive illness and the bipolar spectrum, because both terms recognize that recurrent forms of mood dysregulation run in families and benefit from treatment with mood-stabilizing agents rather than from antidepressants.

Rates of Bipolar Disorder

Mania (BD-I) has been estimated to occur in 1 to 1.5 percent of the general adult population. A similar rate was found in the only epidemiological study of children and adolescents (Lewinsohn, Klein, and Seeley 1995). Estimating the prevalence of mania, however, does not accurately capture the prevalence of hypomania. More recent epidemiological data report rates of hypomania in 5 to 8 percent of the adult population. A study in adolescents suggests that rates of hypomania may be as high as 13 percent (Carlson and Kashani 1988) if arbitrary duration criteria are waived. This incidence rate is a great deal higher than the generally accepted rate of 1 to 1.5 percent cited above for BD in the adult population.

Genetics and Family History

Like most genetically inherited disorders, BD can appear at any age, although most often it does so in late adolescence and early adulthood. Attenuated forms or milder symptoms can be present for months or years before the onset of a diagnosable illness. Much of the current research identifies genetic risk factors as playing a very large role in the development of bipolar disorder, and possibly even more so in younger patients. Family, twin, and adoption studies show that hereditary genetic factors are extremely important. For instance, BD occurs at a rate of 50 to 67 percent in identical twins, whose genetic makeup is exactly the same, compared with a rate of 17 to 24 percent in nonidentical or fraternal twins, who have about half of their genetic makeup in common (Geller and DelBello 2003).

Because of the genetic transmission of bipolar disorder, taking a detailed family history is extremely important for diagnosing BD in your child. Unfortunately, this very important information is not always given adequate weight in assessing children with mood and behavioral disturbances. Misdiagnosis is one of the main obstacles to the proper treatment of BD. If a relative with BD was misdiagnosed as schizophrenic or depressed, or as having a substance abuse problem, then that could affect the diagnosis of a child. If you suspect BD, obtaining detailed medical records for all the members of the family can be helpful.

3

Bipolar Disorder in Children

This chapter will help you to recognize symptoms of bipolar disorder (BD) as they appear in children. Chapter 4 will do the same for adolescents. Using stories from our clinical experience, we will review the signs and symptoms of mania and depression as they appear at different stages of growth and development. Each vignette can be read as if it were the summary of an initial evaluation and follows a developmental sequence, from infancy to childhood, preadolescence, adolescence, and young adulthood (see How Bipolar Disorder Progresses below).

We will discuss examples of BD in children from preschool (ages three to five) to early school (ages six to nine) through preadolescence (ages ten to twelve). In the next chapter we will look at adolescence (ages thirteen to eighteen). As children grow older, particularly when they're in their late teens, the symptoms of BD become more like those observed in adults, including more discrete episodes of mania and depression (clear beginning and end to the phases of the illness), and fewer and slower cycles back and forth between episodes. These features are more typical of adult bipolar disorder (see chapter 2).

HOW BIPOLAR DISORDER PROGRESSES

Under normal circumstances, as the body grows and develops, the child matures cognitively, emotionally, and behaviorally. That is to say, your child is the result of the combined processes of growth (physical and biological), development (mental, emotional, and social), and maturation (the emergence of personal and behavioral characteristics) all in a state of dynamic equilibrium. Because human development is subject to great variability and is influenced by many factors, individual variations are extremely important. Thus, changes in mood, activity, sleep, and ability to concentrate should be compared to your child's own baseline, rather than to that of peers or siblings.

In a child with BD, the progression of the illness runs parallel to ongoing development. The two are closely intertwined, influencing each other in complex and unpredictable ways. On one hand, the unfolding of BD can cause delays or deficits in several areas. On the other hand, problems in one or more developmental areas can exacerbate emotional instability. For example, hyperactivity causes problems with learning and social interactions, while frustration due to delayed language development can trigger angry outbursts.

Developmental factors also play a role in a child's ability to *modulate* (adjust or adapt) his or her emotional responses, contain aggression, channel energy, and focus attention. The onset of the symptoms of BD in a very young child can impair that child's ability to learn effective coping skills and develop problem-solving strategies. This "behavioral immaturity," observed in some children with BD, is in clear contrast to their normal or advanced skills in other areas, and a normal or high IQ. This creates a discrepancy and sharp contrasts between precociousness or talents in some areas and delays or deficits in others.

For these reasons, BD in children and adolescents exhibits several important differences from the "classic" adult forms of the illness. Children are more vulnerable to the effects of mood instability because their ability to adjust their emotional responses is not yet fully developed. For example, consider the effects of depression on cognitive processes, such as poor concentration or slow thinking, in adults and in children.

In an adult, where a baseline level of cognitive functioning is known, a marked change in mental performance is easily recognized. If it cannot be compensated for, it usually leads to a medical evaluation or other intervention. When these symptoms occur in young children, who are still learning language and coping skills, there is no baseline for comparison. The child may appear to be inattentive, "lazy," or lacking in motivation. Unless the depression is recognized and treated, its negative impact on learning and language development can be severe.

BD can manifest with a variety of symptom patterns and at different points along a child's developmental path. During normal development, the central nervous system (CNS) undergoes dramatic transformations. These changes parallel and are necessary for language and cognitive development, emotional regulation, social competency, as well as physical and sexual maturation. Depending on the age of the child at the onset of the illness, developmental changes may affect which symptoms of BD will appear first or will be most prominent.

Normal developmental milestones, like puberty, can have a destabilizing effect on mood, sleep, and activity levels. In a prepubertal child, who has experienced only hypomanic symptoms, the complex hormonal changes of puberty can increase the severity of the symptoms to the threshold of full-blown mania. In fact, we often see eleven-, twelve-, and thirteen-year-old youngsters who are triggered by changes associated with puberty into their first diagnosable manic episode. The progression toward more severe symptoms is the result of a more complete expression, rather than a worsening, of the illness.

■ Andrew: Aggression and Rapid Cycles in a Preschool Boy

Since he was 18-months-old, Andrew, a five-year-old boy, has daily fits of rage. When he is out of control, he starts yelling, arguing, and becomes violent. His parents are concerned about Andrew's extreme emotional changes, and they never know what to expect when he wakes up in the morning. Some days he's gentle, smiles a lot, and is affectionate, compliant, cooperative, and eager to get to kindergarten to play with his friends.

Other days he looks like a restless, caged animal, and says he's not happy or makes statements like, "My mind is coming out of my head." On those days he is angry and upset from the moment he wakes up, and he has no tolerance for any kind of frustration. There have been many episodes of aggression toward his parents (usually his mother), his ten-year-old brother, and even the house pets. On several occasions, his aggression reached the point where he had to be physically restrained by his father.

He has broken things in the house, and once threw a phone across the room, breaking a large window.

Andrew is very bright and he can read very well for a five-year-old, but he refuses to read: he wants his parents to read to him. Sometimes he refuses to go to school, or doesn't leave the house all weekend. When he does go to school, he misbehaves, or worse. At home, he provokes his brother, starts fights, or causes trouble; he has to be kept entertained, catered to in all of his whims, and even then, there are still problems. Basically, he needs one-on-one attention from an adult nearly all of the time.

Andrew can act extremely insecure. He isolates himself from the other children in his class and complains about being worried. His parents have seen him work himself up from very calm to very happy and excited, often accompanied by giggles or gales of laughter and loud singing, resulting in a frenzy of movement and activities. At night, he may get anxious, especially around bedtime, because he is afraid of the dark and of various monsters. At those times, Andrew wears a lion suit he got for Halloween as a shield, and a blanket of the sort that "gives me courage so I can fight my enemies."

Andrew was suspended from school twice in less than two months, once for spitting milk at a peer with his straw, running away, and refusing to admit responsibility. Recently, unprovoked, he kicked a boy and was suspended for one day. When asked about the incident, he explained, "I knew he was going to do something to me, so I hit him first." The teacher who witnessed the incident said the other child was playing with Andrew and wasn't really looking at him, or provoking him. Andrew's possible expulsion from kindergarten and the school psychologist's diagnosis of possible bipolar disorder convinced his parents to seek treatment, even though they feared medication might be needed.

Andrew is a good example of how BD manifests in preschool-age children. Most striking are the dramatic, rapid changes in his mood, activity level, and overall functioning, and especially the shifts in his ability to inhibit aggressive behavior. The intensity of most of his emotional responses is disabling and clearly suggests a form of BD with sudden changes from normal to manic/aggressive, depressed/withdrawn, or anxious/insecure mood states.

■ Audrey: A Bossy First Grader

Audrey is a very slight and beautiful six-year-old girl who was adopted at birth. Her adoptive parents are an intelligent couple struggling with a child they just can't understand, and they don't know what to do to help her. As an infant, Audrey never wanted to be held or to receive affection from either parent. Her mother is still upset about this and interprets Audrey's dislike for physical affection as an indication that she has failed as a parent.

Most mornings Audrey is slow and irritable, and she blows up daily while getting ready for school. She has no tolerance for frustration, is bossy, demanding, and has daily tantrums and rages every time things don't go her way. Audrey is very intense, stubborn, and has a lot of trouble waiting for anything. She often hits and kicks her parents, yet when she does calm down, she is sorry and apologetic for her behavior.

Audrey goes to a school for learning disabled children and says she likes it, but she has some difficulty waiting for her turn, and calls out in class when it isn't her turn. She learns quickly but is very impatient. After school, Audrey becomes very hyper and demanding. She tells us of "shopping sprees" at the mall with her parents when her urge to buy almost everything in sight turns into demands. If these demands are not satisfied, she throws herself on the floor, or hits, kicks, spits, and bites her parents. She can go into a store and come out with an item, but still have a meltdown in the parking lot over the item she wasn't allowed to buy.

An endless variety of activities is necessary to keep her interested and busy. Going to bed is a daily struggle and always requires negotiation. There is always one more thing to do: watching a TV show, using the bathroom, or wanting a sip of water. Since the age of two, she has rarely fallen asleep before 11:30 P.M. Most mornings she can't wake up to go to school.

Audrey's teachers encouraged her parents to have the child evaluated. After being diagnosed with attention-deficit/hyperactivity disorder (ADHD), Audrey was treated with stimulants for one year. Although the school reported that Audrey had become

somewhat more focused, the hours after school were a nightmare
for her parents: more tantrums, more aggression, and less sleep,
all of which made life at home unbearable for her parents.

Audrey's hyperactivity, chronic irritability, low tolerance for frustration, oppositional behavior, and sleep difficulties are all indications that her moodiness might stem from a form of bipolar disorder. Audrey's difficulty maintaining attention is misleading, and has led to the misdiagnosis of ADHD. She has few problems paying attention at the beginning of an activity, but she has a short attention span. She can focus and is able to learn, but is easily bored (loses interests) and moves on to something new, stimulating, or exciting. Unable to wait, she rapidly looses focus in the classroom, and appears to be inattentive and easily distracted.

■ Justine: Diagnosed with BD at Age Eight

Justine has always been hard to handle and very demanding.
She was fussy from birth, cried a lot, and was difficult to calm
down, sleeping only four to five hours a night, and rarely napping.
When she does nap, she is cranky for at least an hour after
waking up. Currently, at eight years old, Justine stays awake
until at least 10 P.M., and often later. Almost every night she
wakes up at about 2 or 3 A.M. and slips into her parents' bed.

Except when attending school, Justine always demands her
mother's full attention. Often, separation from her mom causes
yelling and crying outbursts that last anywhere from a few
minutes to two hours. This still happens, even when her mother
leaves the room to tend to the needs of her younger sister.

Daily home life is a grueling experience. Most mornings,
Justine demands to be dressed by her mother, is extremely fussy
about what she wears, refuses to brush her teeth or her hair, and
is a very picky eater. She's never quite mastered toilet training, and
went back to wearing pull-ups at night, and even at school, when
her younger sister was born two years ago. Transitions are never
smooth, and she gets very upset if plans are changed. Justine has
been impulsive, taking things from school without permission, and
she has run away from her mother into the street. More than
once she has been dangerously close to being hit by a car.

At age three and a half, after four months of nursery school, Justine's teacher reported that she didn't share toys or games with the other kids, and seemed unable to adjust to being in a group. Now as an eight-year-old second grader, Justine can be bossy and demanding, but she is also animated and full of ideas. She can be very calm, sitting in the book corner and entertaining herself, or very difficult and aggressive if she doesn't get her way.

Since the beginning of nursery school to the present time, unprovoked incidents of hitting her peers have occurred several times a year. When asked about these incidents, she says she doesn't have any idea what happened. When Justine and her mother came for an evaluation at the school's request, her mother said that Justine has acted the same way at home for years. When she is out of control, she yells, hits, or kicks anyone who gets near her.

Justine's mother is an intelligent and insightful woman who is treated for bipolar disorder, and worries about her child suffering with the same illness. She has many black and blue bruises because Justine hits and kicks her regularly. Her mom told us of how overwhelmed she feels by the unrelenting difficulties of parenting Justine.

Since infancy, Justine has exhibited moodiness along with sleep disturbances, symptoms of separation anxiety, and severely aggressive behavior. Fussiness about food and clothing may indicate sensitivity to various stimuli, often a factor that can exacerbate irritability. Justine is usually irritable and unhappy at home, in a chronic mixed state that explodes into violent tantrums at the slightest provocation or during transitions.

In school, she is able to contain emotional outbursts most of the time, and her behavior is more variable. For Justine, different degrees of emotional dysregulation are always present, a common manifestation of BD in children. (See chapter 12 to find out more about Justine's development and growth.)

■ Jason: Hope After a Stay at the Hospital

Nine-year-old Jason has just returned home from a psychiatric hospital after having become violent toward his sister. Jason's parents report that before this violent incident took place,

everything seemed to be more or less okay. He was popular with
other boys at school, participated in sports regularly, and was
usually nice to his sister.

According to his parents, Jason has had problems going to
sleep since he was three, and he has intense nightmares that wake
him (and his parents). Since he was five, when he entered
kindergarten in a public school, he has been increasingly irritable.
School reports suggested that in first grade Jason had difficulties
paying attention. A psycho-educational evaluation revealed average
intelligence with difficulties in attention, organization, and subtle
difficulties with expressive language. At age eight, his parents took
him to see a psychiatrist for help with his attention problems.
After the psychiatrist prescribed stimulants, the school supported
this intervention with school accommodations and reported that
he was more attentive.

After-school hours are the most difficult times of the day for
Jason: He often takes hours to complete his homework, especially
on days when his mother works late. He calls her a lot and is
always reluctant to hang up. In the last few months, he has
stopped playing with his friends and prefers individual playdates
or neighborhood play (where he can go inside when he needs to
be indoors).

In the past year, Jason became more irritable at home,
and he began cursing and hitting his sister. After the psychiatrist
increased the dose of stimulants, Jason progressively lost his ability
to calm down when upset, his sleep decreased, he was more and
more "wound up," talking (and cursing) loudly, and full of
explosive rage. At school he was impulsive, and at home he had
lots of meltdowns. After assaulting his sister in a rage over the
use of the TV, he was hospitalized.

Jason's sleep difficulties were the first symptom to appear.
Irritability and difficulties with attention and concentration then
caused difficulties at school; Jason was diagnosed with ADHD
and treated with stimulants. His verbal and physical aggression
and his low tolerance for frustration continued to worsen in spite
of treatment. His dislike for authority and his desire to control
his environment rapidly escalated to conflicts in school (with his
teachers and friends), as well as home (with his parents and
sister). After leaving the hospital, Jason began psychotherapy and

a more modified school program to relieve stress. Gradually, his anger and oppositional behavior decreased, and family life has improved significantly.

■ Greg: Seasonal Depression and Psychotic Mania

Greg's symptoms appeared when he was eleven years old. Viewing a tornado watch on TV triggered excessive fear. Before that, he was scared of thunderstorms and could not stop thinking, talking, and worrying about them. He lost his appetite, did not want to go sailing, his favorite activity, and watched TV in silence for an entire weekend. He remembers his mind racing, as it still does, from time to time. Referred to a therapist and then to a pharmacologist, Greg was treated with antidepressants.

He did well for a year and the medication was tapered off. After a few months, at the beginning of the fall, symptoms of depression and withdrawal reappeared, and his grades started slipping. After consulting the psychiatrist, the antidepressant was restarted. Within a week his symptoms were in remission, and Greg's grades were improving. When he was transferred to a private school, his parents were surprised that he had become very withdrawn, complained of anxiety, and, finally, stopped attending school.

An increase in his medication, within two days, pushed him over the edge. Greg became acutely psychotic and suicidal. He tried to hang himself but was stopped by neighbors who saw him unsupervised and playing with a rope in the backyard. He was agitated, talked fast and loud, was jumping from one subject to the other, which made it hard for people to follow him.

In the following days, Greg didn't sleep much, seemed to always be in a rush, and was very anxious and impulsive, with many ideas and many worries. He had brief episodes (lasting less than one hour) of euphoria (with giddiness and inappropriate laughter), while on other days he seemed fine. After a month, Greg became severely depressed, feeling guilty about past behaviors, and was, again, unable to attend school. He was home-tutored as he was fearful of leaving the house. Greg's parents were not totally surprised when the diagnosis of BD was suggested, as this illness seems to run in the family and several members have been treated for it.

After two years, his depressive symptoms continue to appear at the beginning of every fall when Greg is prone to anxiety and worrying, and manic symptoms resurface every spring.

Recurrent symptoms, especially with a seasonal pattern, are a prominent feature of Greg's difficulties. Anxiety and moodiness seem related, appearing and disappearing at the same time. Although the initial symptoms were those of anxiety and fear of thunderstorms, depressive symptoms often followed or occurred together, justifying the use of antidepressant treatment. This changed when the antidepressant triggered an episode of psychotic mania. This vignette demonstrates how BD can remain latent long after symptoms of depression and anxiety are already clearly recognizable.

MANIC AND DEPRESSIVE SYMPTOMS IN CHILDREN

The child's developmental stage and the phase of the illness play a powerful role in shaping the way BD *presents* (that is, the way it appears or manifests), as you saw in the cases discussed above. However, their effect on a child's course of illness and what the appropriate treatment response should be is not clear. To manage BD effectively is to appreciate that both child and illness are in constant flux and/or transformation. Table 3 summarizes some of the common symptoms found in children with BD. In children and adolescents, comorbidity further complicates both assessment and treatment (see chapters 6 and 7).

Table 3: Frequency of Early Symptoms of BD*

Very Often (90–97%)	Often (60–80%)	Sometimes (20–35%)	Less than 10%
Irritability	Anxiety	Hypersexuality	Homicidal ideas
Mood lability**	Racing thoughts	Psychosis	Suicidal acts
Sleep disorder	Pressured speech	Suicidal ideation	
Anger, rage	Euphoria, grandiosity	Self-harm	
Impulsivity			
Agitation			
Aggression			

* Adapted from Faedda, Baldessarini, Glovinsky, and Austin 2004a.

** *Lability* means being unstable or changeable.

Symptoms of BD in children primarily affect physical activity and behavior, emotions and mood, and cognitive functions. A summary of these symptoms is presented in table 4.

Table 4: Clinical Symptoms of BD in Children

Depression/Dysthymia	Mania/Hypomania
Physical/Behavioral	**Physical/Behavioral**
Increased sleep, tired, inhibited	Energetic, hyper, tireless, overtalkative, loud
Slow movements, quiet, withdrawn	Impulsive, aggressive, violent
Does not feel well, aches, pains, malaise	Feels "great", decreased sleep
Appetite increase, weight gain	Appetite decrease, weight loss
Emotional	**Emotional**
Sadness, guilt, hopelessness, melancholy	Euphoric, humorous, giddy
Irritable, passive-aggressive, easily annoyed	Moody, labile, easily frustrated, explosive
Avoidant, dependent, passive, needy	Irritable, angry, sarcastic, defiant
Insecure, indecisive, cries easily	Argumentative, demanding
Shy, fearful, separation anxiety	Tense, wired, wound-up
Cognitive	**Cognitive**
Anhedonia,* lacks interest, motivation	Racing, crowded thoughts; many plans
Poor memory and/or concentration	Distractible, inattentive, daydreaming
Low self-esteem	Grandiose, overconfident, willful, bossy

* *Anhedonia* means the inability to enjoy normally pleasurable activities.

Mania in Children: *Physical Symptoms*

Mania and its milder variant, *hypomania*, are fundamentally excitatory states; that is, they are the result of activation (or disinhibition) of some or all mental functions. The physical symptoms of mania and hypomania include increased activity, increased speech (logorrhea), sleep and appetite disturbances, increased sexual interest/drive, impulsiveness and aggression.

INCREASED ACTIVITY

An increased level of activity can cause increased goal-oriented activities, when the high energy level is organized and somewhat productive. During increased goal-oriented activities, a child will appear busy, playing, moving objects, organizing belongings, or participating in sports or games). When the increased activity is not organized or focused, the child appears restless, hyperactive, and unable to remain on the same task for long. In this state, a child might be constantly "on the go," changing from activity to activity without completing any, unable to focus or organize his or her activity toward a goal.

Attempts to restrict this activity in a child with BD might cause angry outbursts and even violent defiance. Sometimes, the hyperactivity is so intense that the child might start dancing or cartwheeling, or run into walls or doors, causing self-injury or breaking things. The increased activity can interfere with food intake, as when the child will gorge food in the same frenzied way as he or she runs around aimlessly. Such extreme agitation can interfere with sleep, and result in a lack of cooperation with a bedtime routine or in an inability to lie down long enough to fall asleep. If the child does fall asleep, the increased physical activity, or thrashing, may cause interrupted and/or decreased sleep.

RESTLESSNESS

Restlessness describes an increased level of activity or a need to move. In its most severe presentation, hyperactivity and pacing are common. Seemingly harmless repetitive behaviors like nail-biting, leg-swinging, or finger-tapping, and even motor restlessness during sleep (restless leg syndrome, teeth grinding or *bruxism*) are common examples.

INCREASED SPEECH

Increased speech (or *logorrhea*) is the expression of crowded (too many) or racing (too rapid) thoughts and indicates a certain level of increased energy and disinhibition. Increased speech may vary, ranging from humming to talking to strangers, singing, or reciting a litany of criticisms or complaints, to sometimes talking to oneself. Mania can be associated with elation or *grandiosity* (an exaggerated sense of self-importance, power, talent, or knowledge), or with irritability and *dysphoria* (unpleasant, uncomfortable, or upset mood). The content of speech (what the child is saying) will depend on the quality of mood. During euphoria it can range from joking and mocking to making puns and comical remarks; in dysphoric states it can manifest with endless demands or complaints to insulting remarks or cursing.

Fast speech sometimes leads to impulsive lying, while grandiosity can lead to exaggerations and "big stories." There can be an increase in the speed and volume of speech (pressured speech), greater emphasis is given to words, and the tone of voice can also be affected. The voice is often loud, sometimes with singing, other times with yelling or screaming, an expression of the child's heightened emotional state.

SLEEP DISTURBANCES

Sleep disturbances are very common in BD. They include problems with getting to bed and staying asleep (initiation and continuity of sleep) that lead to inefficient, and/or insufficient, sleep overall. Children often have nightmares, night terrors, bedwetting (*enuresis*), and sleepwalking. Many children, and even some young teenagers, might go to their parents' bedroom to find some comfort and sleep after a nightmare or when they can't sleep through the night.

Because some medications (e.g., stimulants prescribed for ADHD) can induce sleep disorders, a thorough history of sleep disorders before or after any treatment will be helpful for differentiating BD from other causes of such sleep disorders.

APPETITE DISTURBANCES

Appetite can vary a lot, or be disturbed predominantly toward an increase or decrease even before any medication affects it. Appetite disturbances are frequent and include abnormal eating patterns with a decrease or loss of appetite (*anorexia*), decreased caloric intake due to the high levels of hyperactivity, or changes of *circadian* (daily cycle) appetite regulation, with increased appetite or cravings (especially for carbohydrates) and/or binge eating in the evening and at night.

INCREASED SEXUAL DRIVE

Increased sexual drive or hypersexual behavior may be present at any age. Very young children may show increased interest in sexually charged subjects, curiosity or interest in nudity, use of "bathroom language," fascination with childbirth and reproduction, increased spontaneous arousal and self-stimulation, and seductive behavior or exhibitionism.

Young girls might insist on dressing in sexually provocative outfits and young boys might expose themselves, or engage in self-stimulation in public and other inappropriate forms of sexual acting-out.

One mother told us that as early as two years of age, her son seemed unusually curious about her private parts, fondling her or trying to touch her breasts in ways that made her feel uncomfortable. At the age of three, he was engaging in self-stimulation and exposed himself to a cousin. At four, he was found inserting a pencil into his pet's anal orifice, and at five he engaged in mutual oral sexual stimulation with a child in his kindergarten class. This occurred in the absence of any sexual abuse, inappropriate exposure to sexual material, or any other known precipitant.

IMPULSIVITY

In children, as in adults, the most disruptive symptoms are those related to impulsivity, as they are often gestures of aggression that cannot be predicted or prevented. Impulse dyscontrol and aggression are frequent correlates of the irritability, increased energy, and impaired judgment experienced by some children during mania. Manic disinhibition can cause the lack of any impulse control, which leads to dangerous risk-taking behaviors. These often result in self-injury, shoplifting, and bizarre activities.

Poor impulse control manifests with varying degrees of aggression that range from verbal (threats, abusive language, cursing) to physical abuse (aimed at objects, pets/animals, oneself or other people, mostly parents, siblings, or friends). Verbal and physical aggression will occur more frequently among impulsive children or when they are under the influence of substances that decrease impulse control (that is, alcohol and marijuana).

AGGRESSION

Parents frequently report the presence of aggressive impulses toward the attachment figure (generally the mother) beginning as early as the first year of life. As children grow older, aggression is often directed toward both parents and siblings. Manic children (like adults) manifest poor judgment, think they are always right, and do not fear consequences. Reports of aggression by overwhelmed parents are often met with disbelief, negative judgments, suspicions of exaggeration, or as evidence of poor parenting by mental health professionals and relatives alike.

The mood state experienced by the child seems to determine the risk and direction of aggressive acts. If a young boy is in a manic state and is convinced his peers are out to get him, he will be prone to aggressive confrontations or fights. In a depressed or pessimistic mood, that same boy might inflict self-harm as a way to punish himself for losing or breaking a toy. Most of the acts of aggression tend to be purposeful and deliberate, as opposed to the aggression seen in children with ADHD, which is more likely to be the result of impulsivity or inattention (accidental rather than intentional).

As many parents know, much of the time in young children, aggression is contained within the house, and one parent generally gets the brunt of it; usually, but not always, the mother. As the child grows older, aggressive behavior increasingly targets siblings. Sometimes children are also unable to contain themselves with adults, peers, or younger children outside of the house.

Because of their grandiosity, manic children are self-assured and feel special. They may feel untouchable, above consequences, and sometimes above all rules (leading to rebellion), or laws (leading to crime). Clinicians and parents may interpret these behaviors, which are in blatant violation of all rules, as evidence of oppositional defiant disorder or conduct disorder.

Mania in Children: Emotional Symptoms

Emotional symptoms of mania in children include mood instability, euphoria, irritability, and outbursts of anger.

MOOD INSTABILITY

In most children with BD, mood states are very unstable and transient: moods shift frequently with little or no apparent cause. Clinicians describe this as *mood lability* (instability). In most cases of BD in children, these shifts in mood tend to be the most unpredictable and disabling symptoms because they affect learning as well as social and home behavior. Because of the high intensity of emotional reactions, any transition becomes a tremendous shock to the child's unstable system.

EUPHORIA

Many children with BD experience periods of euphoria, often very short-lived, with laughter and elation. Everything causes laughter; this silly, goofy behavior is uncontrollable. The child is joyful and giddy without clear reason: he/she can be the class clown, or act defiant and grandiose. Sometimes the child mocks adults who reprimand or punish him or her by laughing, or making sarcastic and abusive remarks. These are symptoms of mania, not a feature of ADHD.

IRRITABILITY

In many cases, chronic irritability pervades the child's day, provoking negative responses from family members, peers, and school personnel. The child is irritated and annoyed by everything, complains, protests, and fusses. For example, people routinely describe children with BD as rude or as having "an attitude." Superimposed on this chronic irritability are frequent shifts from calm to upset. These changes are unpredictable and confusing both for the children themselves and for those around them. Parents must deal with the consequences of such sudden changes. And, even though the symptoms are not always there, the impairment is chronic.

ANGER AND RAGES

Outbursts of anger and rage can be a really scary sight. The inability to modulate emotional responses can be particularly destructive. Anger attacks, crises, rages, and temper tantrums are some of the names given to these intense emotional states by parents. They range in severity from irritability to angry outbursts, temper tantrums, and rages, sometimes progressing to verbal and physical aggression. At these times, the child can appear as if in a trance, eyes in a gaze that some parents refer to as "the feral look." The child may have no or little recollection of these episodes, especially if he or she is very young. Although other children also experience this spectrum of emotions, children with BD do so with greater intensity and for longer periods of time, which often causes significant impairment.

Episodes of emotional loss of control vary in duration and frequency. Severity is not always an adequate way of assessing the effect of these episodes on a child or on his or her environment. For instance, serious consequences or marked impairment can be the result of mild but frequent outbursts. A child with mild chronic irritability might not be able to get along with peers during playdates or on the playground, leading to social isolation and rejection from those peers. An isolated but severe episode of rage at home might not produce the same consequences on the child's social life.

Mania in Children: Cognitive Symptoms

Cognitive symptoms of mania include distractibility, racing thoughts, rigidity, hyperfocus, and delusions. At the root of these manic symptoms is the fact that there is an excessive acceleration of all cognitive processes.

DISTRACTIBILITY

Distractibility is perhaps the most important sign of the manic activation of a child's cognitive functions. It is also, perhaps, the most disabling symptom, interfering with the completion of tasks and, when extreme, with self-care. Everything is exciting and stimulating, and attention is divided among many competing stimuli. Distractibility interferes with learning and usually causes negative responses toward the child from peers and adults. In a distractible state, the child responds to any new internal (ideas) or external (events) stimuli by switching from one activity to another. This makes it difficult to understand why a child with BD can pay attention and follow directions one day (or one minute), but the next day (or minute) cannot stay on task or even listen.

RACING AND CROWDED THOUGHTS

Children do not know how their minds work. For the most part they do not know what racing or crowded thoughts are. Racing thoughts are similar to fast-forwarded images on a screen; it is like switching channels or having two or more programs on at once. Some children with BD experience increased or accelerated thinking as a crowded or racing mind. The child might say that his or her mind is busy with thoughts, that ideas are "flying off my mind," or that thoughts are too fast to follow. This may be a lifelong condition for children with BD. They don't realize how active their minds are and they consider a running mental commentary normal. Almost always, they will acknowledge daydreaming, because they understand what that is.

RIGIDITY

A child with BD may be extremely sensitive to any change or transition. It is as if his or her emotional balance depends on a static, predictable, unchanging environment. Children with BD almost always have a strong desire to maintain control over their environment, and this can manifest in wanting to be in charge, or have everybody's attention, positive or negative, and opposing every plan that is not self-generated. Therefore, separations from parents or changes in plans or activities precipitate emotional meltdowns. Some transitions are easy, others are not.

The most challenging transitions are daily occurrences: going to sleep, getting up in the morning, going to school (separation), and coming home (homework). Many parents know firsthand what a challenge it can be to get a child with BD to go to sleep, to get up in the morning, and to go to school. There are children with BD who are early risers and good, efficient sleepers, but they are the exception to the rule.

HYPERFOCUS

The capacity to become deeply engrossed in an activity or idea is called *hyperfocus*. This symptom is found in some children and adults with BD. With hyperfocus, a child may get so deeply immersed in activities like reading, watching a movie, or playing a game that he or she looses the ability to stop and/or to switch to another activity. A certain food, toy, place, or object may become the focus of an unrelenting demand. This hyperfocus might appear willful or even *perseverative* (this means continuing to do something, such as repeating a word, even when it is clearly not useful or helpful).

The ability to change from one set of rules to another is often impaired in children with BD (see Executive Functions in chapter 6). This overinvolvement in activities makes it more difficult for the child to go through transitions, and can grossly impair his or her ability to function in school or in a group setting, because the child gets stuck in one activity and cannot change gears.

PSYCHOSIS

Psychosis in a child can manifest as a *delusion*, a false belief not based on factual information; or a *hallucination* (seeing, hearing, smelling, tasting, or feeling touched by something that is not there). These symptoms are affected by the child's mood state. *Euphoric mania* may lead to grandiose delusions such as announcing, "I have found the cure" for a disease. *Dysphoric mania* might lead to paranoid and/or persecutory delusions, like "That kid wants to hurt me." *Grandiose delusions* reflect inflated or very high self-esteem, sometimes with an unshakable belief that one has special powers. For example, delusional children have jumped from roofs, windows, and other great heights believing they could fly. Grandiosity often leads to boasting and exaggerations, but also to risk-taking and daring or impulsive behaviors.

Misunderstanding and misperceptions of verbal and nonverbal (body) language or misinterpretation of a situation also can be disabling. Children with BD often "read" facial expressions incorrectly.

Paranoid children might believe others are hostile or are planning something against them. These children might become aggressive for fear of being attacked. This fear can cause unprovoked, unpredictable aggression.

Depression in Children: Physical Symptoms

Depression in BD can be described as a depleted or low-energy state. The physical symptoms include decreased activity, passivity, increased sleep, appetite disturbances, and decreased speech. During these times, the child moves and talks less, sleeps and eats more, seems more passive and less oppositional, but he or she might become anxious, needy, and very dependent.

DECREASED ACTIVITY

Depression is characterized by low energy and decreased activity. During phases of depression, everything becomes an effort: it is a struggle to start or to complete the simplest activity or task. This leads to a slowing down of all physical activities, including talking, walking, and self-care. Many parents observe these behaviors early in the morning, upon awakening, when their child must get ready for school.

PASSIVITY

During a phase of depression, the child may become unmotivated, passive, given to procrastination, or too fatigued to even complete a task. Nothing seems to be interesting enough, all activities are boring, and the child refuses to engage in all suggested activities.

INCREASED SLEEP

In spite of increased amounts of sleep, the child still might complain of feeling tired. Increased sleep (or intermittent napping with little or no physical activity) is not sufficient to restore the energy of a depressed child. Lethargy is often reported by both the child and his or her parents. This may also explain extended morning grogginess, which often interferes with the morning routine.

APPETITE DISTURBANCES

Appetite disturbances are common during periods of depression. In some cases, especially in the winter months, children show an increase in appetite, mostly with carbohydrate cravings. In other cases, depression can cause nausea, and a decrease in appetite. Appetite disturbances can either lead to weight gain associated with overeating, or to weight loss.

DECREASED SPEECH

During a depressed state, a child might become less talkative (decreased speech) or respond with yes or no answers, refusing to engage in conversation. This might be a marked change for a child who is usually talkative and articulate.

Depression in Children: Emotional Symptoms

Emotional symptoms encountered during periods of depression include sadness, a sense of worthlessness, and suicidal ideation; lack of interest in formerly enjoyed activities (anhedonia); irritability; and low self-esteem.

SADNESS, TEARFULNESS

A pervasive sadness of mood is often a prominent symptom of depression. The child's facial expression is one of sadness, malaise, dissatisfaction, or upset, and he or she might be prone to crying easily. Feeling blue for no reason or because of very small disappointments can bring a child to tears every night.

FEELING WORTHLESS, SUICIDAL IDEATION

Feelings of worthlessness, guilt, self-reproach, and a pessimistic outlook on life are associated with sadness or depressed mood. Sometimes, the child feels hopelessness (no hope for the future), or helplessness (nothing can or will help), or both. Morbid or suicidal thoughts can occur often in children with BD. Suicidal ideation (wishing to be dead, never born, or a desire to actively end life) can be voiced (or communicated in writing), which is usually a sign that the child really has been thinking about this. These thoughts must be taken seriously: they require emergency consultation if the child is not already under psychiatric care.

LACK OF INTEREST AND MOTIVATION

In contrast to adults with BD who primarily experience sadness with depression, children and adolescents more commonly experience a lack or loss of interest, an overall lack of motivation, or an inability to enjoy activities or hobbies that were of great interest before.

IRRITABILITY

Irritability is a common expression of depression in children, but because irritability is also frequent during mania, it is not always helpful for recognizing the phase of the illness or for choosing an effective treatment. Most of the time, demands placed on the patient during periods of depression elicit irritability and hostile refusal. During mania, instead, irritability can be spontaneous and unprovoked, and it is usually more intense.

LOW SELF-ESTEEM

The effect of depression on self-esteem is usually profound, and does not always fully resolve with the remission of depressive symptoms. Low self-esteem can be very disabling, preventing a child from interacting socially with others; causing withdrawal from school or sports; and even isolation from siblings and other family members. A depressed child is unsure, lacks confidence, fears mistakes, and anticipates difficulties. Reluctance to make decisions adds to feelings of inadequacy, further lowering self-esteem.

Depression in Children: Cognitive Symptoms

Cognitive symptoms, characteristic of depression, are the result of a general dulling which slows down all mental functions. These symptoms include confusion or lack of mental clarity, indecisiveness, and poor concentration.

COGNITIVE DULLING

Depression affects most cognitive functions in a profound and negative way, sometimes almost completely shutting down short- and long-term memory, concentration, and attention. Depression can significantly alter IQ scores, lowering the child's ability to perform in most tests. A child with BD can score as much as 30 IQ points lower during an episode of depression; the IQ usually improves toward baseline when the symptoms have remitted. This is one reason we often see fluctuating IQ and other test scores over a child's school years.

When depressed, a child may voice this change in mental functions as self-criticism ("I am stupid") or as grounds for feeling inadequate ("I can never do anything right"). Poor concentration and problems with attention are frequent complaints, as they interfere with academic functioning. Even more frustrating and paralyzing are the child's difficulties in making decisions, often leading to procrastination (especially with homework), sometimes with serious consequences.

Mixed Symptoms and Rapid Cycling

In school-age children, depressive and/or mixed symptoms are usually more prominent than manic symptoms, often becoming more severe around puberty. At puberty, problems with mood dyscontrol, originally worst at home (but not apparent in school), start affecting school behavior and performance, interfering with school functioning and interpersonal relationships. In the majority of cases, depressive symptoms are prominent for several years before manic symptoms are detected. In these cases, parents are mostly concerned with their child's depressive symptoms and many professionals do not consider the possibility that latent bipolar disorder may be the cause of these symptoms.

In such cases, psychiatrists may start antidepressant treatment, inadvertently triggering mania, as happened in Jason and Greg's examples. Compared to adult forms, pediatric BD manifests with unstable periods of mixed symptomatology. This presentation, which can be very hard to diagnose, is often referred to as *subsyndromal* (the full criteria are not met), to distinguish it from *syndromal* BD (the full DSM criteria are met).

Most children with BD have chronic symptoms, so that they are never balanced or calm for very long. The child with BD becomes immersed in this chaos of emotions, tantrums, and unpredictable fluctuations from euphoric joy to thoughts of suicide, from relaxed to irritable or violent.

Waxing and waning symptoms, sometimes with remissions, cause ongoing instability (ultra-ultra-rapid cycling). Regardless of the severity, the type and duration of the symptoms, the final outcome is always markedly uneven functioning, and some level of impairment.

4

Bipolar Disorder
in Adolescents

Distinguishing normal adolescent behaviors from the symptoms of a mood disorder is extremely difficult. Few adolescents are not irritable or oppositional, but this is not necessarily the result of an illness. For this reason, a lot of confusion exists about what is "normal adolescent behavior" as opposed to illness. Determining which behaviors are symptomatic can be difficult for a parent, and can delay treatment, allowing dysfunctional behaviors to persist.

ADOLESCENCE AND BIPOLAR DISORDER

In some cases, a trigger or precipitating life event leads to a marked change in a teenager's behavior and ability to function in school and/or at home. This type of "acute" or sudden onset can be observed both in manic and depressive phases. Much more common is a subtle and insidious onset of symptoms that gradually changes the teen's demeanor and behavior. Sometimes, symptoms fluctuate, waxing and waning over the course of a day (*diurnal mood variations*), a week, or longer periods of time.

When symptoms are present on and off for very long periods (months, years), we call them *subchronic*, to distinguish them from *chronic* symptoms that remain virtually unchanged for a long time. Because of an insidious onset and the subchronic or chronic course of bipolar disorder (BD), parents (and teachers) might become accustomed to manic symptoms such as aggression, disturbed sleep, increased activity, and impaired concentration. As the symptoms of early-onset BD may be intermittent, or may follow a fluctuating pattern, clinicians and parents often misjudge these symptoms as willful, intentional behaviors, or adolescent excesses, and respond with a stern or punitive attitude.

Symptoms of BD, like moodiness, impulsiveness, irritability, and oppositional or defiant behavior, must be distinguished from developmentally appropriate adolescent rebellious behaviors, which can also cause intense power struggles with parents and other authority figures. A teenager's need for independence is an integral part of normal development, including rejection of parental guidance and authority. Parental limits and rules are often ignored or actively broken, which can lead to power struggles and confrontations between parents and their teenage children.

For example, most adolescents struggle with curfews. A "normal" fourteen-year-old might stay out one hour later than agreed upon, while a fourteen-year-old with BD might come home at 4 A.M. after engaging in risky behaviors, such as underage drinking or unprotected sex.

In BD, abnormal behaviors are part of a syndrome, in which other symptoms are also present, like a history or pattern of difficulties with mood, energy, sleep, and/or concentration. This helps to differentiate between isolated instances of adolescent rebellious behavior and the symptoms of a disorder like BD. A family history of BD, as discussed in chapter 2, is also extremely important in trying to differentiate normal from abnormal adolescent behavior.

In adolescents, symptoms of anxiety (panic or social and school phobias), eating disorders, and comorbid substance abuse must be distinguished from normal development, social adjustment, changes in self-esteem, self-image, and predictable experimentation with risk-taking behaviors. A marked degree of variability can be observed among adolescents and this can affect the way BD begins to interfere with home, school, and social life. The following vignettes can help illustrate differences in symptoms or patterns according to age and gender.

■ Amy: Manic, Grandiose, and Hypersexual at Age Thirteen

Amy had just turned thirteen when her cousin died of cancer. He had been sick for several months, and Amy had become increasingly depressed. A moody girl since childhood, Amy had had short bouts of depression or sadness in the past, usually brought on by behavior problems in school: she had been suspended once for hitting a peer, and had received several warnings for stealing pens and pencils and for knocking down the Christmas tree in class.

Amy's pediatrician had suggested starting an antidepressant in anticipation of the imminent death of her cousin. When her cousin died, Amy's depressive symptoms increased. She cried a lot, refused to go to school, and had suicidal thoughts and anxiety attacks. After a few weeks she was doing better, even though she told her mom that her thoughts were still racing through her mind.

Toward the end of the school year, her behavior changed. She started dressing very provocatively, cutting school, and leaving class early to hang out with her boyfriend, a seventeen-year-old from the local high school. At summer camp, Amy, who previously had been well-liked by most of the staff and her peers, "argued with everybody about everything," as she put it herself. After she refused to follow curfews, Amy became agitated and restless. Her parents were asked to take her home when she was verbally and physically abusive to the camp director who had tried to calm her down.

When her parents picked her up, Amy told them in very rapid, pressured speech that she'd been singled out because she was too smart and pretty. She had not been able to sleep for days, had lost a lot of weight, and was so hyper that they had to stop the car several times on the way home to let her stretch her legs, as she felt quite restless.

At our first meeting, Amy was very excited, talked very fast, and jumped from one subject to the other every few seconds, making it difficult for anyone to follow what she was saying. She said she thought about her boyfriend all the time, and had a great idea for a business she could start up with him. She didn't think there was anything wrong with her, except for high anxiety. Amy said that she had engaged in unprotected sex and also wanted to be an "egg donor" because "I am pretty, smart, and healthy."

Advised by the pediatrician, her parents stopped her antidepressant and things seemed to normalize for a while. A few days later, Amy became obsessed with her weight, and started refusing breakfast, avoiding bread, pasta, and rice. She asked to be allowed to eat only salads, and this worried her parents. Six months later Amy was caught with amphetamines in her purse: Amy said she needed them to help her concentrate, but her mother thinks Amy was using them as a way to lose weight.

To summarize, Amy's symptoms began in childhood, with emotional instability, impulsive aggression, and intermittent depressive symptoms. Her cousin's death triggered a depressive episode, and she was treated with antidepressants which initially helped. Amy recovered from the depression, but then she became manic, hypersexual, and grandiose. Even after the antidepressant was discontinued, Amy remained unstable, started manifesting symptoms of an eating disorder, and was abusing stimulants.

■ Philip: Bipolar Depression and Academic Failure

Philip's father called us to inquire about treatment for his fifteen-year-old son's depressive symptoms. Adopted at birth, Philip had always been a quiet child. He was capable of taking six-hour car trips to visit his grandparents without ever saying a word. He just sat quietly in the backseat busy with his thoughts or daydreaming while listening to his music playing.

After a summer spent mostly at home, brooding over a breakup with his girlfriend of ten months, his first year of high school was a complete disaster. His grades, usually A's and B's, dropped to D's and F's. At first, his parents were angry at his lack of effort. As things went from bad to worse, they began to punish Philip by taking away TV and computer time, and they made any social interactions with his peers contingent upon completion of his homework.

When nothing worked, they became resigned to school failure, as Philip became increasingly isolated. At the advice of a school counselor (a family friend), Philip was tested for learning disabilities (LD). His IQ was average, with some evidence of depression but no evidence of a learning disability. The school psychologist said that Philip's school difficulties might be due to symptoms of his depression but also to executive functioning deficits, i.e., difficulties that interfere with organizing, thinking through a task, anticipating problems, mental flexibility, and completing tasks. (See chapter 6 for further discussion of learning disabilities and executive functioning.)

When the testing demonstrated that Philip had significant problems with memory, sustained attention, and keeping ideas in proper sequence, along with depression, Philip's teachers were then able to see why he was so disorganized, lacked initiative to start and/or complete projects, and was forgetful and confused about homework and tests.

At the school psychologist's suggestion, Philip was evaluated by a psychiatrist for antidepressant medications. For nine months now, Philip has been taking an antidepressant but there has been no improvement.

Our first meeting was very productive. As soon as his parents left the room, Philip described problems with concentration, feelings of sadness, and a complete lack of motivation; yet, he does not believe he's depressed. Actually, he doesn't believe in depression: He said, "I feel 'real' only when I'm down; 'happy' is just an act." He still cares about his ex-girlfriend, but he doesn't believe this is affecting him nowadays. He told us he daydreams a lot, and he gets teary very easily if he sees a sad movie.

When asked if his friends would describe him as moody, he smiled and nodded emphatically. Music can make him very happy, or put him down in the dumps. We talked about feeling extremely happy when a certain song is played: the happiness can last for an hour or two. He reported, "I'm just being happy for no reason." It starts with the music and can continue for a while. Sometimes, he finds cartoons so funny he cannot stop laughing. He said he thinks he laughs too much because "those cartoons aren't really that funny." When he's in that "funny mood," he always feels energized and hyper.

His parents have also noticed short periods of "extreme excitement," as when they offered to pay him to clean out the garage. In contrast to his schoolwork, his parents said that Philip was "so efficient and so fast, his eyes were wide open

and excited, the music blasting. . . . He didn't stop for hours."
Philip smiled, listening to his parents' report, and said, "I was
feeling really good."

Over time, Philip's symptoms of hypomania, alternating with depression, are becoming more intense and severe. Antidepressants and strict discipline are not helping him. School failure, possibly due to the deficits in his executive skills, common in adolescents with BD, further complicates the symptoms of depression and further affects his already low self-esteem. His short-lived euphoric hypomanic periods suggest that Philip may be suffering from BD type II (see chapter 2).

■ Anthony: Substance Abuse and School Failure

At sixteen, Anthony feels that he has his own life to live and there is no reason for his parents to interfere. Anthony is increasingly rude, evasive, and angry when his parents make attempts at setting limits. He goes out with his friends "into town" and often doesn't come home until after 11 P.M. on weeknights and much later on weekends. He was caught drinking with his friends in the park several days after a previous drinking incident had occurred at a friend's home.

As an infant, Anthony was excitable, stubborn, and demanding. His mother remembers, with dread, his difficulties with sleep: Anthony fought going to sleep, had trouble falling asleep, and was irritable after taking naps. He did not want to be separated from his mom, and made a scene whenever she was not by his side. In first grade, he was unable to sit still in class, was restless, and seemed to have too much energy.

His parents told us that he cycles: his down periods of sadness can last for as long as a week, bouts of giddiness or temper tantrums last only a few minutes, while restlessness lasts for a day or less. During a temper tantrum, his facial expression becomes distorted and his parents say he looks "evil" and "wild" then. In a tantrum, Anthony screams, curses viciously, slams doors, kicks walls, and makes threatening gestures.

Sometimes, Anthony seems depressed or voices low self-esteem. Periods of withdrawal alternate with short-lived moods of silliness and grandiosity and extended periods of irritability. He annoys his siblings, defies rules, and steals money from his mother and brother. In the last year, he's made several attempts to run away from home. Anthony's father was recently diagnosed with BD and he's doing better. He is hopeful that good treatment will also help Anthony.

During the evaluation, Anthony responded to questions by nodding his head; he didn't know, nor did he want to know, why his parents had brought him to see a psychiatrist. When asked about whether he was getting along at home and at school, he pulled his coat over his head and refused to answer all questions.

Several days after our meeting, Anthony was pulled over and charged with driving at night without a proper license and under the influence of alcohol. The court sentenced him to mandatory psychiatric treatment. During his first week in treatment, Anthony admitted to drinking almost every day for the past several months and experimenting with marijuana and Ecstasy (a synthetic amphetamine) to try to feel better. "Self-medicating behavior," common among youngsters with mood disorders, has the potential to delay diagnosis and decrease response to treatment.

Anthony has a history of early sleep dysregulation, wide mood swings, tantrums, and inability to control his anger, all of which have disruptive consequences on family relations. BD runs in his family. The tantrums and chronic irritability are extremely disabling in terms of personal and social development, and self-medicating is only adding to his problems.

■ Natalie: Mixed Mania and Self-Harm in a Teenager

Natalie, a seventeen-year-old, had always excelled in school, until the end of the last school year. For no obvious reasons, last spring, her grades started to slip and, for the first time, she didn't get straight A's. After the term ended, she was upset and moody for most of the summer. She became withdrawn and irritable.

Her first alarming behavior took place in August, when her father, returning home from a business trip, found Natalie sitting on the fire escape of their four-story building, dangling her legs over the edge. When asked what she was doing, Natalie couldn't give an explanation.

Then, her parents noticed that she wasn't returning any of her friends' calls, always seemed agitated and very irritable, and complained about not being able to sleep because her mind was "too busy thinking." A few days later, while reorganizing Natalie's closet, her mother found a T-shirt covered with blood stains. When confronted by her mom, Natalie became very angry, abusive, and threatened to kill herself.

When she calmed down, she confessed to cutting her thighs and ankles "because it makes me feel better." Her cuts were so deep that her mother, who had studied nursing, brought her to the emergency room at a local hospital. After a psychiatrist spoke to her, it became clear that Natalie couldn't promise she would not hurt herself again, and she was admitted to the psychiatric ward. She told the doctor that she had wanted to kill herself but had not been able to find the courage to jump off the fire escape or to cut her wrists, as she had seen in movies. She had written a suicide note with her own blood which her mother later found underneath her mattress.

In this teenager, a significant change in school functioning and behavior at home, combined with irritability and agitation, were the first symptoms to appear. Social withdrawal, sleep disturbances, and racing thoughts frequently seem to precede suicidal thoughts and self-harm associated with restlessness and hopelessness.

THE CLINICAL PICTURE

Like many hereditary disorders, BD can begin in infancy, childhood, adolescence, young adulthood, or later in life. The manifestations of BD differ depending on several variables. We think it is an important first step to recognize and distinguish individual characteristics and the illness's variables from comorbid illnesses and environmental factors. Table 5 below provides an overview of these variables.

Table 5: Variables Affecting the Clinical Picture

Individual	Illness	Comorbidity	Environmental
Temperament	BD Subtype	Medical, Neurological	Season
Personality	Psychosis	Psychiatric	Diet
Intelligence	Symptoms' severity	Substance abuse	Trauma
Insight	Recurrence rate	Learning disabilities	Medications
Maturity	Symptom-free intervals	Sensory integration	Overstimulation

Individual Characteristics

The effects of BD on a child can be quite different depending on the child's developmental stage at the time of the illness's onset. For example, severe and recurrent forms of BD can have a different effect on the life of an adult as opposed to a child. In an adult, the illness starts causing problems after the individual has completed his or her education, has developed interpersonal relationships, and mastered most, if not all, developmental tasks.

In contrast, the onset of BD during the preschool or school years can severely interfere with a child's ongoing social and educational development. An early onset can have a damaging effect on educational and social development, profoundly affecting self-esteem and impairing interpersonal relationships.

Temperament describes the most basic settings of mood and energy regulation. It can be recognized very early in infancy, well before personality traits are formed. For instance, a child can be born with a high energy level and a pleasant, agreeable mood as opposed to a low energy level and a shy, anxious, or irritable mood. These features might represent temperamental settings affecting how the infant or child interacts with and experiences the world. Temperament can determine how the child perceives the environment: pleasant and reassuring versus unpleasant and threatening.

For this reason, temperament has a profound effect on the symptoms and the clinical presentation of BD. These innate qualities may determine the child's tendency toward manifestations of depression, mania, or anxiety; and they may modify the clinical picture of BD while it is still unfolding.

Personality traits, especially narcissistic and borderline traits, have been associated with BD. Note that some features of BD can be mistaken for personality traits. Narcissistic features, often associated with mania, are prominent in children and adolescents with BD: for example, a lack of empathy and the presence of egocentricity can be characteristic of some children with BD.

Emotional reactivity and a sensitivity to rejection are common features of borderline personality disorder (BPD). There is some overlap between these personality disorders and a subsyndromal or latent form of BD. If symptoms are resolved with pharmacological treatment, that is an indication that these are symptoms of BD rather than features of the child's still developing personality.

Intelligence, as measured by standard IQ testing, can greatly affect the way BD manifests in children, adolescents, and adults. The ability to learn verbal and nonverbal forms of communication can greatly influence social interaction, education, and self-esteem, as well as the development of effective coping skills for dealing with mood instability.

Insight, or the ability to see oneself from another person's perspective, is an extremely important factor in the treatment of BD. Insight sometimes goes hand in hand with cognitive maturation. In other words, the older and more mature the person, the better, usually, is their insight. Of course, there are great individual variations in insight. A child of ten might have great insight, while an intelligent adult might completely lack any insight into his or her problems. Insight helps the child to recognize that something is "wrong," and to ask for help. For this reason, fostering the development of insight, at any age, is essential to the successful treatment of BD.

Illness Variables

Depending on the bipolar disorder subtype, your child might experience symptoms of mania (BP-I) or hypomania (BP-II, BP-NOS, or cyclothymia) that can easily be recognized; they may or may not be associated with depressive symptoms of variable severity. Depressive symptoms can be the most prominent presentation of BD. This is especially true in BP-II forms, but also in many BP-I forms, where the first manic episode might follow one or more episodes of depression.

Manic, depressive, and mixed bipolar phases may cause psychotic symptoms, requiring a *differential diagnosis*, that is, to differentiate BD from schizophrenia and other psychotic disorders, and usually affecting the urgency and type of treatment (see chapter 14). In all phases, the severity of the symptoms of BD can go from very mild to moderate to severe, causing different levels of disability. The severity of the symptom and disability are not always correlated. In other words, mild symptoms may cause severe disability, while severe symptoms might not always be disabling. For instance, a psychotic child will be recognized as "being sick" and referred for treatment, while an irritable teen might be suspended several times and fail the grade, receiving no help at all.

Another important variable is the presence of symptom-free intervals. During such an interval, symptoms might remit and all but disappear. Descriptions of the classic (adult) forms of BD include symptom-free (euthymic) intervals, while subchronic and chronic forms without symptom-free intervals are the norm in early-onset BD.

Comorbid Disorders

Other medical and psychiatric disorders can be present along with BD, posing challenges to both diagnosis and treatment (see chapter 6). Medical comorbidities are common. For instance, a course of steroids for asthma can trigger manic/hypomanic symptoms and, sometimes, even psychosis, in a vulnerable child. Liver, kidney, and thyroid disorders can interfere with the treatment of BD. A decreased thyroid function (*hypothyroidism*) can cause decreased energy, sluggish mental functioning, and increased sleep, all of which can look like depression.

The treatment of a comorbid psychiatric disorder (like panic attacks or obsessive-compulsive disorder) might require antidepressants, which, at times, can exacerbate manic symptoms or increase cycling (see chapter 8). In school-age children, attention-deficit/hyperactivity disorder might require treatment with stimulants; this can cause sleep disturbances, increase irritability and, at times, trigger hypomania or mania (see chapter 8).

In other cases, comorbid substance abuse/dependence disorder can interfere with both diagnosis and treatment of BD by causing mood instability and/or reducing response to treatment (see chapter 6). In preschoolers, sensory dysregulation (hypersensitivity to various stimuli) will cause increased emotional dysregulation (see chapter 6).

Environmental Variables

Changes in the environment can have a profound effect on a child with BD. The birth of a sibling, the separation or divorce of parents, relocation and/or a change of school, recent losses (illness/ death of a relative or friend, school failure), or trauma and/or abuse can trigger the onset of BD in genetically vulnerable, that is, predisposed children.

Parenting style and parental variables (i.e., depression or other medical illness) profoundly affect the environment in which the child grows. Many aspects of a school day (completing tests or assignments on time, being called upon to answer questions, fitting in socially, being teased or bullied) can function as environmental stressors. The child's perspective on his or her environment—that is, how the child sees and understands what is happening in his or her life—will determine which specific circumstances or experiences act as stressors, causing symptoms to surface.

Sleep deprivation (insomnia, sleep interruptions, nightmares), too much caffeine, pharmacological treatments (stimulants or antidepressants, steroids, ephedrine—found in cough and decongestant medication), or discontinuation of medications can all cause mood instability.

In vulnerable individuals, even seasonal changes of light or temperature may be enough to bring about mood instability or new recurrences of the illness. Often the environmental factors lead to an episode of BD through the common pathway of sleep disturbances.

5

Clinical Assessment

As we have seen, bipolar disorder (BD) can present in a multitude of ways, and many children with this disorder can receive several conflicting diagnoses before they are correctly diagnosed. Unfortunately, the same thing happens frequently with adults.

DEREK: MULTIPLE DIAGNOSES IN A SEVENTEEN-YEAR-OLD BOY

Now seventeen, Derek is the "class clown" with a terrific sense of humor and a long list of psychiatric diagnoses. The first diagnosis, made when he was eight years old, was that of "nonverbal learning disability." At age nine, Derek was diagnosed with attention-deficit disorder (ADD), and treated with stimulants. At that time, he was having problems with his studies and with discipline, and complained about anxiety. Since then, he has attended many boarding schools, and seen many psychiatrists, psychologists, and school counselors. The reasons: clowning around in class, starting physical fights, using abusive language, and defying authority.

As a teenager, he's become even more oppositional and abusive. He's also started smoking marijuana and drinking alcohol.

Derek's room is a complete mess with leftover food, empty soda
cans, and dirty clothes piled up on the floor. His sleep patterns
are erratic: during manic periods he's often up till 3 or 4 A.M.
or goes without sleep entirely, but when he becomes depressed,
he can sleep for twenty hours straight.

His parents describe him as "either manic or depressed."
When manic, Derek thinks he's a very talented businessman,
and he has grand schemes for his company's success. When he's
depressed, he loses all interest in it. Then, as soon as he becomes
manic again, he starts making new plans to build his company.

In everyday life, however, he's not able to follow through
with his chores, is verbally abusive to his parents, and openly
steals money from his mother. Socially, he cannot keep friends.
"Nobody is good enough for me," he says, and those peers he
once was friendly with have been alienated, insulted, or attacked.
When he's depressed, he feels guilty about how he treated them.

Derek has dropped out of high school and cannot keep a
job, and his parents are very concerned. They've made a list of
the (DSM) diagnoses he's received over the years: bipolar disorder,
generalized anxiety disorder, oppositional defiant disorder, ADHD,
parent/child relational problem, learning disorder–not otherwise
specified (LD-NOS), and alcohol and marijuana abuse. Nothing
seems to change or help.

Many parents have found themselves in similar diagnostic confusion: does the child suffer from several disorders, or has he or she been
misdiagnosed? These diagnostic uncertainties affect treatment as different diagnoses might lead to different, sometimes opposite treatment
recommendations. To prevent this from happening, a thorough
diagnostic evaluation is a good starting point.

A DIAGNOSTIC PUZZLE

Putting together the many pieces of the diagnostic puzzle has profound implications for reaching a correct diagnosis and prescribing
effective treatment. Both have to take into account the uniqueness of
each child as well as his or her present and future needs. The emphasis must be on a comprehensive assessment of all areas of the child's

functioning: at home, in school, and socially. Developmental and educational histories help us to understand the child's strengths and weaknesses, such as learning or sensory integration difficulties. A history of bipolar disorder in the family confirms a genetic vulnerability, and a thorough history of past medication trials can provide good clues for future treatment. Previously adverse responses to certain medications, for instance, may predict similar responses with other drugs of the same class.

Familiarity with the symptoms of BD varies, but it is not uncommon for the child's parents to be quite knowledgeable about BD. Some have BD themselves, or their spouse does, or they can remember observing symptoms of BD (often undiagnosed) in other family members (often siblings or parents). A lack of familiarity with the symptoms of BD and/or language difficulties in describing the symptoms often delays diagnosis for years.

DIAGNOSTIC EVALUATION

When the child hasn't been diagnosed yet, the most important but delicate task is to gather all the relevant clinical information to help make a diagnosis. Note that all of the subjects called out in the bulleted list below should be discussed during the initial evaluation of the child. This will guarantee a thorough diagnostic assessment.

- Child's prenatal (before birth), perinatal (around delivery/ birth), and developmental history

- Pre-school and school functioning

- Psychosocial history (family structure, parents' marital/work history, the circumstances the child is raised in)

- Medical history

- Family history of psychiatric and substance use disorders

- Symptoms' frequency (how often), severity (how severe), duration (how long), and disability (how impairing)

- Chronological history of the symptoms and their severity, from their initial presentation throughout the child's life

- The effect of environmental factors on symptoms, including seasonal changes, sleep deprivation, overstimulation, sugar, caffeine, and/or illicit drugs

- Psychological and neuropsychological assessment

- Pharmacotherapy history, i.e., response to treatment with mood stabilizers, atypical antipsychotics, antidepressants, stimulants, and steroids

The following section offers suggestions for gathering all the relevant information for the initial assessment of a child or adolescent. There isn't a right or wrong way to conduct an evaluation, because different clinicians do things differently. There are, however, some minimum standards that are professionally accepted and are followed by most clinicians.

At the end of the evaluation, parents and clinicians should have an initial idea about the following: primary diagnosis (the main problem affecting the child); secondary or comorbid diagnoses (other diagnoses affecting the child, both medical and psychiatric); precipitants or triggers (medications, life events or traumas, including family, social, or school issues); strengths and weaknesses (talents, interests, developmental delays); and the child's overall functioning in school, at home, and in social settings.

GATHERING CLINICAL INFORMATION

From the very first communication with a family, a clinician should try to understand and decide whether the child can be evaluated in an outpatient setting (usually the case) or requires an emergency evaluation (usually in a psychiatric emergency room). If this cannot be determined through a telephone conversation, the clinician should meet both parent(s) and child in order to assess the child's current needs. Regardless of the circumstances, the clinician should assess, with your input, what type of treatment your child needs.

First and foremost: Is the child safe at home? Are the other family members safe? Is crisis intervention necessary? The clinician must get a sense of the situation and will then be able to suggest a suitable evaluation process for the child.

Parent Interview

The most important element of the initial parent interview is for the parent to feel heard and understood. Regardless of your child's symptoms, many of you have never told anyone about your worries, hopes, and isolation. Unless the clinician can provide you with the opportunity to discuss the painful details about living with a bipolar child, you may never be fully comfortable with your child's treatment.

Despite their short lives, most bipolar children have complicated histories of multiple evaluations, treatments, and interventions. Before your first appointment, a clinician might ask you to fill out questionnaires (used to gather background information). This will help you to think about your child's whole life, both past and current symptoms and behaviors, and to put things into a chronological perspective. The information on the questionnaires will also help you to keep the focus on your main concerns during the initial interview.

A parent's perspective is very helpful to a clinician for gaining a deeper understanding of the child's difficulties as well as his or her strengths. The clinician learns important details about weaknesses, strengths, and problems by reviewing the completed questionnaires during the parent interview. We encourage you to work with your clinician to learn about BD, as this will certainly improve your understanding of what you have witnessed over the years and what you are observing currently.

The clinician should also obtain from you extensive family histories of any psychiatric disorders, on both the maternal and paternal sides of the family (blood relatives only), including substance and/or alcohol abuse, psychoses, mood disorders, and learning disabilities.

During the interview, your responses help a clinician to confirm or exclude the presence of certain symptoms; this advances both the clinician's and your own understanding of your child's difficulties. Examining your child's symptoms with the clinician will help you to become familiar with some psychiatric terms and symptomatology. The emphasis of this approach is to develop a common language, using terms you both understand, as an important step in developing a close collaboration and exchange between child, parent, and clinician.

Ideally, a clinician should collect information on your child's prenatal care, birth, and early development; current family makeup (who lives with whom and where); history of trauma; medical and neurological history; allergies; school and learning issues, focusing on cognitive strengths and weaknesses; and details about the symptoms, especially their course over time, as well as current and past treatment history.

Questionnaires

In order to make the assessment as thorough and time-efficient as possible, we use some questionnaires (see below). These questionnaires are filled out before the parent interview, so they can be discussed during the interview. Note that you should always review your answers to questionnaires with a clinician, to avoid any misunderstandings that might occur. Some of the questionnaires used at our Mood Disorders Center include the following:

THE MOOD DISORDERS CENTER QUESTIONNAIRE-CHILD VERSION (MDCQ-C)

Over the years, many questionnaires have been developed to assist in screening children and adolescents for psychiatric symptoms. The MDCQ-C, developed by Dr. Faedda, gathers specific details about symptoms, including the age when the disorder first appeared; its severity, duration, frequency; and its effects on everyday life. We focus your attention on the particular ways that symptoms first manifested early in the child's life: which symptom(s) appeared first and which followed, and their fluctuating patterns of recurrence.

THE CHILD BEHAVIOR CHECKLIST (CBCL)

Clinicians use the CBCL in the assessment of children with emotional or behavioral difficulties. This instrument provides a profile that highlights several areas of psychopathology: high scores on some CBCL scales (delinquent and aggressive behavior, somatic complaints, anxious/depressed, and thought problems) have been associated with mania in prepubertal children. The CBCL is not, however, a diagnostic instrument, but rather a well-established, efficient screening tool for child psychopathology. As such, the CBCL is helpful in the comprehensive assessment of children with BD.

THE OVERT AGGRESSION SCALE (OAS)

The OAS is a survey of aggressive behaviors that can provide important details and is easily rated. Aggression is frequent in children with BD, and it is useful to clearly document past or current incidents. Clinicians use the OAS to assess symptoms at baseline and as a follow-up measure. In fact, effective treatment usually reduces or stops aggression.

YALE-BROWN OBSESSIVE COMPULSIVE SCALE (YBOCS)

The Yale-Brown Obsessive Compulsive Scale rates your child's obsessive thoughts and/or compulsive behaviors. Obsessions and compulsions can have a negative impact on a child's functioning, and may require additional treatment.

SENSORY PROFILE, CHILD VERSION

The Sensory Profile, developed by Dr. Winnie Dunn, an occupational therapist, measures your child's sensitivity to different types of sensory input, and how the information is processed in the different sensory modalities. This tool helps clinicians identify your child's sensitivities and behavioral and processing difficulties with various stimuli.

Child Interview

An interview with your child offers the clinician an opportunity to understand how your child experiences and says about what you see as a problem. It is also an opportunity to learn about your child's personality, self-esteem, interests, wishes, and fears. In addition, the interview is useful for determining your child's capacity to observe and identify his or her own symptoms and the consequences they cause. Depending on the child's age, the interview will rely more or less on play and dialogue.

During the interview, the therapist can observe how the child separates from his or her parent(s), and assess the child's anxiety level, shyness, and/or self-confidence. These can all be evaluated by the way the child plays, relates to parents and other adults, in addition to verbal and social skills, impulse control, activity level, mood and *affect* (see chapter 2), as well as attention span and distractibility.

In young children and adolescents, the Upset Scale (see chapter 11) developed by Dr. Austin can be used to determine how aware, how comfortable, or how defensive your child is when talking about moodiness and anger. These are some of the variables a professional will try to assess during an initial diagnostic evaluation.

Mood Charting (MoodLog)

Daily mood charting is the most reliable and efficient way to monitor symptoms of BD over time. The goal of keeping track of your child's moods is to identify patterns of mood instability. This information can then be used to help predict or prevent recurrences by means of early intervention. For example, if you observe that every spring your child's sleep decreases and his or her symptoms worsen, your child's doctor might prescribe something to help your child sleep well.

In some cases, only *longitudinal monitoring*, i.e., monitoring that goes on for several weeks, months, or years, will reveal a recurrence pattern according to the season or in response to environmental stressors (homework, caffeine use, sleep deprivation), which are otherwise difficult to recognize.

Many instruments and charts are used for longitudinal monitoring of symptoms and sleep. Most also keep track of medications' type and dose. We use the MoodLog™; developed by Dr. Faedda as a diary for patients with BD, it provides a simple way to organize and record information (see appendix II).

Monitoring Levels of Activity

Actigraphy (the recording and analysis of activity levels) is a noninvasive tool for the assessment of activity, sleep, and circadian rhythms. Preliminary data suggest that activity patterns may differ according to diagnosis and phase of illness. Besides providing objective measures of daily activity, actigraphy appears to provide some helpful data that might one day refine diagnostic practices (Faedda and Teicher 2005).

Educational Assessment

School reports, educational, psychological, and neuropsychological evaluations will help assess your child's present levels of cognitive and academic functioning. A significant difference between current cognitive potential (as measured by IQ in a psychological evaluation) and academic functioning may be caused by a mood disorder, attention-deficit or anxiety disorder, as well as a number of learning disabilities. Learning can be negatively affected by difficulties with attention, memory, and executive functions; problems with auditory and visual processing; and impaired fine or gross motor skills (see chapter 6). Cognitive functions, especially executive skills are often impaired by BD, causing deterioration of academic performance. A change in your child's school and intellectual functioning may suggest that BD and other potential comorbid deficits interfere with learning.

The negative impact on cognitive functions and the degree of alertness can be detected during episodes of illness as well as partial remissions. The possible side effect of cognitive deterioration due to medication may add to the negative affect of mood instability and produce learning difficulties. On the other hand, remission of symptoms can be usually associated with recovery of premorbid (before the illness's onset) levels of cognitive functioning.

NEUROPSYCHOLOGICAL EVALUATION

A neuropsychological evaluation is a systematic and comprehensive assessment of a person's current mental, emotional, and behavioral functioning, administered by a trained psychologist. For children with BD who also have learning difficulties, a neuropsychological evaluation can determine which aspects of brain functioning, mentioned above, affect daily functioning. One outcome of such an evaluation would be recommendations for specific, useful interventions. We often encourage this assessment which can also serve as a baseline to assess progress (or lack thereof) in the future. (More about the specifics of neuropsychological evaluation are in chapter 13, School Decisions.)

Parent/Child Communication

An important part of the clinician's assessment is to observe how you and your child interact, the level of emotional intensity of your interactions, and your ability to understand and help your child when his or her emotions become too intense. Clinicians also observe your ability to avoid or prevent the escalation of a disagreement into an emotionally charged argument, and whether your child views you as a source of help or upset (or both). This is, of course, relative, especially because distorted perceptions are a symptom of BD, and your child might distort your words, actions, and motives depending on his or her mood state. For these reasons, the parent/child relationship needs to be observed over time and in different situations.

For the most part, children recognize the balancing, supportive role of their parents, but sometimes a child may be intensely adversarial with one or both parents, refusing their help and support. If the parent has enough emotional stability to tolerate the child's mood swings, he or she will be able to fulfill the role of co-regulator of the child's mood state. In this role the parent is able to help the child return to a state of emotional balance.

Treatment History and Medical Records

In spite of their young age, many of the children with BD have extensive and complex treatment histories. Often, many clinicians across different disciplines have evaluated one or more aspects of the child's problems, sometimes reaching conflicting conclusions or diagnoses. Valuable information about the child's illness can be obtained from sources as diverse as school or hospital records, or records of previous courses of treatment and other interventions.

It is always helpful for clinicians to obtain permission to communicate with other current and past treatment team members. Sometimes, important information (a side effect, a symptom) needs to be shared with the other members of the treatment team. Regular contact between you and all of your child's clinicians is beneficial to the overall success of treatment; ongoing, open communication can guide and support both stabilization and remission.

6

Diagnostic Overlap and Multiple Diagnoses

Elias is a four-year-old boy who becomes aggressive, yells, and kicks when his mother asks him to put on a clean shirt, unless it is the soft, blue cotton T-shirt he wants to wear every day. He's a poor sleeper and very fussy with food: he wants only chicken fingers for lunch and dinner. He hates to put on his jacket to go outside, even in the middle of winter, and his mother says he "never listens." For example, when he goes outside to play, he gets so involved in play that he ignores his mother when she calls him to come inside.

Other times, he won't even go outside, or can't find any thing to do, becoming so irritable that his mother leaves him alone to watch cartoons or a video. In preschool, Elias has difficulty completing puzzles and hates to draw. In the classroom and on the playground, he bumps into others and falls a lot. The teacher describes him as "accident prone." At times, Elias is very interested in books and stories and talks a lot. At other times, he's withdrawn, stares into space, and seems to be in his own world. Elias's parents are very concerned because of his aggressive reaction when they try to hold or comfort him. Elias becomes wild and full of rage, and he pushes his parents away yelling, "I hate you."

DIAGNOSTIC ACCURACY

As we have seen in the previous chapter, diagnosing bipolar disorder (BD) is like a lengthy scientific investigation. It involves searching for, and putting together, information from different sources: the child, the family, school records, and interviews with school and mental health professionals. The diagnosis is the key to effective treatment and its starting point, directing all therapeutic interventions. A thorough diagnostic evaluation improves accuracy and usually leads to a successful treatment plan. Many of you might know from personal experience that, if the diagnosis is incorrect, your child will not benefit from treatment.

The clinician has the responsibility to correctly identify BD, but also to exclude the presence of other disorders. Two major obstacles interfere with the correct identification of BD: first, the symptoms of many psychiatric disorders overlap, making it difficult to differentiate BD from other conditions; second, several psychiatric disorders can also occur in combination with bipolar disorder, a phenomenon called *comorbidity*.

We distinguish true from false comorbidity in the following ways: *True comorbidity* requires the presence of two distinct diagnoses in the same child. For instance, a child may suffer with both BD and attention-deficit/hyperactivity disorder (ADHD). False comorbidity occurs when the symptoms of one disorder mimic the presence of a second disorder.

Comorbidity of Untreated BD

Untreated BD is fertile ground for the development of co-occurring (comorbid) disorders. These independent disorders, most often substance abuse and/or attention-deficit or anxiety disorders, might be the reason for a referral, or the main focus of treatment. In fact, BD without any comorbidity (medical or psychiatric) is the exception rather than the rule. For the most part, children and adolescents with BD show symptoms that overlap with other diagnoses, or meet the criteria for two or more diagnoses at the same time.

Depending on the age of the child, different problems might require diagnosis and treatment. In preschool children, developmental delays, sensory integration difficulties, comorbid medical (e.g., deafness), neurological (e.g., seizure disorder), or psychiatric (e.g., separation anxiety) conditions must be considered. In school-age children, learning (e.g., dyslexia), behavioral, and anxiety disorders must be evaluated. In teenagers, substance abuse, eating disorders, and anxiety disorders need to be considered in the differential diagnosis. Comorbidity can complicate diagnosis, treatment, and prognosis.

Comorbidity in Preschool Children

During growth and development, different disorders can become apparent and their symptoms might overlap with BD. Quite often, language delays, anxiety, or aggressive behavior attract the attention of parents and early-development specialists at an early age. Mental retardation, developmental delays (e.g., autism or Asperger's disorder), anxiety disorders, congenital disorders, or sensory integration difficulties can first become diagnosable during the preschool years. Hyperactivity, for instance, might be caused either by ADHD or by BD; other symptoms, like distractibility, excessive talking, and impulsive behavior might also be present in both disorders. In these cases, the clinician will rely on symptoms that do not overlap (i.e., moodiness, sleep disturbances, grandiosity, and hypersexual behavior) to determine whether the child suffers from either disorder, neither, or both.

Separation anxiety can begin to manifest as the child makes the transition from home to nursery school or daycare, and might become more and more disabling as the child is expected to separate from his parents more readily (including sleeping in his or her own room) as he or she grows older. At this time, phobic symptoms may also make their first appearance, either in the form of fear of the dark, pets, or strangers.

Motor skills, communication, and pervasive developmental disorders can be associated with, or might exacerbate, mood dysregulation in young children, and must be addressed with specific interventions (e.g., speech and language, or occupational therapy).

Comorbidity in School-Age Children

The most common comorbidities in children of school age include attention-deficit/hyperactivity disorder (ADHD) and disruptive behavior disorders (oppositional defiant disorder [ODD], and conduct disorder [CD]; see below), as well as learning and anxiety disorders. All these disorders manifest with symptoms that overlap, or are comorbid, with BD.

Hyperactivity, oppositional behavior, arguing, or becoming hostile could signal either a mood or a behavioral disorder. In these cases, a careful analysis of the symptoms, their course over time, associated features, and the family history of psychiatric disorders can help both to diagnose the child and to select proper treatment.

During the early school years (ages six to twelve), learning disorders (LD) and/or communication disorders can interfere with education and school performance, causing significant stress and self-esteem problems. When a child with BD also has to cope with a learning disorder, his or her ability to manage through the school day (and after-school homework) is diminished, thereby causing additional stress and impairment.

At this age, symptoms of separation anxiety and phobias might become more severe. In some children with BD, anxiety symptoms can also manifest as school or social phobia, obsessive-compulsive disorder (OCD), or generalized anxiety disorder. Less frequent are tics (motor, verbal, complex) and migraine headaches. These symptoms can lead to school tardiness, poor attendance, and school failure.

Comorbidity in Teenagers

During their teenage years, along with ADHD, disruptive behavior, and anxiety disorders, many children with BD suffer from a comorbid eating or substance abuse disorder. Cutting, burning, and other types of self-injury, seen mostly in girls, are frequent expressions of aggressive impulses. Other self-destructive, impulsive, and risk-taking behaviors—ranging from sexual promiscuity and acting-out to shoplifting, reckless driving, and experimenting with illegal substances—are often reported in adolescents and young adults with BD.

Attention-Deficit and Disruptive Behavior Disorders

Attention-deficit/hyperactivity disorder can be described as a persistent (six months or longer) pattern of inattention and/or hyperactivity that is not consistent with development, has an early onset (before age seven), and causes impairment of normal functioning in at least two settings (i.e., home and school). Although most children with mania will meet the criteria for ADHD, only a minority of children with ADHD meet the criteria for mania. More common in boys than girls, ADHD may affect 3 to 5 percent of all prepubertal elementary school children (Shaffer et al. 1996).

Oppositional defiant disorder is defined in the DSM-IV as "a pattern of negativistic, defiant, disobedient, and hostile behaviors toward authority figures." It is usually associated with temper tantrums, anger, and resentment (American Psychiatric Association 2000, p. 100).

Conduct disorder is defined in the DSM-IV as "A repetitive and persistent pattern of behavior in which the basic rights of others or major age-appropriate societal norms or rules are violated." To qualify as a conduct disorder, symptoms must have lasted for at least twelve months (American Psychiatric Association 2000, p. 98).

Anxiety Disorders

Fear of separation from caretakers, day and/or night worries about attachment figures getting hurt or dying, as well as phobias are common anxiety disorders in children with BD. School phobia (fear of going to school), social phobia (fear of strangers and of social situations), generalized anxiety (excessive anxiety about events and activities), panic (discrete episodes of intense fear of dying or losing control), and obsessive-compulsive disorder (recurrent and intrusive thoughts and/or ritualistic behaviors) often can be prominent in the clinical picture.

Substance Abuse

Teenage (or childhood) use of alcohol and tobacco is hardly diagnostic- or illness-specific; these and other drugs (amphetamine, cocaine, heroin, Ecstasy, and hallucinogens) are so widely used and abused that the problem has been called an epidemic. Although many adolescents experiment with various drugs without developing an addiction, adolescents with latent or diagnosable BD are at greater risk of using more drugs, more often, at an earlier age, and developing substance abuse or dependence.

Among adults with BD, the rate of comorbid alcohol and/or substance abuse is very high, and the rate of BD among alcohol abusers is much higher than in the general population. Certainly a substance abuse disorder destabilizes BD. When that substance abuse is not treated and is comorbid with BD, it can:

- prevent a beneficial response to mood stabilizers,

- worsen mood symptoms, and

- require adjunctive specialized treatment.

However, when alcohol, drug, tobacco, and caffeine dependence are adequately treated, stabilizing mood swings is much easier. Untreated BD with comorbid substance abuse can be extremely severe, and can be associated with violence, psychosis, and suicidal behavior.

Most stimulants, from caffeine to amphetamines and cocaine, are more likely to be abused during mania and hypomania. Stimulants can reduce sleep, induce hypomania or mania, produce psychosis in vulnerable children, and interfere with long-term stabilization. The abuse of stimulants, especially caffeine, is further encouraged by their effects on two areas of interest to patients with BD: attention span (increased) and weight (decreased).

Parents should be watchful of any suspicious behaviors that might suggest alcohol or drug use, although too often, substance abuse can come as a total surprise to the family. Most of the time, parents can detect signs of substance abuse easily if they remain vigilant, and monitor the child adequately. When parents suspect substance abuse, they must get the cooperation of the pediatrician and obtain a urine toxic screen, a test that can confirm or exclude the use of most commonly used drugs.

Eating Disorders

Eating disorders include anorexia nervosa, bulimia nervosa, and binge eating. *Anorexia nervosa* refers to the refusal, incapacity, or fear of maintaining a normal weight. This is usually associated with a distortion of one's body image (seeing oneself as overweight in spite of a very low body weight). The two variants, the restricting type and the bingeing/purging type, differ mostly in the methods used to lower or keep a low body weight. Just like other obsessive symptoms, weight can become a preoccupation in youngsters with mood swings, especially if reinforced by social and cultural factors.

The obsessive preoccupation to maintain control over body weight during a time of physical development (like adolescence) can lead to unhealthy expectations about weight or dietary restrictions with or without compulsive physical exercise. Anorexia can lead to malnutrition, with significant medical complications as a result of electrolyte imbalance, endocrinological abnormalities, osteoporosis, as well as dental and cardiac complications.

Bulimia nervosa, usually associated with bingeing and purging, results from food cravings—often for carbohydrates—and can be uncontrollable. Sometimes episodes of bingeing can leave a child feeling completely helpless, guilt-ridden, and depressed. Usually, the child is very secretive about these behaviors, and only careful and gentle questioning, as well as monitoring of dietary intake, can reveal their presence.

More common in females, concerns about weight can have a powerful role in leading to, or maintaining, stimulant abuse and dependence. Note, however, that appetite changes associated with mood changes or their treatment are not necessarily a sign of an eating disorder. The child's pediatrician can help parents explore their concerns about an eating disorder, by monitoring weight, overall health and growth, diet, or by referring the child to an eating disorder specialist.

Psychotic Disorders

Psychosis is a broad term used to describe delusions, hallucinations, and disorganized or bizarre speech and/or behavior.

Delusions are false beliefs that are fixed and inconsistent with the patient's cultural background. An example is a child's belief that he or she can fly or read someone's mind. Most delusions are grandiose or paranoid, but many others can be observed in children and adolescents.

Hallucinations are faulty perceptions affecting one of the senses, most often hearing and vision. A child might hear sounds or noises, music, voices calling, or pieces of conversation (auditory hallucinations), and even orders (command hallucinations), or see objects, animals, or people (visual hallucinations).

Incoherent speech or newly created words, odd or bizarre behaviors (acting like an animal, i.e., meowing instead of talking), or catatonia (rigid immobility without a physical cause) may signal the presence of psychotic symptoms.

Psychotic symptoms are not specific to a single diagnosis. Mood disorders, substance abuse, and schizophrenia are the most common causes of psychosis, if we exclude cases precipitated by drug use.

SENSORY INTEGRATION

Sensory integration is a relatively new area of research developed by occupational therapists. An occupational therapist (OT) is trained to help children and adults with common tasks requiring fine motor skills (handling utensils, buttoning clothes, holding a pencil and writing letters, etc.), gross motor coordination (walking, running, jumping, and skipping, and so forth), and motor planning.

Sensory integration examines the individual differences in the way children (and adults) respond to the following seven sensory modalities:

1. Sight

2. Hearing

3. Touch

4. Taste

5. Smell

6. Sense of position in space (*proprioception*), which organizes multiple sensations registered through joints and muscles to help develop learned movements, such as jumping, running, and climbing

7. Balance and equilibrium (through the vestibular system in the inner ear), which help maintain balance while moving

Sensory integration is the mechanism by which the central nervous system (CNS) acquires and analyzes basic sensory information and translates it into meaningful action through one or more motor systems. For example, when an infant hears his mother's voice, the infant may turn and smile. When a toddler sees a toy, he or she reaches for it to play. When a three-year-old hears his parent or nursery-school teacher say it's time to go to the playground, he or she may smile and jump up and down with excitement. When a child tastes something, if it is liked, the child may smile, bite, chew, and swallow. If the child doesn't like the taste, he or she might spit it out. All these simple responses, as well as talking, have a motor component to them.

Normal sensory integration helps the individual to function in the world and to relate to others. A normal child is able to modulate responses to sensory stimuli. This means the child can take in essential information and screen out excess information to avoid sensory overload. As the CNS matures, children are required to process more complex stimuli, and this poses additional challenges.

Styles of Processing Sensory Information

The way sensory information is processed depends also on the person's "thresholds of arousal." A child with a normal threshold of arousal can screen out unnecessary stimulation in the environment, remain alert and focused on age-appropriate activities, such as school tasks, and can transition to other activities easily, even when overstimulated. For example, if a child with a normal threshold of arousal is listening to an interesting story in a kindergarten classroom and is interrupted by an unexpected fire drill, that child will come back to the classroom after the fire drill is over and will be eager for the teacher to continue the story.

A child born with a low threshold of arousal is easily overstimulated and overwhelmed. The child may have difficulty screening out environmental noises, such as traffic or classroom noise. This child can focus and participate in activities when the environment is quiet. Because they can become overstimulated with less input than "normal" kids, they tend to manage transitions by slowing down or resisting change. When overstimulated, these children may become anxious or may withdraw as a way of calming down, and will then be able to transition to another activity. If there is a fire drill during story time, these children might need a longer time to calm down before rejoining the class or they may become anxious about another fire drill in the future.

At the other end of the arousal spectrum, a child with a high threshold of arousal (hyperaroused) will be considered *sensory-seeking*, which means such children need novel and exciting activities to attract their attention. Because they also tend to screen out many aspects of daily life, they crave excitement and are easily bored by the daily class-room activities. In kindergarten, these children may not pay attention to a story, unless it excites them. The novelty of a fire drill will delight children with a high threshold of arousal and they will prefer to stay outside and play, ignoring the bell that signals the transition back to the classroom. In an overstimulated state, rather than calming down, such children will continue to crave excitement, and may become aggressive if they're not allowed to continue an exciting activity.

Sensory Integration Disorder (SID)

Difficulty processing input from one or more of the sources of sensory input is described as a *sensory integration disorder* (SID). For example, children who run away from the vacuum cleaner may be overwhelmed because their perception of the noise is exaggerated and they react with fear. Elias (see the beginning of this chapter), who shuns the touch of his parents and resists new kinds of food or cloth-ing, may be easily overwhelmed by sensory input. A poor sense of balance explains his tendency to bump into others and his frequent falls on the playground (accident prone). Because Elias has a low threshold of arousal, he gets easily overwhelmed, causing avoidant behavior.

On the other hand, some children have a high threshold of arousal and don't notice the sensation unless it is very intense. Imagine Elias with the same sensitivities but with a high threshold of arousal. He would crave the affectionate touch of his parents, or he might fall over a noisy vacuum even while it is in use. In spite of coordination and balance problems, he would be fearless and climb high on the jungle gym, craving stimulation (sensory-seeking).

SENSORY INTEGRATION AND BD

In a child with both BD and SID, minimal stimulation provokes a reaction of far greater intensity and duration than in other children. In their book *Bipolar Patterns in Children: New Perspectives on Developmental*

Pathways and a Comprehensive Approach to Prevention and Treatment (2002), Stanley Greenspan, a psychiatrist, and Ira Glovinsky, a psychologist, suggest that in a low threshold state, a child with BD is easily overwhelmed, but does not (or cannot) withdraw, often becoming irritable. In children with BD, overstimulation accelerates with lightning speed from irritability into angry, aggressive, and disorganized responses. These children respond in a similar way as a child who craves excitement (sensory-seeking).

Simply put, if there is sensory overload, a child with BD may not be able to "put on the brakes" and you will see out-of-control responses, such as aggression and rages. This may be the case with Elias, who is sensitive to touch and does not (or cannot) withdraw, resulting in a tantrum when his parents try to hold him.

RED FLAGS

Craving or avoiding certain foods or smells, insisting on certain clothes, hypersensitivity to heat or cold temperatures, or feeling that the volume of the TV or the radio is too low or too high can be signs of SID. Poor balance, excessive falling, or being "accident prone" compared to others of the same age may be another sign. Here are some examples:

- When a four-year-old girl pulled off her new jeans and shirt, her mom thought she was being stubborn and oppositional because she was in a hurry. But her daughter was sensitive to the tags in the new clothes, which may have felt like nails scratching the back of her neck and waist. A seven-year-old insisted that her sneakers were so tight that her feet had marks and her circulation was impaired. When her mother refused to loosen them, she threw a tantrum and refused to go to school, so often that she was medically excused from her physical education class.

- A nine-year-old pulled off his socks and sneakers at the beginning of the initial evaluation, much to the distress of his parents, who thought he was being deliberately rude. The boy said, "My feet have claustrophobia," meaning he was extremely uncomfortable due to the heat generated by his sneakers.

- An adolescent has difficulty sitting straight on a soft couch or chair and sits in a slumped or slouched posture; or he literally slips onto the floor while talking. He seems floppy and this may also be a sign of low muscular tone in his upper body, while his parents may think this is avoidant, rude, or oppositional behavior.

Occupational therapists (OT) have taken the lead in assessment and intervention for SID, and no child is too young to be evaluated by an OT. Although there is no formal measure of the impact of early intervention in children with BD, anecdotal reports suggest that it can be helpful. Occupational therapists know how to help you develop what is called a "sensory diet" for your child, and thus help your child to avoid too much or too little stimulation. In chapter 13, we will guide you in how to gain access to the services of an OT.

LEARNING, PROCESSING, AND EXECUTIVE FUNCTION DIFFICULTIES

Elias is now in second grade. Diagnosed with BD, he is responding well to a mood stabilizer. Having worked with an occupational therapist since kindergarten, he is now able to write (with difficulty), run, throw, and catch a ball. Elias seems bright and he tries hard, but he's often the last to hand in his schoolwork. The teacher is concerned because he can't read. His mom is also concerned because Elias is very disorganized and forgetful. Every day Elias misplaces or loses something, even though the teacher helps him pack his backpack. Every morning before he leaves for school, Elias's mother has to make sure he has his homework, pencils, and lunch.

Entering elementary school, children are faced with the challenges of learning. Like Elias, many children with BD have co-occurring learning difficulties. He is behind in reading, slow in completing assignments, forgetful, disorganized, and inefficient. Elias's difficulties are not caused by BD, as he's responding well to treatment. His school difficulties, however, seem to originate from a separate, diagnosable learning disability (true comorbidity).

In the following section, we'll define learning disabilities, processing difficulties, and executive functioning difficulties, and we'll review how they can affect learning.

Learning Disorders

When it comes to learning, we all have strengths and weaknesses. Learning disorders (LD) affect acquiring, understanding, retaining, recalling, and using new information in a purposeful way. When the brain's ability to acquire, memorize, process, or communicate information is compromised, learning is affected.

"Learning disability" is a legal definition from the Individuals with Disabilities Education Act, 1997 (IDEA 1997), currently used in the classification for special education services (see chapter 13). It states that a child with a learning disability has

> "a disorder in one or more of the basic psychological processes involved in understanding or in using language, spoken or written, that may manifest itself in an imperfect ability to listen, think, speak, write, spell or do mathematical calculations." (Public Law 94-142, section 300.7, 1997)

This definition of learning disability refers to children with average intellectual functioning (IQ) and does not include children who have learning problems which are primarily the result of visual, hearing, or motor handicaps, mental retardation, emotional disturbance, or disadvantage stemming from the child's environment, culture, or economic status.

Types of Learning Disorders

Learning disorders (a category that includes learning disabilities) can affect any child. They are classified as follows:

- Reading disorders affect reading in a way that cannot be explained by age, deficits of intelligence, or age-appropriate education. *Examples:* reads "b" as "d," or reads "I see the cat" as "The cat sees."

■ Mathematics disorders may affect mathematical abilities that cannot be explained by age, deficits of intelligence, or age-appropriate education. *Examples:* problems learning to count by two's; mixing up addition and subtraction facts; problems with making change from a one dollar bill.

■ Disorders of written expression affect handwriting, spelling, and writing. Writing is among the most complex of tasks. It requires the development of motor skills and an integrated utilization of cognitive skills (thinking and reasoning), language skills (vocabulary, grammar, punctuation), and motor skills (writing).

    Although some children have difficulties with legible handwriting, other have difficulty organizing their ideas. Taking notes is essential for adequate functioning in school. In the early years, it requires copying and attention to details. Note-taking becomes more challenging in the upper grades when it requires simultaneous listening, comprehending, memorizing, and summarizing important points into a useful format. Writing notes has to take place while listening attentively and it has to be done quickly, almost automatically. If the process is successful, the result is a legible note; ideally a summary of the relevant concepts heard while listening to a lesson. If any aspect of this process is faulty, the result will be frustration, confusion, and a lost opportunity to learn new information.

■ Motor skills disorders affect basic coordination and agility in a way that cannot be explained by age or deficits of intelligence, and they interfere with learning (penmanship) or daily activities. *Examples:* poor ability to use zippers, to button clothes, to draw, and/or to use scissors.

■ Communication disorders affect the ability to express oneself through spoken language (expressive language disorder), to understand and express through spoken words (mixed receptive-expressive language disorder), to articulate language into clear speech (phonological disorder), or to speak fluently (stuttering). These disorders must impair academic, social, or occupational activities in the absence of intellectual or neurological deficits.

Processing Disorders

Within the formal definition of learning disabilities, there are no specific categories for "information processing deficits." Information processing, like learning, depends on an intact central nervous system.

Information processing is affected by long- and short-term memory, attention span, and *sequencing* (keeping things in proper order). Different types and levels of processing can be affected as described below:

- *Auditory processing* (the ability to interpret sounds) affects the basic development of language understanding and reading. *Examples:* problems understanding verbal directions that require more than one or two steps; a child who appears to hear, but does not respond, "doesn't listen;" and problems with recalling or spelling words.

- *Visual processing* (the ability to interpret visual stimuli) affects reading, writing, and mathematics. *Examples:* problems distinguishing "h" from "n" or "x" from "+"; does not pay attention to details; mixes up the sequence of words in a sentence; mixes up numbers, such as "85" for "58"; difficulty identifying facial expressions.

Executive Functions

Executive functions, including selective attention, behavioral planning, strategic thinking, response inhibition, and manipulation of data, serve the purpose of solving problems and completing tasks. Included in this category are: working memory, abstract thinking, creative problem solving, following a sequence of tasks, self-monitoring, and mental flexibility. A child with poor executive skills seems disorganized, inefficient, and forgetful, appearing unable to plan ahead or to follow a sequence of actions, or incapable of completing a task.

EXECUTIVE FUNCTIONS AND BD

As we have pointed out throughout this book, one important feature of children with BD is the difficulty inhibiting their emotional, behavioral, and cognitive responses—an inability to "put on the brakes."

Moreover, children with BD, especially when their mood symptoms are active, have problems with attention and memory, which affect their ability to stay on task. It is very common to find children and teens with BD who also have difficulty with executive functioning.

HOW BD AFFECTS LEARNING

Many children with BD, like Elias, have co-occurring learning disabilities that may or may not be addressed by the school before the diagnosis of BD has been made. Difficulties in reading, writing, arithmetic, speaking, and understanding what is said in the classroom and at home (especially when asked to do homework) can be stressors, hidden or obvious, that may exacerbate the symptoms of BD. On the other hand, as we saw in chapter 3, when the symptoms of bipolar disorder are active, they can adversely affect attention, concentration, and memory. Many children and adolescents with BD have difficulty with visual-spatial tasks, verbal learning and memory, and, specifically in adolescents, poor achievement in mathematics.

RED FLAGS

Consider the possibility that your child may have a learning problem (for which accommodations in school may be helpful) if one or more of the following behaviors occurs frequently:

- Your child comes home from school unhappy and complains about how "hard the work is," how "mean and unfair the teacher is," and you know for a fact that the teacher is understanding and the work is within your child's abilities.

- Your child is inconsistent in completing assignments in class and at home.

- Your young child has difficulty with articulation.

- Your child takes a long time to copy assignments from the board.

- Your child has trouble listening to directions in class.

- Your child overreacts when asked about school or test grades.

- Your child is disorganized and constantly loses work (and may lie about it).

Many children with both an LD and/or BD are relaxed in the summertime, when school demands are absent, but they may have problems in the new school year, no matter how understanding the teacher is. If you are concerned, it is time to get the help of professionals. In the previous chapter, we reviewed the usefulness of a neuropsychological evaluation. In chapter 13, School Decisions, we will take you through the steps for getting an extensive evaluation.

MISDIAGNOSIS: A COMMON PROBLEM

As we have previously mentioned, children with BD are commonly misdiagnosed with a host of other disorders before receiving a correct diagnosis. There are many reasons for this phenomenon, the principal ones being the lack of an objective diagnosis, poor recognition of BD's symptoms, language barriers, stigma and denial, professionals' beliefs (i.e., BD does not manifest in children), and different manifestations from those seen in adult forms of BD.

Attention-deficit disorders with hyperactivity can look like mania, and mania can look like ADHD, and the two can also occur together. In the absence of reliable and objective ways of distinguishing these two conditions, diagnostic errors are bound to confuse parents and professionals alike. Ongoing research may help resolve this problem in the future.

Language issues may interfere with the reporting of symptoms and with effective communication with professionals, thus interfering with diagnostic accuracy.

Stigma (shame of, and discrimination against, mental illness) or denial of symptoms are common because illnesses like BD are not accepted by parents, peers, and sometimes even by professionals.

Some professionals deny the existence of BD in children or are unwilling to diagnose it and treat it. Some clinicians refuse to consider BD among possible diagnoses, or favor other diagnoses (e.g., depression or ADHD) when symptoms of another disorder overlap. Some professionals encourage or pressure parents and young patients to discontinue necessary treatment (mostly pharmacological, because they believe BD is a "trendy" diagnosis). This does not happen to children treated for seizure disorders, asthma, or insulin-dependent diabetes, but it is a common occurrence in BD.

Misdiagnosis can lead to a series of ineffective, or potentially detrimental, interventions. At best, it causes a delay in beginning proper treatment, and in the worst cases, it leads to complications from untreated BD and inadequate treatment.

Research shows that among adult patients with BD there is often a long delay between the onset of symptoms and its diagnosis (Lish et al. 1994). Sometimes, this delay can result in inappropriate or a lack of treatment for months or years. Too often, the journey of diagnosis and effective treatment is a difficult and frustrating experience. After several evaluations, conflicting diagnoses or treatment recommendations, along with trials of medications or psychotherapy, many are still looking for help.

When an incorrect diagnosis leads to ineffective interventions or strategies, the most common outcome is the absence of improvement. Disillusionment with treatment can lead to gaps in treatment because "nothing works." Unstable BD forces families to coexist with symptoms and behaviors that disrupt family life and relationships, often leaving family members feeling hopeless about the possibility of change.

Quite often BD remains undiagnosed and untreated for many years. The absence of vigorous treatment for several years can lead to serious consequences, such as self-harm, resistance to treatment, and comorbidity, placing a tremendous burden on the patients, their families, and ultimately on society.

Early treatment can prevent or correct many obstacles that BD places on your child's development and education. In the next chapters we discuss how a multidisciplinary approach is helpful in addressing different aspects of this complex disorder, allowing your child's strengths and talents to emerge.

7

Treatment Overview

"I'm so upset. Bobby just hit my one-year-old toddler for no reason, and he's been tormenting the dog. He's so mean. . . . He was doing so well. I was always afraid that the medication would stop working," a mother told us, breaking into tears. Bobby, a five-year-old, had been stable for several months, but a growth spurt and the change of season were causing an exacerbation of his symptoms, and it looked as if the medication had lost its efficacy.

Successful treatment requires the parents' active participation in a treatment team. This ongoing collaboration begins with the diagnostic evaluation, continues with planning and implementing a treatment strategy, and extends to the ongoing monitoring of responses and side effects. For this reason, a clear understanding of all aspects of the disorder and its treatment is absolutely necessary.

As discussed in chapter 5, the first step in planning treatment for your child with bipolar disorder (BD) is determining the appropriate level of care—whether outpatient or inpatient treatment is needed. In this chapter, the emphasis is on outpatient treatment; chapter 14 will discuss inpatient treatment. Each treatment plan is individualized to address each child's specific, unique needs; however, some basic principles apply to all children and families. Those are reviewed here.

BASIC PRINCIPLES

Several areas of intervention must be addressed in designing and implementing a comprehensive treatment plan for your child with BD. There are three targets for treatment: the child, the parents, and the child's environment. All of these must be addressed for the plan to succeed.

Several interventions focus on the child, such as controlling symptoms with medication, restoring normal sleep patterns, helping the child first to observe and report his or her symptoms, and, later on, to modulate his or her reactions.

Parents, in this initial phase of treatment, learn about the symptoms and how to best deal with them. They receive support and guidance for implementing changes in the child's sleep routine, and for reinforcing compliance with medications and school attendance. Interventions that modify home and school environments are crucial.

Emotional and physical overload caused by too many family or social commitments. For instance, if the child has a birthday party to attend one afternoon, a family function the following day, and asks permission to have a friend visit for a sleepover, parents should intervene to "pace" (or slow down) family and social interactions. Rather than allowing the child to become overstimulated, they can allow a sleepover the following weekend. That way they would not be adding to the overstimulation of a birthday party (including the excess sugar and caffeine) the sleep deprivation that is often part of a sleepover and the stress and excitement of a family gathering.

Pacing or slowing down activities is often a crucial part of how parents can help their child: pacing allows the child adequate time to transition from one activity to another, as well as time to rest and recover from stimulating or stressful school, social, or family activities. Parents must support a healthy diet and regular exercise schedule. With the direction and help of qualified clinicians, the order and/or emphasis of specific interventions can (and should) be modified according to each child's unique needs including, addressing comorbid diagnoses.

In most cases, however, the following seven interventions should be considered:

1. Medical stabilization of mood, activity, and sleep

2. Lifestyle changes, including diet, exercise, and sleep hygiene

3. Educating parents and child about BD (psycho-education)

4. Parent guidance and support

5. Monitoring symptoms

6. School intervention, occupational, speech and language therapy

7. Individual, group, and family psychotherapy

STAGES OF ILLNESS

Before we get into specifics about treatment, it is important for you to understand what stage of the illness your child is in at the present time. We find it helpful to distinguish three stages of BD: acute illness, partial remission, and full remission. Depending on the stage of illness, your child will need different types of interventions. In other words, different stages of illness correspond to different phases of treatment.

Table 6 is adapted for children and adolescents and expanded from *Bipolar Disorder: A Family-Focused Treatment Approach* (1997) written for adults by psychologists David Miklowitz and Michael Goldstein. It outlines treatment phases in children and adolescents, and the goals for each stage of the illness.

Table 6: Stages of Illness and Phase of Treatment*

Phase and Duration	Illness's Symptoms	Treatment Goals
Acute 1–6 months	**Severe to Moderate** Home, school, social life are compromised by severe or frequent symptoms May be hospitalized	Medication trials, adjustments Reduce severity of symptoms and side effects If hospitalized, discharge to a partial hospital day-treatment program or outpatient care
Stabilization 6–18 months	**Moderate to Mild** Home, school, social life is improved but not back to baseline functioning, mild or infrequent symptoms	Medication adjustments Remission of acute symptoms Regulate sleep, mood, cope with side effects Lower stress Social rehabilitation Outpatient, partial hospital
Maintenance **Indefinite**	**Mild or in Remission** Attends school Home, social functioning returns to normal	Maintain remission, prevention of recurrences, compliance w/meds Self-monitoring of symptoms, side effects Improve self-esteem

* Adapted from Miklowitz, D. J., and M. J. Goldstein. 1997. *Bipolar Disorder: A Family-Focused Treatment Approach.* NY: Guilford Press, page 36.

An episode or crisis might be triggered by an argument escalating out of control, a romantic breakup, substance abuse, self-harm, suicidal ideation, or school problems. Other times, new medication can produce an adverse reaction (see chapter 8). The acute onset or exacerbation of the symptoms of BD may occur suddenly, and can require that your child be hospitalized.

Acute phase.   Regardless of what led to the crisis, during the acute phase your child must be shielded from all unnecessary stress (including school), whether the child stays at home, is hospitalized, or requires a partial hospital program. Many parents expect their child to go to school and do well even when they are unstable. This is unreasonable, similar to expecting the child to attend school during a serious medical illness or after major surgery. Family life, sports, and social or recreational activities can seem overwhelming: these activities must be adjusted to manageable levels and monitored closely.

Most of the time, acute symptoms can be controlled effectively with medication prescribed in an outpatient setting. Sometimes, however, more expert or professional supervision is needed. This might require a brief stay in a hospital, a partial hospital program, or therapeutic school. The goal of acute treatment is coping with the crisis, reducing the symptoms' severity, and keeping your child safe.

Stabilization phase.   The goal of the stabilization phase is to consolidate the gains made during the acute phase of treatment, facilitating a gradual recovery, and remission of symptoms. Partial hospital programs are often used to provide support, supervision, and some schooling during this phase of stabilization. Additionally, a partial hospital program can provide, together with ongoing supervision and treatment, a gradual transition home, a gentle return to a school routine, and some socialization.

In the meantime, an appropriate school setting must be located and a transition to outpatient treatment is arranged. Even with open communication between the inpatient and the outpatient treatment teams, this transition can take several months. Sometimes a period of homeschooling is the best option available, if no suitable school can be found.

After an acute episode, the period of stabilization may take from several months to one or two years to complete and is often fraught with unevenness, setbacks, and pitfalls. At this point in the course of treatment, both you and your child might have been traumatized by what happened during the acute phase, especially if a hospitalization was needed (the child made a suicide attempt, was aggressive, or experienced psychotic symptoms). The disruption in home, school, and social life may be a source of guilt, shame, and concern about the future for you and your child.

The treatment team can provide support, offer you a better understanding of the symptoms and their course, and a hopeful long-term perspective on future treatment. At this time, gentle reassurance and help putting things into perspective can give both you and your child a break from feeling at the mercy of bipolar disorder.

Maintenance phase.   In the maintenance phase, you and your child will continue monitoring and rebalancing your child's shifts in mood and energy as they occur, making this work part of your everyday life. This can be very helpful when known stressors, such as seasonal changes, transitions back to school after holidays, overstimulating events (for example, birthdays), disruptions of routine, growth spurts, or pubertal changes, cause an increase in symptoms.

Relapse Versus Recurrence

Sometimes, when your child seems to have reached a steady improvement, things can start deteriorating again for a number of reasons. This can trigger what are called "catastrophic reactions," when the progress you and your child worked so hard for seems lost forever. A recurrence occurs when a child, after going through an acute phase of the illness, does well for at least a month, and then gets sick again. This is to distinguish it from a *relapse*. In a relapse, the child falls ill again before reaching and/or maintaining stability for an entire month. The example at the beginning of this chapter is an example of recurrence because the child was completely well for a time before getting sick again. The difference between recurrence and relapse is shown below:

Recurrence:

Acute illness–Remission (four weeks or more)–Acute illness

Relapse:

Acute illness–Improvement (less than four weeks)–Acute illness

In either situation, besides changes in medications or inpatient treatment, this is a time when psychotherapy for your child, parental guidance for you, and education for both can be most useful. If a recurrence or relapse occurs, you and your child will need support and coaching to understand what has happened, how to deal with it, and how to prevent it in the future. At this time, you will need to work with your treatment team on monitoring symptoms, adjusting medications as required by the situation, and helping your child recompensate, using the tools you've learned about during the course of treatment.

THE TREATMENT TEAM

The treatment team is a source of support, guidance, and expertise that empowers parents and children in their struggle with BD. Sometimes a group of professionals working together provides families and children with a ready-made, experienced team. Other times, you have to find ways of working with different professionals, creating your own team to help your child and the whole family.

Members of the Treatment Team

The main participants in a treatment team provide medical treatment, psychotherapy, family support and/or family therapy, school educational assessment, school support, and recommended accommodations. The roles of the participants are different and complementary, and sometimes one or two members of the treatment team will take on more than one role. When necessary, a member of the team may also function as your child's (and family's) advocate.

THE MEDICAL DOCTOR (MD)

This is usually a psychiatrist, child psychiatrist, or neurologist, but in more rural areas, the MD may be a pediatrician or general practitioner. The MD is ultimately responsible for diagnosing the disorder, prescribing and monitoring medications, and often overseeing the entire treatment.

THE THERAPIST

Often a psychologist or another mental health professional, such as a social worker or school counselor, may initially suspect, recognize, or diagnose BD. Psychologists may identify or suspect bipolar disorder while administering a psycho-educational or neuropsychological evaluation. Because many medical conditions can mimic the symptoms of bipolar disorder, an MD, preferably a psychiatrist, should be consulted to confirm the diagnosis. A psychologist or a social worker may be the child's primary therapist and family advocate, may address family and sibling issues, maintain contact with the school, and help coordinate treatment with other team members, like a case manager.

THE SCHOOL STAFF

One member of the team is often a school psychologist or a master's level mental health professional. This person can play a very important role in suggesting and implementing specific school accommodations for the child in collaboration with other professionals. The counselor provides emotional support and guidance in the school setting and monitors the child's progress in school. When the school counselor is the child's primary therapist, especially in residential school settings or partial hospital/day treatment programs, he or she may also help with family issues. Especially in the younger grades, your child's teacher and an occupational therapist and/or speech and language therapist can also contribute to the effectiveness of the treatment team.

There are times when a professional educational advocate and/or educational attorney will become a member of the treatment team (see chapter 13).

AN INTEGRATED, MULTIDISCIPLINARY APPROACH

As outlined in chapter 1, our approach involves intervention for the child, his or her parents, and the environment. Focusing on the treatment of manic or excitatory symptoms, we work simultaneously on improving and regulating sleep and reducing all sources of stimulation. Among the sources of distress are conflicts with parents, siblings, peers, or school-related stressors (learning disabilities). Working with children and parents, we support collaborative work, using education about BD and observation of symptoms as an initial common goal.

Medical Stabilization of Mood, Activity, and Sleep

The first step in the course of treatment is to medically address the prominent symptoms of BD early and aggressively.

MOOD REGULATION

Mood regulation requires specific interventions based on the unique combination of symptoms that your child experiences. Superimposed on, or parallel to, medical stabilization of BD, your treatment team will work with you and your child to implement other interventions at home or school and to address other (learning, sensory, developmental, and medical) issues. One exception would be substance abuse, which usually needs to be addressed first, as it interferes with treatment and stabilization of BD.

Without the foundation of a proper pharmacological stabilization, most interventions can have short-term benefits, but they are usually doomed to fail.

For example, your child may focus on the stress caused by school, including "mean" teachers, "nasty" peers, "unfair" tests, and homework. Under these circumstances your child might temporarily benefit from school accommodations (for instance, extended time for testing and/or a transfer to a smaller classroom) made before adequate medical stabilization, but this will not help in the long run. This is because the symptoms of BD affect learning (restlessness, short attention span) and/or peer relations (aggression). If these symptoms are not addressed, as the novelty of school accommodations wears off, BD will again wreak havoc on your child's school day.

In another situation, you might be working on implementing a good sleep routine, but, without using a sleeping medication, your child doesn't fall asleep until midnight or 1 A.M. Decreased sleep leads to greater mood instability and *activation* (when the child cannot fall asleep and becomes hyper), and you might find yourself in a vicious cycle of sleep disturbances leading to activation, exacerbation of mania, and more sleep disturbances. To break this cycle without medication can be difficult or impossible.

Similarly, attempts to control or reduce aggression with counseling or behavioral therapy will likely fail if pharmacological intervention doesn't help to reduce the underlying symptoms of impulsivity and irritability.

Mood regulation is critical because the instability caused by mood swings produces a conflictual environment that maintains or activates symptoms. It is hard to say what triggers the child or another family member (parent, sibling) already under the stress of previous highly emotional, conflictual interaction with the patient. Let's just say that too often family life is ruined by ongoing arguments, animosity, and anger.

Furthermore, mood instability prevents your child from understanding and benefiting from other interventions. Once medical treatment successfully regulates mood, activity and sleep, then school interventions and other nonmedical treatments (such as psychotherapy, tutoring, speech and language, or occupational therapy) can begin to address any comorbid disorders or developmental delays that might be present.

As seen in the clinical vignettes in chapters 3 and 4, mood instability causes extremely intense periods of elation, irritability, anxiety, or sadness. Usually, the goal of pharmacological intervention is to reduce the frequency, duration, and intensity of these mood changes. For instance, if your child has three to four meltdowns a day, lasting thirty minutes each, with yelling, screaming, and loss of control, you and your doctor will probably target these meltdowns. Improvement can be compared to a "lowering of the volume" of these meltdowns or temper tantrums, or a decrease in the reactivity to habitual triggers (a sibling, waiting for something, a transition, or change of plans).

If treatment is effective, you (and perhaps your child) will start noticing that the duration and intensity of these meltdowns decreases, or that the meltdowns are not as frequent. Note that some children are more sensitive to certain medications than others, and in some cases, it takes some time to find the right medication or the right dose.

ACTIVITY AND SLEEP

Early in treatment, along with mood stabilization, we focus on decreasing hyperactivity or restlessness and providing adequate sleep. The two goals are closely connected; both activity and sleep usually benefit from the same interventions that help stabilize mood. You might have observed that when your child doesn't get enough sleep, his or her mood is unstable (for example, "the fuse is shorter," tantrums are more frequent or severe), and restlessness is increased. When treatment is effective, mood, energy, and sleep all improve, although not always to the same degree or even at the same time.

Sleep regulation is both very complex and very challenging. A central part of our treatment approach requires an integrated approach of pharmacological treatment, behavioral management, time, and patience (see chapter 9). Both sleep quantity (hours of sleep) and/or quality (restful, restorative sleep) can be affected. That is, your child can be sleeping too much or too little, the child's timing might be off, or sleep events, such as nightmares or bedwetting, might interfere. If your child is experiencing depression, sleep might increase, while it is usually decreased in manic or mixed states, as well as in some forms of agitated depression.

The timing of sleep can also be off due to disturbances of *circadian rhythms* (biological activities occurring in approximately twenty-four hour cycles), sometimes with sleep-wake reversal (sleeping during the day, up at night). Your child may have problems falling asleep (*early insomnia*), experience sleep interruptions (*middle insomnia*), or early awakenings (*up early*, or *late insomnia*). Sleep events, such as nightmares, night terrors, *sleep apnea* (holding the breath), bedwetting, sleepwalking, and teeth-grinding can be present (at different times) and can have severe consequences.

The timing of sleep is often dysregulated in BD and it is equally important. There is a tendency for manic symptoms to grow more intense in the evening hours, encouraging more and more activities in the evening. This is because of greater energy and mental clarity, which often interfere with bedtime. This can lead to a progressive shift toward night wakefulness and daytime sleep (naps).

For instance, your adolescent may stay up till 4 or 5 A.M., and then sleep till 2 or 3 in the afternoon. This schedule interferes with school and home functioning, isolates your child socially, and infuriates you, as this behavior seems entirely willful. Regardless of age, the struggle over bedtime and proper sleep habits is usually a lifelong problem that can be improved by educating yourself and your child about the importance of sleep.

Lifestyle Changes, Diet, and Exercise

In combination with sleep regulation, several additional interventions in the areas of diet and exercise can lead to significant, beneficial lifestyle changes. For instance, sleep regulation requires adequate levels of activity during the day, avoiding naps, and removing caffeine from the diet. In other words, in order to regulate sleep, paying attention to all aspects of a child's life is essential.

EXERCISE

Physical exercise can help sleep regulation by tiring the body. Morning or daytime exercise is preferable to evening exercise. A regular exercise schedule is important, but exercise should not take place in the late evening, as it may produce stimulation and arousal at the very time when your child needs to unwind and prepare for bedtime. Regular exercise contributes to maintaining a normal weight and it may have an antidepressant effect, brought about by a release of *endorphins* (brain neurotransmitters similar to opiates that make people feel especially well). The so-called "runner's high" is produced by endorphins.

Your child with BD may have fluctuating levels of motivation, and/or be oversensitive to criticism. Fear of failure and extreme competitiveness may lead to an inconsistent effort, or a tendency to drop out at the first difficulty or failure, adding to the child's social isolation. Without treatment, only effortless success (sometimes due to a natural talent or skill) is acceptable to a child with BD.

As soon as the child is asked to train, or to work on his or her weaknesses, the emotional response of anger and refusal can cause an abrupt withdrawal. Many children with BD refuse to continue playing a sport they once enjoyed after a poor showing, a disagreement with a coach or teammate, or because of an isolated incident (for example, teasing).

However, you may be able to ease your child into sports even if he or she has significant problems with motivation, stress, and/or interpersonal relationships. Following your child's interests, you can begin with one-on-one instruction, as team sports might be intimidating and competitiveness might be too stimulating when your child has not been stable. Also, motivation is often lacking and the undivided attention of a trainer might be required for support, socialization, and encouragement. As the child becomes more stable, parallel tutoring with another student-tutor team, then with another peer are useful for gradual transitions. Some children may go on to play team sports, but most will choose individual sports.

Engaging in sports can help your child understand the need for rules and boundaries, the value of teamwork and sportsmanship, and sports can serve as a strong motivation to do well at schoolwork (especially when academic success is required for game participation). Sometimes, playing a musical instrument can provide a healthy physical outlet (for example, drums); playing in an orchestra, band, or small group ensemble, singing in a chorus, or attending acting classes can also provide opportunities for physical movement and socialization along with an increased sense of competency.

Psycho-education: Parents and Child Learn About BD

At times, parents become confused when they don't understand the reasons for the clinician's suggestions. Without an understanding of its purpose, you may find yourself unable or unwilling to follow through with a specific intervention. On the other hand, understanding the necessity of a certain intervention, its potential benefits, and a sense of control rooted in purposeful action can motivate you to comply fully with treatment suggestions. The treatment team's willingness to listen to and address doubts, questions, and concerns that you (or your child) might have will also be of great help.

Parents often research the many resources available, sometimes join online support groups, or develop a good understanding of BD, its symptoms, and available treatments. Many of you are ready to take in a lot of new information and participate in ongoing parent-education groups. In these settings, many of you, regardless of knowledge or experience, share and learn from each other's valuable information on medical, psychological, school, and home interventions. You can share the pain of a relapse, support each other in a crisis, exchange impressions about hospitals, doctors, schools, arrange playdates for your children, and sometimes find new friends who share your experience. (See appendix III for resources.)

However, despite extensive knowledge and understanding of BD, many of you may feel unable to communicate effectively with your child (especially an adolescent) with BD. That's because children with BD often have a conflictual relationship with authority (that is, you). They may be unwilling or unable to listen to you because they feel bad about being out of control and blame you for it. They can also feel blamed, put down, or criticized by you for something they cannot control.

Many children refuse to listen to or participate in any discussion of BD, as they perceive BD as your way of criticizing them, or as their personal failure. Often this progresses to a standstill, where nothing gets done and nothing gets better. In these circumstances, an experienced clinician can help move your child past this initial resistance. Ideally, a clinician will listen, observe, and use language that is best suited for the child. The clinician will be able to meet your child where he or she is developmentally and emotionally, without making any judgments or assumptions.

While you and your child learn about BD, you can begin observing symptoms and behaviors in everyday life. Starting from a discussion of a shared experience (an argument, perhaps) allows both you and your child to look at how the problem started, progressed, and was resolved. The two of you can begin to recognize patterns, and with the help of your treatment team, you can develop a common language to help you communicate more effectively with each other and with the clinician.

Sometimes, this can greatly reduce the tension in the household, decreasing conflict and emotional upsets. This way you and the treatment team can develop closer relationships with your child, and provide support and guidance when he or she exhibits uncontrollable, abnormal behavior.

You can also *model* desirable behaviors, demonstrating healthy responses that can have a positive effect on your child's experience. For example, if you avoid eye contact and respond calmly when he or she starts to yell, you might prevent the situation from escalating. In contrast, if you loose your temper, lock into eye contact, yell back or threaten punishment, this will only make matters worse by allowing the interaction to escalate into a full-fledged confrontation.

Clinicians can also help by observing how interactions with family members affect the child's symptoms, and by identifying potential triggers of emotional instability at home. By examining a specific event (often a tantrum, or an argument) with a clinician, you and your child can work together on making sense of what went wrong. Together, you can think about alternative ways you both could have dealt with the problem; and you can look for better ways to solve problems. By emphasizing communication and collaboration on solving problems or reducing conflict, you engage your child in the team effort that is most likely to produce results. You and your child are usually in agreement on one thing: You both want the fighting to stop.

Thanks to psycho-education, you can teach your child not only about medications' benefits, side effects, and compliance, but also the importance of sleep hygiene, exercise, and diet. You can support your child's efforts to maintain emotional balance, implement suggested changes in sleep and homework routines, and advocate effectively for necessary school accommodations. Efforts to decrease symptoms can help reduce distress, sometimes quite rapidly. Reducing emotional conflict brings calm to the household, improves everyday functioning, and restores hope to both of you.

Parent Guidance

For families struggling with a child with BD, a simplified and focused plan to address the most troubling current problems is most helpful. Your needs change as your child's condition improves. During acute phases of illness and in emergencies, it is helpful to be able to reach out to the treatment team: you may want to report symptoms, side effects, or request additional medication in a crisis. During less acute periods, you might need advice regarding a medical problem, a school issue, test results, summer plans, or medication issues.

Family issues, especially problems with marriage or the siblings of a child with BD, can also benefit from ongoing support and reinforcement of healthy coping strategies. Sometimes, in order to continue to be effective, you may need a place just to talk about the stressful experience of parenting a child with BD and have that experience validated.

Monitoring Symptoms

Monitoring the course of BD in a child requires knowledge of the symptoms and sufficient understanding of the range of variability of each symptom. Long-term follow-up shows that symptoms fluctuate, and sometimes even disappear, over time. Against this backdrop of fluctuating symptoms, ongoing monitoring helps you define a baseline and assess the benefits of treatment.

Some symptoms appear or become more severe as the seasons change. They may even vary in intensity during the course of the day, with irritability and hyperactivity worsening in the evening and depressive symptoms (like cognitive sluggishness) usually worsening in the morning.

This knowledge is important for all school interventions, and parents' handling of the child should be in tune with the circadian variations of mood, energy, motivation, and concentration. For instance, mornings are the worst times to rush your child; on the other hand, the best time for academic work is late morning and early afternoon. The time in the late evening should be used for relaxing and unwinding, in preparation for sleep.

Knowledge of baseline symptoms can avoid misunderstanding a sudden change (either positive or negative) as the result of medication. Most of the time, clinicians and parents can distinguish patterns of temporary fluctuations from the effects of a drug by closely observing symptoms over time. Such observations enable parents to predict (and even to prevent or control) an episode by alerting the psychiatrist and facilitating a rapid intervention. Close monitoring also helps reduce the severity and duration of medications' side effects and contributes to long-term compliance with treatment.

The *MoodLog*™ (see chapter 5 and appendix II) provides a simple way for you to keep track of your child's symptoms. Monitoring symptoms in a chart provides a clear measure of the child's distress. Observing can also help you remain in control and, with time, you can learn to maintain an emotionally neutral state, even during crises. If you can remember that a tantrum is a symptom, then you can maintain a therapeutic stance.

You can understand your child's needs and respond in a helpful way only when you're in an emotionally neutral, empathic state. When calm and in control, you will be able to observe "being cursed at" as a symptom of BD, rather than becoming offended. Instead of reacting with anger, or escalating the crisis, you can remember that you are witnessing a symptom of the illness.

One parent wrote: "I see it coming. He asks me a question, and if I don't answer right away, he starts in with me. He'll ask the same question over and over, and louder. I remind myself: 'Look at the watch. How long is this tantrum going to last?' Breathe. 'What are the symptoms?' Breathe. 'He's restless, yelling, cursing, threatening; I think it's best to say nothing.' Breathe. 'I must avoid eye contact, and put something to eat on the table; maybe eating will help him calm down.' I breathe deeper; he seems to be calming down. Maybe I will leave him alone. I left the room, and came back in two minutes, and he was eating. I looked at my watch; it lasted less than five minutes. The medication must be working!"

For a child with BD, the ideal parent is consistent, calm, firm on safety and compliance with treatment, but fairly flexible on other issues. A child with BD also needs a warm and supportive style of parenting, with positive reinforcements and encouragement. When you see signs of instability, avoid negative responses (blaming, criticizing, berating, or being sarcastic); this way a tantrum is less likely to escalate, and often it will be shortened.

Over time, it will become clear that your child needs to be engaged, occupied, and active. Most professionals will refer to this important aspect of treatment as "structure." *Structure*, the planning of activities, breaks, school, homework, social events, sports, meals, and family activities can be most effective with the therapist's input, as it addresses the important variable of "pacing" the child's activities. Slowly, as you and your child learn to tag behaviors to symptoms (for example, caffeine causes sleep problems), you will adopt lifestyle changes that help to prevent or mitigate symptoms. With greater stability comes a sense of competence, mastery, and hope.

School Intervention

As discussed in chapter 3, there are cognitive symptoms of BD that cause learning and social problems. After an acute episode of BD, some parents describe their child as no longer able to concentrate sufficiently to read and comprehend a paragraph, let alone a chapter for a book report. For a child whose pride is academic success, to be unable to keep up with classmates can be emotionally devastating. Although you want your child to excel in school, academics must wait until your child is medically and emotionally stable.

Most children require a low-stress school environment to help with the stabilization of BD. As the disorder becomes more apparent, both the academic and the social aspects of being in school can become overwhelming, and school accommodations can make a big difference in the stabilization process. Chapter 13 provides more details on how to make decisions for your child when school accommodations are necessary.

Child Therapy

Individual child therapy can be a helpful bridge between the child and the treatment team, providing a forum for your child to learn about BD, and to monitor and report symptoms that interfere with functioning. In addition, child-therapy sessions are a safe haven in which your child can use play and/or words to express the pain of dealing with the symptoms, work with the therapist to find creative solutions, and offer an opportunity to overcome the many difficulties of living with BD.

In addition to the psychiatric and psycho-educational aspects of the treatment plan, therapy can provide an opportunity for a child to develop skills that have been delayed by BD. In order to "catch up," your child needs to identify what gets in his or her way. This includes ideas and feelings as well as outward behaviors, like outbursts or mood shifts that are part and parcel of BD. This is easiest to learn within an atmosphere of safety, warmth, and understanding.

With therapy, your child learns to identify the warning signs and intensity of the distress, and becomes interested in learning how to calm down. Gradually, your child develops effective ways of coping with school problems and/or siblings. Therapy can also help your child to develop or maintain effective communication not only with you and the treatment team, but also with siblings, peers, and teachers.

Group Therapy

Placing children into a small therapy group (two to four children maximum) occurs later in treatment, after a child has developed the skills to communicate about the symptoms and can manage the intensity of social interactions. These small groups meet one to two times per month along with individual sessions. The groups provide a safe, controlled opportunity for children to learn how to manage the stress of social interactions. In this forum, children can learn again, or learn for the first time, how to get along with their peers.

Family Therapy

Family therapy is useful for keeping all family members on task. Generally, open-ended questions addressed to all the members keep everyone interested. Open-ended questions help everyone understand their experience and address their questions and concerns. For example, respect of physical boundaries (touching others, entering bedrooms without asking) can trigger frequent and even vicious fights between siblings, and can be easily dealt with by the therapist and the parents by setting clear limits and consequences for violating whatever agreement is put in place.

Family therapy is also useful for reinforcing basic rules of mutual respect, collaborative problem solving, planning family activities, and helping parents modulate family interactions effectively and consistently. The therapist can use these meetings as a forum for family members to "try out" pacing their interactions, or to uncover dysfunctional interactions or triggers to the child's symptoms.

8

Medication Choices

*Bea is a six-year-old girl in first grade. Her school requested
a psychiatric evaluation because of her difficulties with paying
attention, hyperactivity, and fighting with peers. In class, Bea is
impatient and restless: with her peers she often yells or is bossy,
stubborn, and verbally abusive. Bea defies rules. She is loud,
intrusive, and interrupts constantly. According to her mother,
Bea has severe temper tantrums several times a day. The tantrums
last for ten to fifteen minutes. During these tantrums, Bea becomes
very agitated (crying, cursing, stomping, spitting, punching, kicking,
head-banging, or impulsively running away).*

    *She also has problems with sleep: she needs the TV on to
fall asleep, wakes up every night with nightmares of being chased
by monsters, and goes to her mother's bed. Occasionally Bea wets
the bed, but she gets very angry if her mother tells anyone about
it. At the age of four, her pediatrician suggested a trial of Ritalin
for hyperactivity, but her parents were too frightened to put a
child so young on medication.*

This chapter does not make treatment recommendations but rather
illustrates how some medication can be used by professionals and the
child's parents to treat bipolar disorder (BD). We explicitly advise you
to make treatment decisions (including starting, changing a dosage, or
discontinuing a medication) only with the advice and supervision of
your physician of choice.

PHARMACOTHERAPY

For parents of a child with bipolar disorder, the issue of using medication is a difficult subject that can be a source of shame for some, and a source of hope for others. If symptoms are mild or intermittent, and other approaches have not been used, medication might not seem the best or first option. Some parents recognize early on that trying to manage without medication is equivalent to allowing a child with seizures to go unmedicated. If everything else has failed, and nothing reduces the suffering of your child, medication is a last option. As a parent, you may even feel that you've failed your child, or that your child has failed you. These are all natural reactions, but there is a more positive, productive way to think about medication for BD. For many parents, there are some expectations: it is assumed the treatment will be short term, is addictive, fast-acting, and always effective.

If you think about your child's symptoms as a sign of suffering, using medication loses its negative connotation. Sometimes, the response is so rapid and dramatic that it appears nothing short of miraculous and convinces everybody of the need for medications. More often, however, the response is more gradual and subtle in its effects.

Tremendous progress has been made in the ability of clinicians to recognize and diagnose BD. In turn, its clinical management has improved thanks to growing familiarity with childhood BD, its course, and the growing experience with available treatments.

In spite of great progress, prescribing medication for children with BD continues to pose several challenges. Just as with a diagnostic assessment, pharmacological treatment is often complicated by unclear boundaries, and by the extensive overlap between the symptoms of BD and the symptoms of other psychiatric, medical, and neurological disorders. The urgent need to intervene often prevails over doubts about efficacy, potential side effects, and concerns about short- and long-term safety.

This chapter provides basic information on commonly prescribed medications for BD and, with the advice of a knowledgeable physician, it will help you to make more informed decisions. For all pediatric age groups, however, the data is scarce: most studies have been conducted with adolescents, and only a few focus on younger children.

Do all drugs work well in all age groups? Unfortunately, the relationship between the child's age and the response to a specific treatment is unclear. For this reason, the response of adults and adolescents to treatment with drugs is often used to guide treatment decisions for younger children.

Furthermore, the knowledge derived from research studies, even those conducted under rigorous double-blind, placebo-controlled conditions, doesn't necessarily apply to every child. Research can give us only an estimate of a specific medication's safety, effectiveness, and tolerability. Decisions about treatment are based, within the context of limited scientific studies, on trial and error.

In other words, there is no known way of predicting which drug will be effective or well-tolerated by your child other than by actually trying it. You may feel that this is too much of a gamble, and, certainly, you don't want your child used as a guinea pig. However, the choice of treatment is not a random guess as there are several ways to predict and choose the best option for your child at any given time.

It is also useful to remember that, in most cases, doing nothing (that is, no meds at all) is not an option, and leaving BD untreated will create its own set of problems. That's why we invite you and your doctor to discuss the risks and benefits of each treatment.

Sometimes, the parents' response to a medication predicts a positive response in their child (see the discussion on lithium below). However, since neither a positive response nor adverse reactions and side effects can be predicted with certainty, parents and the treatment team must be aware of the risks and benefits of any medication and closely monitor the child during a medication trial.

Parental Monitoring

Once you and your treatment team have made the decision to try a medication, it will be useful to become familiar with the medication dosage, side effects, adverse reactions, and potential interactions with other drugs. After some time, as you become more comfortable with recognizing and managing side effects, you'll be better able to judge what you need to do, and when to call the prescribing doctor. Especially at the beginning of a new medication trial, if you are in doubt about whether you should call your doctor, call, leave a message, and let him or her decide.

Depending on the medication, you might be asked to monitor different aspects of your child's physical and psychological functioning.

Your doctor might want you to keep an eye on your child's appetite, weight, thirst, sleep, skin appearance, balance, activity level, attention span, and memory. If you don't understand why, or what you are looking for, just ask.

The normalization of brain functions that is provided by medical treatment is necessary for normal development. Unless your child can overcome challenges to his or her emotional balance, the child's maturation and modulation of responses will be compromised. Holding BD in remission allows a smooth return to normal development.

Under these circumstances, your child has a real chance at benefiting from other interventions. Medication doesn't work alone, and its use must be part of a comprehensive treatment plan, as discussed in chapter 7. When medications are used correctly, all the other approaches become more effective, and the gains consolidate. However, progressive stabilization and compliance with treatment can be negatively affected by mood instability and/or exacerbations of BD. Noncompliance with treatment is common during hypomania, when impaired judgment often leads to discontinuation of treatment, and a worsening of symptoms.

The proper pharmacological management of BD requires the active involvement of all: child, parent(s), clinician(s), and school staff. The process begins with *psycho-education*, which is the ongoing process of learning about BD and its treatment. A collaborative approach encourages reporting and managing side effects and provides continuous assessment of the response to treatment and the monitoring of *treatment compliance* (that is, taking the medication as prescribed).

Everyone has an important, mutually supportive role to play. Such an integrated therapeutic effort offers the best opportunity for success by overcoming common challenges (initial side effects, forgetfulness, slow response, and sedation) along the way.

GENERAL PRINCIPLES

Almost all of the parents and children we've worked with share questions and worries about medication use. Common concerns are side effects, the long-term risks, and the potential for becoming addictive. Many parents ask, "Is medication really necessary?" or "Will it change my child?" Other parents worry about issues like these: "Will my child become addicted to it?" or "Are medications limiting my child's options?" Finally, "What if the medication(s) works but the child/teen doesn't want to take it?"

First of all, *medication treats abnormal brain functioning.* Effective medications help because normal brain functioning is derailed by BD. If there weren't a chemical imbalance, there would be no symptoms or the need for treatment. Furthermore, when medication helps, a child has the opportunity to learn healthy behaviors and coping skills. Your child will then have a chance to live free of the constant intrusion of symptoms.

Medications cannot fix or cure BD, but they can help to control (more or less completely) its symptoms. By doing that, medication removes the obstacles that BD puts in the way of your child's normal development, and it neutralizes the negative effects on frustration tolerance, self-esteem, interpersonal relations, education, and normal adjustment.

The following questions and answers address many of the most common, and absolutely valid, concerns regarding the use of medication:

Q: How does my child start taking the medication?

A: Your child will start taking a low dose of a specific medication, or in some cases, a combination of medications. Often, a clinician will increase the dosage slowly until it becomes effective, or side effects develop. The effective dose of a medication is called the *therapeutic dose.* As your child grows, the therapeutic dose might change (increase). It will remain fairly stable when growth is completed, usually in early adulthood. If body weight decreases substantially, the medication's dose might need to be reduced.

Q: Will there be side effects, and if so, what can we do to minimize them?

A: A strategy that starts your child with small doses will minimize unwanted but expected side effects such as nausea, headaches, itching, and sedation. This strategy will also reduce the risk of adverse reactions. Adverse reactions, unlike side effects, are unexpected.

Q: When will side effects begin and will they go away?

A: Some side effects develop early in the course of treatment (for example, a rash) while other side effects develop only over time (weight gain). Some side effects are mild and can even disappear on their own, but, in some rare instances, side effects can be severe and permanent (for example, impaired liver or kidney function, tics, or other movement disorders).

Q: What if my child has an adverse reaction or severe side effects?

A: In this case, you need to tell your clinician immediately. At that point, the clinician is likely to stop the trial of the medication.

Q: When will we know whether a specific medication is the right one? How long before we see results?

A: If your child tolerates the therapeutic dosage of a medication and takes it long enough to see any results, your clinician will help determine whether the medication is working. Some medications act fast, and their beneficial effect is readily apparent. Other medications take longer to act. With these, your child may begin to have a beneficial response only after several weeks or months of treatment.

Q: How will we know if a specific medication is effective in the short term?

A: To assess the short-term efficacy of a treatment, you and your clinician will have to monitor one or more symptoms and assess their impact on your child's daily life before and after a medication is started. For instance, if the target symptom is insomnia, an effective treatment would shorten the time your child needs to fall asleep, or the number of sleep interruptions. If sleep improves, your child will feel more rested and may be able to function better in school.

Q: How will we know if a specific medication is effective in the long term?

A: It can take several months (or even years) of treatment to determine whether ongoing use of a medication is effective. Success with maintenance treatment means preventing recurrences of the illness and often relates, in part, to the medication's impact on the typical cycle of the illness before and after treatment. An overall improvement in school, home, and social functioning often reflects the effectiveness of a specific treatment. For instance, if your child experiences a seasonal episode of mania (or depression), you might not be able to judge the efficacy of a medication until the child goes through a risk period (e.g., autumn) without recurrences. In this case, this length of time might be one year, but it is usually shorter.

USING MEDICATIONS FOR BD

Two main approaches can be recognized in the treatment of bipolar disorder in all ages: for the purpose of simplification we'll refer to the two as symptomatic treatment and stabilization treatment.

In *symptomatic treatment*, medications are prescribed to address the most significant symptoms present, including depression (stabilizing from "below") or mania (stabilizing from "above"). In this approach, antidepressants are often used, both as acute and maintenance treatment, following the hypothesis that guarding against the risk of depression will reduce morbidity and recurrence rate in bipolar disorder. Antidepressant treatments are often combined with mood stabilizers and/or atypical antipsychotic agents or stimulants during maintenance treatment.

We favor the alternative approach of *stabilization treatment*, which aims at the treatment and prevention of excitatory states (manic or mixed) as a way of preventing cycling and recurrences. Antidepressants and stimulants are avoided whenever possible, as they carry the potential to induce mania and increase cycling (see Antidepressants and Bipolar Disorder below). Rather than treating the illness's phase or phases, priority is given to the long-term stabilization of the illness.

RESEARCH ON EFFICACY

Do medications really work with BD? Some research gives us positive support for many medications. However, research on the use of medications with children lags behind studies involving adults. Therefore, for some medications, clinicians base their recommendations on evidence from adult studies and anecdotal case reports. Table 7 summarizes the scientific evidence for the benefits of various medications in the different phases of treatment. This information applies to specific mood states (mania, depression, mixed states) and maintenance treatment. A question mark indicates that no conclusive evidence has been reported.

Table 7: Medications' Efficacy by Mood State and for Maintenance*

Medication**	Mania	Depression	Mixed States	Maintenance
Lithium salts Lithobid, Eskalith	Yes	Yes	Yes	Yes
Valproic Acid and salts Depakote	Yes	Yes/No	Yes	Yes
Carbamazepine Tegretol, Equetro	Yes	No	Yes	Yes
Oxcarbazepine Trileptal	?/Yes	?/Yes	?/Yes	?/Yes
Lamotrigine Lamictal	No	Yes	?/No	Yes/No
Gabapentin Neurontin	Yes/No	Yes/No	Yes/No	Yes/No
Antipsychotics	Yes	Yes/No	Yes	Yes
Benzodiazepines	Yes	Yes/No	Yes	Yes
Hypnotics	Yes	Yes	Yes	Yes/No
Antidepressants	No	Yes	No	No
Stimulants	No	Yes	No	No

* Reproduced from G. L. Faedda. 2004. Childhood onset bipolar disorder: Pharmacological treatment overview. *Journal of Developmental and Learning Disorders* 8:37–64.

** Medications shown in bold face type are the generic names. Medications shown in regular type are the brand-names.

TYPES OF MEDICATION

As you can see from table 7, there are many different types of medications. Sometimes they are used alone (*monotherapy*), other times in
combination (*polytherapy*). The following sections describe each type of
medication and provide some in-depth technical information. Probably
the best way to absorb this information is to scan through the sections,
read those that are relevant for your child, and use the others as
references.

Mood Stabilizers

The term *mood stabilizer* applies to different types of drugs that
share the ability to reduce the intensity and frequency of mood swings.
Common mood stabilizers include lithium salts, some anticonvulsants,
and some antipsychotic medications. This class of medication can treat
manic and mixed states. Mood stabilizers can also prevent recurrences or
relapses.

Some of the mood-stabilizing agents (lithium and lamotrigine,
possibly others) may also have antidepressant effects. Controlled trials
and clinical case reports with both adults and children support the
relative efficacy and safety of mood stabilizers. However, to date, little
scientific data exists on the use of mood stabilizers in children either in
monotherapy or in combination (a combination might consist of two
mood stabilizers or a mood stabilizer with an atypical antipsychotic).

Lithium Salts

Discovered by the Australian psychiatrist John Cade in 1949,
lithium remains the gold standard for the pharmacological treatment of
BD in adults. Lithium is effective in mania and for prevention of manic
and depressive recurrences. There is limited data on the efficacy of
lithium in the acute treatment of manic or mixed states in children and
adolescents.

EFFICACY

The vast majority (more than 80 percent) of patients in placebo-controlled and open trials responded to treatment with lithium. The response to lithium is higher in cases of "pure" BD than in cases with a comorbid disorder (for example, attention-deficit/hyperactivity disorder [ADHD] or alcohol abuse). Open trials and case histories show similar rates of response in mostly outpatient populations. Although these are mainly uncontrolled studies, the efficacy of lithium seems well-established. Note that discontinuing lithium treatment in patients who have responded positively often results in a high risk of recurrence.

PREDICTORS OF RESPONSE TO LITHIUM

Predictors of a good response to lithium include cycles in which mania/hypomania occur *before* depression, the lack of ADHD symptoms before adolescence, and a family history of response to lithium. A personality disorder during symptom-free intervals, mixed or dysphoric states, and a cycle where depression occurs *before* mania/hypomania seem to be associated with a poor response to lithium.

Used under experienced supervision, lithium is safe and usually well-tolerated. Nonetheless, treatment with lithium is delicate, as the therapeutic and toxic levels are very close. Clinicians sometimes estimate the total daily dose of lithium for acute treatment of mania either by body weight or using a formula. However, because neither method is always accurate, close monitoring of lithium blood levels and side effects is essential for safety.

Lithium concentrations used therapeutically (0.6–1.2 milli-equivalent/liter) can rise rapidly to toxic levels (1.2 and higher) caused by dehydration due to sweating, exercise, heat, fever, vomiting, or diarrhea. Great caution should be used when first using lithium to treat young children, when the child has a medical illness (particularly fever and fluid or electrolyte imbalance), and when using the higher doses and serum levels. It is common for toxicity to occur with serum lithium concentrations above 1.2 mEq/L, and severe toxicity is very likely to occur above 2.0 mEq/L.

Before starting treatment with lithium it is helpful to obtain the following baseline information about the child: height, weight, vital signs, a complete blood count (CBC), electrolytes and urinalysis, liver (LFTs), kidney (BUN, creatinine), and thyroid function tests. A baseline electrocardiogram (EKG) is often requested.

Routine monitoring of blood lithium levels, renal (kidney), and thyroid function is required for safe long-term or maintenance use. Lithium levels should be measured approximately twelve hours after the last dose; for instance, after an evening dose at 8 P.M. of the first day, a morning blood test at 8 A.M. on the following day (before taking the morning dose) will provide the desired time interval. The child doesn't need to fast before taking a lithium level test. Lithium levels are obtained more often at the beginning of treatment, as a therapeutic dose is gradually reached and measured for consistency.

The frequency of blood monitoring decreases with stabilization of the symptoms and during maintenance treatment, but becomes more frequent during periods of rapid growth. Following a change in lithium dosage, an interval of three to four days is recommended before checking the new blood level.

LITHIUM'S SIDE EFFECTS

Most patients treated with lithium experience some side effects. Young patients seem to experience side effects that are both less frequent and less severe than adults and the elderly experience, possibly because young patients' kidneys are more efficient at eliminating lithium. There are, however, exceptions due to individual sensitivity and differences in how fast each person's body eliminates lithium. Note that continued use of lithium tends to reduce the severity of some side effects.

In most cases, clinicians prescribe a twice a day (called BID) dosage, after breakfast and dinner. Lithium is best tolerated after a meal because it can cause irritation of the upper gastrointestinal tract. At the beginning of treatment, common complaints about side effects include the following:

- Stomach and abdominal cramps or discomfort

- Indigestion

- Heartburn

- Nausea (initially, even when taken after a meal)

- Vomiting

- Loose bowel movements or diarrhea

These side effects are usually milder after the first days or weeks of treatment. Increased thirst and frequent urination are also common and, in children, this can lead to bedwetting. Tremor, muscle weakness, fatigue or tiredness, and poor balance are also frequent complaints. Less common side effects are weight gain, a metallic taste, hair loss, and swelling of the extremities. Skin problems may be exacerbated, especially acne in adolescents and psoriasis, and can further limit the use of lithium in children.

Lithium can have long-term effects on several organs and systems, primarily the central nervous system (CNS), kidneys, and thyroid. The frequency of these adverse effects among children remains understudied, and their impact on treatment compliance and discontinuation is unknown.

Lithium's effects on CNS functions range from a fine resting tremor (an involuntary, barely perceptible shaking when the body is at rest) and poor coordination (relatively common) to cognitive slowing and memory impairment (fortunately, rare). Memory and cognitive difficulties may require discontinuation of maintenance treatment. Lithium's CNS toxicity usually occurs at blood levels two or more times higher than therapeutic levels, and necessitates emergency treatment. Acute poisoning causes confusion, seizures, and coma.

Prolonged treatment with lithium does not alter kidney function, yet toxic levels of lithium, even brief ones, can cause damage to the kidneys. There appears to be an association between lithium treatment and thyroid function, either as enlargement (goiter) or slowing of thyroid activity (hypothyroidism), and the development of thyroid autoimmune antibodies. Mild, treatable hypothyroidism is common and rarely requires discontinuing lithium; it is sometimes reversible upon lithium discontinuation. Hypothyroidism is treated with thyroid hormones (synthetic or natural).

If it becomes necessary to stop lithium in order to avoid destabilizing BD, the doctor should avoid abrupt discontinuation by tapering the dosage, and closely supervising the child. The increased risk of recurrence or relapse soon after discontinuing lithium (and possibly other agents) can be eliminated by slowly reducing the dosage over the course of several weeks.

LITHIUM PREPARATIONS

Lithium is available in several different preparations: a liquid form (citrate), a tablet or capsule form (carbonate), and several slow-release or controlled-release preparations, in both brand-name and generic forms. Controlled-release preparations usually cause fewer side effects and produce more consistent blood levels.

Anticonvulsants

Among the anticonvulsants used in children with BD, sodium divalproex (Depakote) and carbamazepine (Tegretol and others) are best known and commonly used.

The use of anticonvulsants to treat children and adolescents with bipolar disorder is "off-label" because the FDA has not approved the use of these medications for the treatment of BD before age eighteen.

SODIUM DIVALPROEX (DEPAKOTE) AND VALPROIC ACID (VPA)

Sodium divalproex (Depakote) is metabolized or broken up into valproic acid (VPA), the active principle, which has been found to be effective in more than half of adolescents with acute mania (see table 7). Depakote and VPA differ in some aspects, including absorption, metabolism, and side effects. VPA seems to be just as effective, but, sometimes, it is less well-tolerated.

Clinicians commonly prescribe dosages that result in blood levels of 50–120 mg/L. These levels are based on the effective treatment of epilepsy. The dose-response relationship for treatment of BD in children and adolescents is unknown. Aggressive rapid titration (also called *oral loading*, giving the estimated daily dose all at once, to produce therapeutic levels quickly) has been used to control seizures and can produce a rapid (within days) antimanic effect.

Side effects of valproic acid. Side effects reported with VPA, and somewhat less often with Divalproex, include the following:

- Sedation

- Gastrointestinal upset

- Nausea

- Vomiting and loose bowel movements

- Increased appetite and weight gain (quite common; may reduce compliance and/or lead to discontinuation of treatment)

There are also reports of the following:

- Reversible hair loss

- Decreased serum carnitine (a liver and muscle chemical that promotes normal cell function) levels

- Hyperglycemia (high blood sugar)

- Increased ammonia serum levels and menstrual irregularities

Parents are often concerned about liver (hepatic) toxicity, which is rare, or acute liver failure, which is even more rare. However, liver failure has been reported in very young children (less than two years of age) treated with VPA *in combination* with other anticonvulsants for epilepsy. Pancreatitis and aplastic anemia (a rare form of anemia) or other blood-count abnormalities are also rare occurrences.

In adolescents, high testosterone levels have been reported during long-term treatment with VPA. In girls, this has been associated with *polycystic* (having many cysts) changes in the ovaries, menstrual irregularities or interruption (amenorrhea), masculinization, and increased insulin resistance. These changes are usually reversible, and because this data is derived primarily from children with seizure disorders, it may not necessarily generalize to children with BD.

CARBAMAZEPINE (TEGRETOL AND OTHERS)

Carbamazepine (CBZ), an anticonvulsant used for seizure disorders and pain syndromes, is effective in the treatment of adults with mania, and may be effective in childhood BD. Carbamazepine has been used to treat a host of emotional, behavioral, and neuropsychiatric disorders in children, including ADHD, conduct disorder, and aggression. Several case reports support the efficacy of CBZ for aggression and ADHD-like behavioral disorders in children.

For both adults and children, CBZ seems to be most helpful in mixed states or dysphoric mania. Anti-epileptic therapeutic blood levels (6–12 mg/L) measured twelve hours after the last dose are used in maintenance treatment for BD, although the relationship between blood levels and antimanic efficacy is unclear.

Side effects of carbamazepine.   Side effects of CBZ in adolescents with seizures were similar to those found in adults, including the following:

- Excessive sedation

- Vertigo or poor balance

- Mild CNS toxicity (tremor, slurred speech, double vision) or headache

- Nausea, vomiting, or gastrointestinal complaints

- Rashes

Rare but serious reactions to CBZ include blood-count abnormalities or, much less often, anemia or blood-platelet deficiencies. These reactions, usually mild, do not differ in frequency or severity between children and adults. However, for this reason, regular blood-count monitoring is required. CBZ stimulates liver enzymes that metabolize several drugs, including CBZ. A high metabolic rate can decrease CBZ blood levels; combined with other treatment, it requires closer monitoring of blood levels.

OXCARBAZEPINE (TRILEPTAL)

The anticonvulsant oxcarbazepine (OXC), structurally related to CBZ, is metabolized differently, and many drug interactions found with CBZ are less likely to occur with OXC. Compared to CBZ, oxcarbazepine also has a more benign side-effect profile, including sleepiness, headache, dizziness, double vision, unsteady gait, vomiting, rash, and abdominal pain. OXC is not known to cause aplastic anemia or liver toxicity, but can significantly reduce sodium blood levels.

There have been no controlled trials of OXC in children with BD. However, anecdotal experience and controlled trials in adults indicate that OXC has antimanic effects. Its broad spectrum of action, relatively benign side effects, reported safety in children, and ease of use (no drug-to-drug interactions or blood-level monitoring) contribute to the growing use of OXC as a mood stabilizer. In spite of the limited scientific support for its effectiveness in children, OXC alone or in combination with other mood stabilizers or antipsychotics has become a first-line agent in the treatment of childhood BD.

LAMOTRIGINE (LAMICTAL)

Lamotrigine (LTG) has been used successfully to stabilize adults with BD. Compared to other mood stabilizers, LTG seems to be effective in preventing depressive symptoms as well as or better than other medications, but it lacks antimanic effects and can, on rare occasion, induce mania or cause activation. Its efficacy in children with BD remains unknown. It is effective for ameliorating depressive symptoms and some mixed/rapid cycling states in adults, so it appears to be a promising addition to the available treatments for childhood BD.

Side effects of lamotrigine.   Because LTG has the potential to cause skin rashes, clinicians commonly increase the dosage very slowly. Most of the rashes are benign and disappear on their own, or after the medication is discontinued. Rarely, these rashes can progress to a potentially lethal shedding of skin (Stevens-Johnson syndrome). A slow increase in dosage can markedly reduce and usually prevent such reactions.

Common side effects may include dizziness, unsteadiness, somnolence, headache, double or blurred vision, nausea, vomiting, and rash. Many side effects are dose-related; therefore, slow, careful titration of LTG may help to avoid these effects. LTG does not appear to cause weight gain, but it does interfere with other commonly used mood-stabilizing treatments.

OTHER ANTICONVULSANTS

Anticonvulsants of potential interest in the treatment of BD include gabapentin (Neurontin), levitiracetam (Keppra), tiagabine (Gabitril), topiramate (Topamax), and zonisamide (Zonegran). To date, there have been no controlled trials on the use of any of these medications in children with BD. The only data supporting their use come from case reports, or clinical experience and trials in adults with BD.

Gabapentin is sometimes used as an add-on agent in adults with BD. However, the reports in children with seizure disorders of activity and behavior changes encourage caution. The child might seem drunk, confused, or activated with a complete loss of inhibitions.

Topiramate and zonisamide are of interest as they do not cause weight gain in long-term use, but their status as an effective antimanic or mood-stabilizing agent has not been proved. These medications are often prescribed as an "add-on," when greater control of mood swings is desirable, or because they suppress appetite. Levitiracetam has anti-anxiety effects in adults, but systematic studies in adults or children with BD are lacking. The antimanic or mood-stabilizing activity of tiagabine, doubtful in adults, has yet to be studied in children with BD.

Antipsychotics

Antipsychotic medications include traditional antipsychotics (neuroleptics) and atypical antipsychotics (AAPs). AAPs have almost completely replaced the older neuroleptic drugs. Neuroleptics are rarely used since they can induce parkinsonism (stiffness and tremor), dystonia, tardive dyskinesia (TD), and other movement disorders. AAPs are often used in the treatment of BD because of their powerful antimanic effects and sedating properties. In addition, these medications provide clinical benefits very quickly. AAPs are particularly useful in managing psychotic symptoms found in childhood BD. The mechanism of action of AAPs is not clear, but it is probably related to their effect on the neurotransmitter dopamine.

AAP medications are grouped based on their chemical structure: the *benzepines* include clozapine (Clozaril and generic), olanzapine (Zyprexa, and rapidly dissolving Zydis), and quetiapine (Seroquel) and the *benzisoxazoles* include risperidone (Risperdal, long-acting Consta), ziprasidone (Geodon), and aripiprazole (Abilify).

OLANZAPINE (ZYPREXA)

The FDA has approved olanzapine (OLZ) for acute treatment of mania as well as for long-term maintenance treatment of BD in adults.

Its use in child psychiatry as an antimanic and/or mood-stabilizing agent has rapidly increased, in spite of concerns about weight gain, sedation, increased insulin blood levels, and the development of type II diabetes. The long-term benefits and metabolic risks of OLZ in young patients are still unclear. However, high rates of discontinuation due to long-term adverse effects (mostly weight gain and sedation) reduce its appeal for long-term use in treating children with BD.

QUETIAPINE (SEROQUEL)

Evidence of quetiapine's (QTP's) efficacy in mania is provided by the adult literature, case reports of its efficacy in childhood mania, and a controlled study in hospitalized adolescents (adding QTP to divalproex produced some improvement). In a study) comparing efficacy and rapid onset of action, QTP did better than VPA (DelBello et al. 2006. A small percentage of the patients treated with QTP had elevated liver function tests compared to patients treated with other AAPs. This effect, readily detected, resolves spontaneously within the first month of treatment in most cases. High doses of QTP are associated with weight gain and excessive sedation.

CLOZAPINE (CLOZARIL AND OTHERS)

The use of clozapine (CLZ) is limited by the requirement of frequent monitoring of white blood cell count. Such intensive monitoring lowers the risk of a potentially fatal decrease of white blood cells (agranulocytosis) during the first six months of treatment. FDA-mandated monitoring guidelines now allow for blood monitoring every four weeks after extended monitoring has been negative.

CLZ can work well in juveniles with mixed states, and in acute or long-term maintenance of prepubertal cases of BD that have not responded to neuroleptics or other agents. Common side effects include weight gain, excessive salivation, sedation, lowering of seizure threshold, and constipation.

RISPERIDONE (RISPERDAL)

The only controlled study of risperidone (RIS) in children proved its efficacy for the treatment of aggression (a common symptom of mania), although the group had not been diagnosed with BD. Some children with manic or mixed BD showed a significant reduction of manic and aggressive symptoms with risperidone.

Risperidone can have some significant side effects. It can prolong the QTc interval on an EKG, possibly increasing the risk for arrhythmias. Therefore, this medication should not be used in patients with an abnormal EKG or with other agents that prolong the QTc interval, such as thioridazine (Mellaril, generic) or tricyclic antidepressants.

Among modern antipsychotic agents, risperidone has a high risk of inducing severe *hyperprolactinemia* (high prolactin blood levels). Hyperprolactinemia causes milk production (*galactorrhea*), swelling breasts (*gynecomastia*), and stops menstruation (*amenorrhea*). It might predispose individuals to osteoporosis and cardiovascular disease. Long-term treatment with risperidone should be monitored for the development of hyperprolactinemia, as the risk is much higher than with other AAPs.

ARIPIPRAZOLE (ABILIFY)

Aripiprazole (Abilify) has been approved for treatment of mania in adults, and is increasingly popular due to the lower risk of weight gain and diabetes compared to other agents. Aripiprazole lacks, like most agents, controlled data from the pediatric population. Although its sedative effects are not as prominent as with other AAPs, aripiprazole is used as an antimanic and for maintenance treatment. Adult doses range from 2.5 mg to 20 mg daily. This range is also used in children and adolescents. Among adults, the most common adverse effects include headache, anxiety, and insomnia; nausea and vomiting; dizziness, constipation, and restlessness. Sleepiness is usually a complaint with higher doses.

ZIPRASIDONE (GEODON)

Ziprasidone has shown efficacy in the acute treatment and long-term prevention of mania in adults. The use of ziprasidone increases the risk of elevated prolactin levels and EKG changes, especially an increase in the QTc interval. There is no evidence of significant weight gain, and common side effects include somnolence, nausea, and tiredness.

Combined Treatment

Various combinations of mood-stabilizing medications, involving those proven or assumed to be effective, are prescribed when one medication (*monotherapy*) does not adequately treat BD. This empirical, off-label use of combined treatment is supported by some open trials as well as by limited clinical experience. Lithium, the standard and longest-established treatment for BD, has far more research support than any other treatment. Therefore, most research has been focused on the benefits of adding an anticonvulsant or a second-generation antipsychotic agent to lithium when monotherapy proves ineffective.

Miscellaneous Treatments

Several other medications are sometimes used in treating children with BD. Antihistamines (diphenhydramine; Benadryl) can work as a mild sedative and safe sleep aid. Antihypertensive agents, which lower blood pressure, including clonidine (Catapres), have sedating properties. Benzodiazepines, especially lorazepam (Ativan) and clonazepam (Klonopin), are widely used as sedatives and for additional management of mania. Occasionally, they can produce disinhibition in young children, and they carry a potential for addiction, abuse, and trafficking in contraband among adolescents.

Other benzodiazepines and typical antipsychotics, including chlorpromazine (Thorazine and generics), haloperidol (Haldol and generics), and others, are used for the treatment of mania. Calcium-channel blockers, briefly studied after some anecdotal reports of efficacy, remain an option in cases where more traditional treatments have failed. Hypnotic agents including zolpidem (Ambien), zaleplon (Sonata), eszopiclone (Lunesta), or melatonin (over-the-counter medication) may also be useful in the management of insomnia in childhood BD.

Omega-3 fatty acids (O3FA), particularly eicosapentaenoic acid (EPA) and perhaps docosahexaenoic acid (DHA), found in fish oils or linseed oil, were more effective than a placebo as an add-on for adults with BD. They appear to be particularly helpful in managing bipolar depression and mood instability. To date, there have been no published studies of O3FA in children, and its value in the treatment of BD is questionable.

Mood-Elevating Medications

Two groups of medication are discussed here, antidepressant agents (AD) and stimulants. Although some stimulants are used for treatment of depression in adults, in children their use is usually for ADHD either alone or comorbid with BD and other conditions.

ANTIDEPRESSANTS

The use of an AD in children is often required by the presence of depressive symptoms during bipolar depressive or mixed episodes, as well as for the treatment of comorbid ADHD or anxiety disorders. Symptoms of depression, anxiety, or school problems often prompt an evaluation. Clinicians easily identify major depression, with its potentially devastating effects on home and school functioning, but they may not always rule out the possibility of BD. Also, since the diagnosis of depression is more socially acceptable, many parents feel comfortable accepting a trial of AD agent.

Although the efficacy of AD in depression and anxiety disorders seems fairly well-established, recently their safety has been the object of intense scrutiny. In children with BD, a history of AD trials is quite common. Although the efficacy of these medications is established in major depression and anxiety disorders, their efficacy and safety in BD have been questioned. In patients with diagnosed or latent BD, these medications sometimes cause insomnia, increased anxiety and agitation, or lead to a switch from depression to hypomania or mania. (For Treatment-Emergent Mania, see below.)

Antidepressant agents can be grouped according to chemical structure (tricyclic; TCA), mechanism of action (selective serotonin reuptake inhibitors [SSRIs] such as fluoxetine [Prozac] and others; norepinephrine reuptake inhibitors [NRIs] like desipramine [Norpramin] and others; monoamine oxidase inhibitors [MAOIs] like tranylcypromine [Parnate]; and serotonin and norepinephrine reuptake inhibitors [SNRIs] such as venlafaxine [Effexor] and duloxetine [Cymbalta]), or atypical agents such as bupropion (Wellbutrin) and mirtazapine (Remeron).

The efficacy of antidepressants in children with major depression (MD) has been established for fluoxetine (Prozac), paroxetine (Paxil), and sertraline (Zoloft), but only fluoxetine is FDA-approved. Rigorous research has not found the older tricyclic AD (TCA) to be effective for childhood depression. These agents are less commonly prescribed because of their relatively high toxicity in an overdose. In contrast, other agents like the SSRIs, which are FDA-approved for the treatment of obsessive-compulsive disorder (OCD) or other anxiety disorders, are commonly prescribed for treatment of depression.

In children and adolescents with BD we use AD sparingly, starting with small doses and increasing the dose very gradually; reducing or discontinuing the AD as soon as clinically feasible has rarely resulted in adverse reactions or manic symptoms. Starting with a low dose and increasing the dose slowly seems to avoid (in most cases) dramatic changes in the child's mental state.

Close supervision by parents and treatment team members of mood, sleep, energy, and cognitive changes is required to prevent sleep or mood disturbances. Before resorting to the use of AD, we believe it is important to determine if the depressive symptoms are occurring in the course of mood instability, as this might be better treated with mood-stabilizing agents.

Depression needs to be distinguished from discouragement due to school failure or family conflict, as well as from low self-esteem, a common issue in children and adolescents with mood disorders in general and BD especially. Only a deep understanding of the child's issues and the course of his or her illness can help tease apart depressive symptoms requiring pharmacological treatment with AD from other causes. Sleep deprivation can be associated with daytime somnolence, inefficient school functioning, impaired concentration, poor executive functions, and irritability, and can be easily mistaken for depression.

In some seasonal forms of BD, the use of exercise, light therapy (using a light box), and AD during episodes of depression can help the child maintain adequate functioning at home and school. Interventions at school and in the home to reduce the amount of stress put on the child. They can be most helpful in keeping the child from feeling overwhelmed, unable to function, or a school failure, as these can further decrease self-esteem, and make the child feel guilty or hopeless.

A supportive home and school environment, and help from the therapist addressing cognitive distortions associated with depression ("I am a failure." "Nobody likes me." "Nothing will ever be better.") can help the child manage through mild to moderate depressive mood swings.

Side effects of antidepressants. Antidepressants may affect how other drugs are metabolized by the liver. Side effects commonly encountered with SSRIs include the following:

- Nausea

- Diarrhea

- Changes in appetite and weight

- Tremor, jitteriness

- Excessive sweating

- Vivid dreams

- Sexual dysfunctions

- Headaches and migraines (in those predisposed)

- Weight gain in varying degrees of frequency and severity

The SSRIs offer many advantages compared to tricyclics and to the MAOIs, including safety in case of overdose, ease of administration (single instead of multiple daily doses), and milder side effects. A routine medical evaluation (but no blood testing) is usually recommended before an antidepressant's trial in a child. Antidepressants usually require a trial of several weeks' duration before a full response is obtained. Treatment usually continues for several months, to help prevent a relapse or recurrence of depression. This practice, however, is not based on scientific evidence in children or adults with BD, as discussed in the next section.

ANTIDEPRESSANTS AND BIPOLAR DISORDER

Recent reports of aggressive or violent and suicidal behaviors among children and teenagers exposed to SSRIs have stimulated careful scrutiny of the efficacy, safety, and adverse-effect profile of antidepressants. The widespread use of the SSRIs, prompted by their ease of use and relative safety in case of overdose is also a concern, especially since close supervision by a mental health specialist has often been replaced (for economic reasons) by infrequent visits to the pediatrician. Serious concerns about the effects of exposure to antidepressants in bipolar disorder stem from the following substantial evidence in adults:

- Mania may be induced or worsened.

- Cycling can be induced or accelerated.

- Response to mood stabilizers is diminished or impaired.

All antidepressants and stimulants seem capable of inducing (hypo)mania, although their ability to do so may vary depending on the class and specific agent. Extreme caution with antidepressants (and stimulants) is advisable, especially for children of adults who have been diagnosed with BD, or when BD is suspected. In fact, many cases of childhood-onset depression and dysthymia eventually evolve or convert into BD, sometimes after several years of recurrences of depression.

Common predictors of later spontaneous or medication-induced "conversion" from depression to BD include: early and/or acute (sudden) onset of depression, slowing down of psychomotor functions (retardation), psychotic features during depression, a multigenerational family history of mood disorders, and multiple recurrences. An increase in emotional instability or disinhibited behaviors with antidepressants or other mood-elevating agents should be considered a possible indicator of latent BD.

How often manic symptoms occur during treatment of children with antidepressants and other mood-elevating treatments remains unclear. Some depressed children, not previously diagnosed with BD, become manic or hypomanic when treated with antidepressants. In children who manifest symptoms of bipolar disorder while on antidepressants, sleep disturbances, dysphoric irritability, moodiness, explosive outbursts, aggression, and oppositional-defiant behaviors are common.

STIMULANTS

Indicated for the treatment of ADHD, stimulants such as Ritalin, Adderall, Dexedrine, and Concerta are used extensively with children and adolescents. Given the high rates of comorbidity of ADHD and BD in children, along with misdiagnosis, many young people with BD are treated with stimulants.

At present, the American Academy of Child and Adolescent Psychiatry (McClellan and Werry 1997) recommends that: "Psychostimulants must be used with caution in patients with Bipolar Disorder and are best avoided during acute manic phases" (p. 166).

More recently, an article entitled the "Practice Parameters for the Use of Stimulant Medications in the Treatment of Children, Adolescents, and Adults" concluded that "Stimulants do not precipitate young adult Bipolar Disorders in boys comorbid for both Attention Deficit Hyperactivity Disorder and nonpsychotic Bipolar Disorder on mood stabilizers, either acutely or later on" (Carlson et al. 2000, quoted in Greenhill, Pliska, and Dulcan 2002, p. 32). These statements imply that for children with BD, stimulant treatment is quite safe. However, this point of view remains controversial and must be reconsidered in the light of clinical wisdom and emerging research findings.

Some reports suggest there is the potential for specific adverse psychiatric responses among patients with known or latent BD, particularly during treatment with stimulants or other mood-elevating agents, especially when those agents are unopposed by a mood stabilizer. Moreover, adverse psychiatric consequences may include a worsening course of BD long after stimulant treatment has been discontinued. These observations indicate that the problem of pharmacologically induced mania in children and adolescents with unrecognized BD is not sufficiently appreciated.

Treatment-Emergent Mania (TEM)

The development of new, or the worsening of preexisting manic symptoms with psychotropic drugs (*treatment-emergent mania* or TEM; Faedda et al. 2004b) is an important clinical phenomenon, and a devastating and traumatic event for the child and the entire family. When this change is related to medical treatment, it is important for the treatment team to recognize it and manage it promptly, advising the family on what to do.

Usually, TEM is a dramatic occurrence, and requires interventions such as stopping the medication associated with this reaction, and often sedating treatment or hospitalization. During a TEM, parents may observe sleep disturbances, restlessness or agitation, anxiety, and confusion with too many thoughts racing through the child's mind. During this time, the child is very emotional, overly sensitive, cries or angers easily, suddenly becoming explosive, abusive, and occasionally violent or aggressive. For parents who have never seen these symptoms before, TEM can be very alarming and disturbing.

In other cases, existing symptoms are made worse by treatment, as if "the volume has been turned up." In some cases, the reaction occurs within a day or two after starting a new medication. At other times, it takes a few weeks before symptoms appear. Less often, the gradual emergence of mania may take several months, or it may coincide with a seasonal pattern of switching from depression to mania. Sometimes, trouble falling asleep or sleep interruptions and restlessness may be the only indications that the medication might be destabilizing bipolar disorder. When manic symptoms reach their full intensity, the child may be so out of control (or psychotic) that a visit to the emergency room or even hospitalization might be required.

Adverse reactions to medications in childhood BD are often attributed to antidepressants, less often to stimulants, or to a combination of both types of drug. It is alarming that stimulants and antidepressants are the two most commonly prescribed psychotropic drugs in the United States.

Given the lack of data indicating the short- and long-term safety of antidepressants and stimulants for children with bipolar disorder, if either type of drug is prescribed, treatment should be started with low doses and closely monitored. Until safety data become available, we recommend that antidepressants be used only in combination with a mood stabilizer, under close supervision. Moreover, it is important to educate parents to recognize and report promptly any suspicious change in a young patient with known or suspected bipolar disorder.

As soon as the desired effect is obtained, an attempt should be made to reduce the dose of the antidepressant and, when possible, to discontinue it gradually. At the same time, the patient should continue to take the mood stabilizers in order to maintain remission of symptoms. This slow process allows assessment of the need to continue the antidepressant while decreasing exposure to a potentially destabilizing treatment.

9

Sleep Disorders

Sleep is a natural mood stabilizer and is essential to the successful treatment of bipolar disorder (BD) in children and adults. If your child suffers with bipolar disorder, sleep disturbances have likely been a problem, sometimes since birth. In the majority of cases, even when BD is in remission, patients experience and need to be treated for sleep disturbances. Some children with BD, however, do not experience prominent sleep disturbances. The relationship between sleep and BD is twofold: BD causes sleep disturbances, and sleep disturbances can destabilize BD. For instance, sleep deprivation can precipitate hypomania or mania which, in turn, can cause further sleep deprivation.

For many children with BD, going to sleep is a challenge. Many reasons contribute to this: First, sleep is a transition; it requires shifting from activity to rest. Second, fear of darkness, anxiety about separation from parent(s), and sometimes the fear of nightmares can cause a significant amount of anxiety and arousal. Third, disturbances of circadian rhythms produce a sense of increased energy and well-being in the child in the afternoon and evening hours, just when it is time for the child to settle down to sleep. Fourth, late evening TV programming, use of telephone, computer, e-mail, instant messaging, and various electronic gadgets may add to the child's dislike for bedtime, especially if older siblings are allowed to stay up. Conflict with parents over bedtime can easily escalate into arguments, further interfering with a good sleep schedule.

NORMAL SLEEP

Normal sleep follows a sequence of stages or phases, as described below:

Non-REM (nonrapid eye movement) sleep is associated with the progressive slowing of electrical brain activity. It represents slightly more than three-quarters of our total sleep time, and is divided into four stages of progressively deeper sleep.

- Stage I: falling asleep

- Stage II: the sleep baseline, 45 to 60 percent of our sleep, with very rapid brain waves (alpha waves)

- Stages III and IV: phases of deep sleep, or slow-wave sleep (SWS), because brain waves are very slow and deep (delta waves)

SWS is called "restorative" sleep: during this phase, the heart rate and breathing slow down, muscle tone decreases, and growth hormone is secreted. During these dreamless sleep phases, the body can rest, giving a sense of being refreshed and reinvigorated.

REM (rapid eye movement) or "dream sleep" takes up to 20 percent of our total sleep time, and occurs in cycles approximately every ninety minutes. Besides the eye movement, it is characterized by increased brain activity, dreaming, and paralysis of the voluntary muscles. Its duration increases over the course of the night from five minutes in the first cycle to thirty minutes by morning. Sleep deprivation disproportionately decreases both SWS and REM sleep.

SLEEP DISTURBANCES

Sleep can be disturbed in quantity (too much or too little), in its quality (continuous or interrupted), or its timing (advanced or delayed). In some forms of depression, the duration of sleep may increase; whereas it usually decreases in manic and mixed states, as well as in some forms of (agitated) depression. Sleep can be disturbed because of problems with the following:

- Falling asleep (early insomnia)

- Awakenings (middle insomnia)

- Waking up early (late insomnia)

- Sleep events

Sleep events, such as nightmares, night terrors, restless leg syndrome, sleepwalking, teeth-grinding (bruxism), and bedwetting (enuresis) can interfere with restorative sleep, disrupting both the quality and duration (quantity) of sleep.

Sleep Disturbances in Children with BD

Sleep disturbances are a consistent finding in BD at all ages. Some children manifest problems with sleep as early as infancy, waking up the moment they are put down in their crib. Many are short sleepers, do not take naps, or wake up extremely irritable after a nap and prefer to be constantly rocking or moving (in a stroller, car, or just being held in their parent's arms).

Later on, difficulty falling asleep, sleep interruptions, and early awakening can decrease sleep efficiency (hours of sleep/hours in bed). Sleep deprivation, often the result of inefficient sleep, can trigger instability in a child (or adult) with BD. Disrupted sleep may be one of the first symptoms of mania, depression, or a mixed state, or signal that BD is not completely stabilized.

Many children and adolescents with BD are "night owls"—they don't get to sleep before 11 P.M. or later, most nights. As children grow older, the demands of school interfere with their desire to stay up late, causing children and adolescents to argue with their parents over the issue of sleep. Since sleep disturbances are usually present long before the child has developed an interest in television, computer, or other electronic gadgets, it is easier to recognize them as biologically based problems. Many parents with BD know from their own experience, that their children are overinvolved in activities when it is time to go to sleep. Objective sleep measures obtained in sleep studies confirm that children with BD are "poor sleepers."

Causes of Sleep Disturbances

Many factors can affect sleep. They can be grouped into four categories:

1. **Medical and psychological:** can include cough, headaches, itching, cramps, or pain; anxiety, racing thoughts, restlessness; caffeine, medications (stimulants), or drugs

2. **Genetic and biological:** sleep disorders, disturbances of circadian rhythms

3. **Environmental:** such as noise, vibrations, light, high or low temperatures, lack of safety

4. **Social factors:** schoolwork, late-evening activities including TV, music, and telephones

In most cases, more than one factor contributes to the sleep disturbance. For instance, a child might be having too much caffeine (sodas, coffee, iced tea, chocolate), sleep in a noisy part of the house, and experience nightmares.

Activity Levels and Circadian Rhythms

For most children and adults, it's normal for activity levels to fluctuate throughout the day. Normal *circadian rhythms* produce a gradual increase in energy and activity from morning to early afternoon. This is followed by a gradual decrease in the evening that coincides with bedtime and a restful, restorative sleep. In a child with BD, this smooth rhythm is disturbed, with a so-called "phase delay." Everything is shifted forward. Morning wakefulness is delayed and midday activation occurs later, interfering with sleep. The result is the child goes to sleep late, wakes up late, is very tired and groggy in the morning, and has trouble keeping up with the school's schedule and work.

Further disturbing the baseline daily rhythm are the faster, half-day (or *hemicircadian*) rhythms with peaks every twelve hours. Strong hemicircadian rhythms, often found in children with BD, cause activity levels to cycle faster, fluctuating from high to low. The result can be sluggishness in the morning with impaired school functioning, and activation around the time the school day is ending. When your child returns home, it's time for homework. As bedtime approaches, your child might enjoy an increase in his or her physical and mental energy, or become aroused and anxious about going to sleep. Either way, going to sleep gradually becomes an unfair parental demand, an end to playing or having fun, as well as an anxiety-provoking transition.

Sleep Difficulties Caused by Anxiety and Arousal

Other reasons can produce an aversion to sleep. Children with BD may be afraid of the dark, easily fall prey to their vivid imagination, worry about monsters under the bed, darkness, and so forth. Many children have been traumatized by nightmares experienced since a young age. It appears that children (and adults) with BD experience their dreams more vividly and are more aroused and scared by them.

The dreams are quite gory or pose significant threats to the individual's safety (being taken away, catastrophic events occurring, loved ones being harmed). These dreams cause intense anxiety and a state of high arousal (palpitations, high blood pressure, increased body temperature, flushing and sweating, screaming).

Difficulty Falling Asleep

In addition to an increased activity level at bedtime, children who have difficulty settling into sleep tend to be more concerned with separation anxiety, worries about homework, or events (such as tests) occurring the following day in school. Environmental factors can play a significant role: noise, light, vibrations, extreme temperatures (too hot or too cold), uncomfortable bedding, or the absence of a sense of safety can prevent normal restorative sleep.

Some children will be able to sleep only with "white noise" in the background, as this masks other noises, is relatively constant, and helps slow down racing or crowded thoughts. Some children need a night-light due to a fear of the dark, others might need to have a very cold room to be able to fall and stay asleep. Fear of burglars or terrorists can maintain a state of hypervigilance and arousal in these highly impressionable children. Exposure to upsetting material in movies or TV can interfere with their sense of safety and delay sleep initiation. Medication used to treat comorbid ADHD (stimulants) or anxiety disorders (antidepressants) can also interfere with sleep initiation and continuity.

Interrupted Sleep

Interrupted sleep is a frequent problem: if your child wakes up in the middle of the night feeling anxious and in need of reassurance, he or she might want to retreat to your bedroom or your bed. Sometimes this can occur even in their teens, as the reassuring presence of a parent helps them return quickly to sleep.

Sleep interruptions can be caused by restlessness, nightmares, snoring, sleep apnea, or loss of bladder control and bedwetting. Increased activity levels during sleep in children with BD may be reported as restless or fitful sleep, with signs of activation, such as talking, grinding teeth, thrashing, or sleepwalking.

Bedwetting causes significant problems with self-esteem, along with interfering with age-appropriate social activities such as sleepovers and sleep-away camps. The use of pull-ups might be needed until teenage years.

Siblings, parents, and neighbors can be a source of disturbance to the child's sleep. Identifying and removing all possible causes of sleep problems is the key to providing your child with good sleep.

Note that your child's sleep interruptions may cause you to suffer from sleep deprivation, and thus negatively affect your ability to parent effectively. Sometimes, this can add pressure on a strained marital relationship, especially if your child needs to be in your room to go back to sleep.

INTERVENTIONS

Setting up a routine to facilitate a smooth transition to sleep requires flexibility and close attention to the many problems of children with BD.

Sleep Schedule

Creating a calm and relaxing environment with a predictable routine leading to sleep is extremely important. This could lead to changes affecting the whole family and their lifestyle. A child will want to do what his or her older siblings or peers do; adolescents will try to emancipate themselves from parental control, or imitate their parents' poor sleep habit (or symptom) of staying up late.

Having interesting activities scheduled in the morning, and arranging for slow, relaxing evening routines will facilitate putting in place a more balanced schedule. Also, sports can help maintain a better sleep schedule because of the positive effect of regular physical activity. (As mentioned earlier, regular physical activity should take place earlier in the day to avoid activation.)

To help regulate a grossly disturbed and unstable sleep pattern, it is essential to slowly and gradually shift the timing of sleep, while helping the child settle down for sleep. This is usually accomplished through changes in both lifestyle and sleep routine. Pharmacological intervention is generally helpful.

How Much Sleep?

Every individual has a certain sleep requirement, varying according to age and individual features (like temperament). As many as ten or more hours of sleep might be required, especially during childhood and teenage years. Having less sleep than necessary is called *sleep deprivation* or "sleep loss." And contrary to popular belief, lost sleep cannot be made up for. Weekend nights are the times when your child sleeps later and catches up on sleep. Unfortunately, competing social and environmental pressures lead to later bedtimes: a sibling staying up late, often with friends, is very stimulating, and so are late-night TV programming, movies, computer games, and phones.

For these reasons, your child might not get enough sleep on those nights, especially if you insist on an early wake-up schedule, as this only adds to the sleep deprivation. In addition to sleep problems caused by a manic or depressive episode, your child may be chronically sleep-deprived. A good way to find out is to determine how many hours your child sleeps when left undisturbed. If it is more than on any school night, it is likely that your child is sleep-deprived. Often a teen can sleep ten or more hours on a weekend or during vacations, but may sleep only six or seven hours a night during the school week.

Bedtime Routine

An ideal sleep schedule is formulated with the help of a clinician and takes into consideration school schedule, medication side effects, and individual factors. The goals of the sleep schedule should be implemented in small increments with the coordinated and collaborative effort of parents and child. It is not possible to shift rapidly from a very disturbed sleep schedule to a regular one, so you and your child will have to compromise. The clinician will help you set up a workable schedule. Keeping wake-up time fixed, at a time that allows for sufficient sleep and regular school attendance, we concentrate our efforts on anticipating bedtime, until the routine allows for sufficient sleep.

For instance, first-grader Annie's wake-up time has to be 8 A.M. if school starts at 9 A.M. She needs about twelve hours of sleep, but her bedtime is 10 P.M.: she is only sleeping ten hours a night and seems exhausted. Sleeping time can be gradually increased by trying to get Annie to fall asleep by 8 P.M., and by rearranging her activities. Changing into pajamas at 7 P.M. helps create a slow, quiet, bedtime routine to prepare for an earlier bedtime, thus moving it from 10 P.M. to 8 P.M. over the course of several weeks. Sometimes, by using a pharmacological intervention, the sleep schedule can be changed more rapidly.

A teenager who's going to sleep at 1 A.M. would not be able to fall asleep at 10 P.M. just because his or her parents ask, even if the teen wanted to fall asleep at that hour. Rather, a motivated parent/child team can work together in progressive, incremental steps toward a more desirable schedule, as bedtime is gradually shifted. For example, a realistic goal may be adjusting bedtime by thirty minutes each week, while wake-up time remains the same.

Reducing Stimulation

Dietary factors such as caffeine or alcohol, eating late, or environmental factors such as late-evening exercise, stimulating music, Internet or television programming (scary movies), telephone use, or heated discussions around bedtime may interfere with falling asleep and should, therefore, be avoided.

Getting to Sleep

The sleep-wake cycle is complex and still incompletely understood. Among the brain structures involved is the supra-chiasmatic nucleus (SCN) in the hypothalamus, which regulates sleep onset by modifying the body temperature. *Sleep latency*, which is the time required to fall asleep, is shortened by a rapid decrease of the body temperature. Lowering the body temperature facilitates sleep onset, and the old recommendation of a hot bath before sleep may be effective because the *vasodilation* (relaxation of blood vessels) that follows a hot bath increases blood flow and heat loss, which leads to a lowering of core body temperature.

Racing or crowded thoughts, physical restlessness, and a sense of overarousal and anxiety related to darkness and fear of separation are the most prominent obstacles to sleep initiation. The therapist might want to teach or reinforce the use of relaxation techniques to deal with racing thoughts, anxiety about sleep, fear of darkness, and ease the separation from caretakers. To overcome the sense of anxiety that precedes sleep, you can help by simply being physically present. Parents might read to their child or lie beside the child until he or she is asleep.

A white-noise machine, a fan, or a radio softly playing some relaxing music can help your child to overcome racing thoughts.

In most cases, a pharmacological aid can provide rapid onset of sleep, reducing the child and the parents' stress around bedtime (see chapter 8).

Staying Asleep

Factors affecting continuity of sleep, such as noise, temperature, air quality, bathroom use, thirst, hunger, pets, and so forth need to be addressed on an individual basis, as they often make the difference between adequate restorative sleep and sleep deprivation. Medical problems like obstructive sleep apnea (due to enlarged tonsils, or secondary to weight gain) can cause sleep interruptions and result in sleep loss.

Sleep events like nightmares may require a parent to intervene, provide reassurance, and often stay with the child until he or she falls asleep again. Although it is always better to help distressed children to settle back to sleep in their own bed, at times they will want to sleep in the parents' bed. Occasionally, this can be helpful to minimize sleep disruption until the child's sleep pattern has improved sufficiently and the child can get used to sleeping in his or her own bed.

Morning Sluggishness

Morning awakening is a feared daily event for most parents of a child with BD. Awakening is controlled in part by the SCN through a gradual increase in the body's temperature. Grogginess upon awakening can cause significant irritability and is worsened by sleep deprivation. The transition from sleep to wakefulness is slower if your child is awakened while in a phase of slow-wave sleep, or when the core body temperature is at its lowest.

A child with BD, often activated at bedtime, might fall asleep late, and be sleep-deprived on school days because of an early wake-up time. During the later part of a night's sleep, deep and REM sleep are more concentrated, so that the chances of a child with BD being awakened from a deep sleep state in the morning are increased.

This might contribute to the problem of *sleep inertia* (SI). SI is a transient episode of incomplete awakening, with confusion, low awareness, and automatic (not fully willful) behavior that immediately follows awakening. SI can last from minutes to hours, and can be associated with impaired cognitive and sensory-motor performance. It occurs immediately after awakening from sleep, and greatly impairs the child's ability to function, slowing down or interfering with most activities.

Parents are often frustrated with what seems an exaggerated, prolonged, painfully slow awakening. If they push, the child becomes increasingly upset and frequently oppositional. This, in turn, is met by a parent's stern discipline and can easily escalate into major arguments every morning. Some children can tell the exact time when SI lifts. This can help school personnel better understand and modify the child's schedule to address early-morning slowness.

MEDICAL INTERVENTIONS

Having excluded other medical causes for the sleep disturbance, it is usually helpful to assist the child in this difficult transition using medication that induces sleep. These medications, often referred to as hypnotics (from the Greek word "hypnos," meaning sleep), can be necessary to restore a normal sleep pattern, and can be necessary for maintenance treatment, as well.

Hypnotics

In chapter 8 on the pharmacological treatment of BD, you saw how mood stabilizers can be more or less sedating. We often take advantage of this by using the larger, or only, dose of medication at bedtime. Sometimes this solves the problem of putting the child to sleep, helping significantly and quickly to alter an abnormal sleep schedule. Quite often, however, this is not easily accomplished, and other medications are used for this purpose, including clonidine, benadryl, zolpidem, and zaleplon; or hypnotic benzodiazepines like flurazepam, nitrazepam, or triazolam. Most of these interventions are not approved for use in children, but they are often used when other interventions have failed. A careful assessment of risks and benefits should be the basis for using any of these medications.

Melatonin

Biological clocks (our internal timekeepers) regulate the secretion of melatonin and other hormones like cortisol, as well as rest-activity patterns, changes of body temperature, and the tone of blood vessels (vasodilation). *Melatonin* has a special place among sleep aids, being a natural hormone, produced and released according to circadian rhythms in preparation for sleep. Melatonin is secreted by the pineal gland and signals the onset of sleep, helping sleep initiation, and sometimes sleep continuity.

A potential predictor of bipolar disorder is the ability to suppress the secretion of melatonin with bright light. Melatonin has been used to treat insomnia in manic patients, reducing sleep latency: variable doses are dispensed either in the late afternoon (6 P.M.) or twenty to thirty minutes before bedtime. Melatonin can be an extremely effective way of rebalancing a profoundly disturbed sleep cycle. Although there are no studies on long-term use or safety, parents have reported that melatonin is helpful for maintaining a regular bedtime and sleep schedule. Besides allowing for improved wakefulness and functioning during the day, the most dramatic effect of an improved sleep cycle seems to be the marked reduction in irritability and emotional dysregulation.

SLEEP HYGIENE CHECKLIST

Avoid the following:

- Caffeine and alcohol intake

- Meals before bedtime (acid reflux)

- Bright light before bedtime

- Exercise two to three hours before bedtime

- Emotional upset before bedtime

- Violent or upsetting TV programs

- Naps; if necessary, limit to ten to fifteen minutes

- Clocks or checking the time (increases anxiety)

What to do:

- Keep the same bedtime/wake-up schedule (holidays and weekends included)

- Use the bed only for sleep, as it will behaviorally facilitate sleep initiation

- Develop bedtime routines like a warm bath, reading, or relaxing activities before turning out the lights

- Sleep in a completely dark and quiet environment

- A cool environment promotes sleep onset and continuity

- Soft foam earplugs help in a noisy environment

- A fan or white-noise machine can help block out sounds

10

Living with a Bipolar Child

The parents of ten-year-old Will bribe him for everything. His father says, "The worst part is we have no control over the house. Will does what he wants when he wants, and he goes to sleep when he feels like it. We don't know how we'll get him to your office. Will is in control, and even his older brother lets him get his way when they're not fighting." To get Will to the initial evaluation, his parents pleaded and bargained. The final cost was a new Ipod so Will can listen to the music he wants, when he wants.

Bipolar disorder (BD) can severely interfere with the child's develop-ment and education as well as disrupt family life. The stress on all family members can be very substantial and, at times, lead to serious consequences, including parental and siblings' illness, parental discord, and divorce. Sometimes the strain is so great that one parent has to give up a job and/or other activities in order to care for the child. This can have a negative impact on the family both emotionally and finan-cially. The stress is not alleviated by one parent taking over the caretaking of a child with BD, often a thankless and demanding job.

This chapter will show you how to reduce conflict in the house-hold, while focusing on the most essential need, that of maintaining safety and decreasing angry outbursts. Gradually, this will help you transform a chaotic situation into a relatively orderly family life.

Creating a daily routine or schedule will help to structure most activities in your home. This reduces both the need for reminders or prompts and opportunities for oppositional or defiant behavior. This is done by clearly defining what is expected of the child with BD as well as his or her siblings. Rather than micromanaging all daily activities and routines, clear rewards and consequences for compliance with the daily schedule are discussed with the child. This encourages children to become increasingly more responsible for their behavior, while earning rewards motivates them to consistently choose adaptive behaviors.

Each family will be at a different stage of developing and following through on daily routines. A focused approach will help you to build a reliable home schedule based on the most essential features of your child's treatment plan: medication, sleep, and school attendance. Teaching your child to comply and ultimately to self-monitor these adaptive behaviors is based on the principles of behavioral modification, and requires a team effort.

THE PARENT AND CHILD TEAM

From birth on, parent and child work together as a team to help the child adjust and adapt to the environment. Observing the parent/child team is to assess the attachment style; that is, the type of interaction that develops between parent and child. *Attachment theory* was initially proposed by Dr. John Bowlby in the 1940s. Bowlby was able to link children's symptoms to their histories of maternal deprivation and separation. He suggested that in the early phase of development, although the child needs to acquire the capacity for self-regulation, the mother is the child's ego (desires) and superego (Bowlby 1940, 1944).

> It is not surprising that during infancy and early childhood these functions are either not operating at all or are doing so most imperfectly. During this phase of life, the child is therefore dependent on his mother performing them for him. She orients him in space and time, provides his environment, permits the satisfaction of some impulses, and restricts others. She is his ego and his super-ego. Gradually

he learns these arts himself, and as he does, the skilled parent transfers the roles to him. This is a slow, subtle and continuous process, beginning when he first learns to walk and feed himself, and not ending completely until maturity is reached. (Bowlby 1951)

Bowlby strongly advocated treatment for the mother to benefit the child. Attachment theory was further expanded by Mary Ainsworth and colleagues (1978) defining differences in the quality of mother-infant interactions. Patterns of infant attachment can be recognized based on how an infant reacts to unexpected separation and then reunion with the mother (mother leaves the room and returns after a few minutes).

Infants who are not yet attached appear indifferent to their mother's presence or absence. Securely attached infants cry little, and are content to explore the world even when their mother is away. When their mother returns, they are able to adjust easily and continue playing. Insecurely attached infants have a harder time playing even while their mother is present. When mother leaves and then returns, insecure infants react by avoiding the mother or being tearful and clinging to her. They can be so disorganized that they cannot settle back into play. The significant observation is whether a parent/child team can work effectively to help an upset child calm down.

The Attachment Process

It is generally accepted that by the time a child is eighteen-months old, the parent/child unit is developing a secure or insecure attachment. Clinicians consider attachment to be a lifetime phenomenon unless there is some "significant" interference. The quality of the attachment depends on both the child and the parent's participation in the process of coregulating the child when he or she is feeling overwhelmed. When upset by a stressful event, securely attached young children can use their parent(s) as a source of reassurance to rapidly overcome their fear and calm down. These children can then safely return to play.

An insecurely attached child cannot benefit from the presence of parents or caretakers to calm down. When there is an unexpected event, the parent will see the child become intensely upset and the child will withdraw (flight response), become aggressive (fight response), or exhibit a mixture of both behaviors. Insecurely attached children cannot use parent(s) as a way to reregulate their emotional responses.

In "disorganized attachment," the child's need for security is expressed by bizarre and unpredictable behaviors, such as running around, yelling, kicking, cursing, throwing, biting, and so forth; they are unable to "use" the parent to calm down. For example, one mother was chatting with a friend while waiting to pick up her daughter from nursery school. When the child didn't see her mother in the usual place, she began shouting, running wildly, and, when her mother tried to console her, she bit her hand instead of taking hold of it.

If BD is active during the first few years of life, the attachment process is derailed, because the child cannot participate fully in the process. The parent may have to take over more of the "comforting" functions than is usually required.

Even when the attachment has developed normally, mood instability can create what we call a "fluctuating attachment." In this case, when the child is *asymptomatic* (that is, symptom-free), a secure attachment is present. However, during periods of decompensation, the child might revert to more insecure forms of attachment. When manic, the child appears to have a pseudosecure attachment, and can become overconfident. Suddenly, fears, anxieties, and insecurities are easily overcome: social or school phobia or OCD might resolve over the course of weeks, especially around seasonal changes. Nonetheless, the confidence displayed at these times is sometimes quite fragile and might crumble in the late afternoon or early evening with nightfall anxiety, often landing the child in his or her parents' bedroom if he or she is awakened at night.

During periods of depression, the child might be more likely to show separation anxiety and an insecure attachment. The chronic strain of this interaction causes secondary maladaptive patterns in the parent, and might exacerbate medical and psychiatric problems.

One aspect of the parent/child team to be considered is this: When you, the parent, are emotionally off-balance or unable to understand the distress signals sent out by your child, you may not respond in a supportive manner. For example, when Will was told a new baby-sitter was coming that evening, just a few minutes before she arrived, he had a fit, and yelled and cursed. Will's tired and overwhelmed mother yelled back, saying, "I can't take it anymore. You never give me a break." When his parents came home, Will was up watching TV, and his parents had not enjoyed their night out.

Full-fledged attachment, the primary emotional connection between parent and child, is complete by three years of age and is considered a lifetime phenomenon. This relationship may be considered the model for other relationships. With secure attachment, the child develops the ability to self-soothe, accepts help from other caregivers when necessary, and is more able to engage in play and school tasks. When the parent/child team is ineffective at helping the child calm down in those early years, at future stages of development, the child will not be able to:

- Learn how to self-soothe.

- Accept help from others (relatives, babysitters, teachers) in order to calm down when stressed.

- Be successful in basic developmental tasks such as socializing with peers and academic functioning.

FOSTERING A MORE SECURE ATTACHMENT BETWEEN PARENTS AND BIPOLAR CHILDREN

With the onset of BD, a parent may have to take over more of the "comforting" functions for his or her child than is developmentally normal. Treatment can help parents and child extend the healthy and trustful attachment to those times when the child is symptomatic and needs direction. Once a parent/child team is better regulated and strengthened, healthy interactions can begin to take place. These exchanges, and opportunities for cooperation, foster understanding and support between parent and child, rather than producing conflict.

We help parents to recognize that having BD, by definition, means the child (especially if oversensitive and/or poorly regulated) cannot participate fully in the parent/child team. If a child's auditory processing is faulty, the parent feels the child does not listen. When a child is unable to read the parent's facial expression, they both may become confused and angry. When a child is unable to modulate emotions, he or she may respond with anxiety or aggression.

With a fuller understanding of your child's symptoms and of the areas in which your child struggles, or is delayed, it will be easier to help your child cope with the symptoms of BD rather than seeing him or her as a "bad child." This will further strengthen your role in the parent/child team. As your child gains an increased understanding and is supported in his or her attempts to calm down, he or she will learn how to self-soothe, which is essential for greater independence and more adaptive behavior.

GENERAL PRINCIPLES OF PARENTAL INTERVENTION

Bipolar disorder is quite complex, and we have found that simple, responses are the most effective. The following principles can be applied to many situations and are sure to increase the effectiveness of the parent/child team:

1. Stay calm

2. Address stressors

3. Plan ahead

4. Proceed step by step

5. Pace responses

6. Comfort your child when necessary

7. Solve problems together

8. Monitor

Stay Calm

When you appear calm, you are not adding to your child's emotional or sensory overload. Keeping a clear head so you can be more effective in all aspects of the difficult job of parenting your child. You also serve as a role model for everyone else in the family when you demonstrate how to stay in control and make good decisions in a stressful, potentially combative situation.

Address Stressors

When an understanding parent prevents stressors before they appear, the chances of overload diminish and opportunities for success increase. Success in daily tasks is what helps improve your child's self-esteem. If going grocery shopping causes sensory or emotional overload for your child, consider shopping during school hours. When your child is overactive on the playground, or causes trouble with other kids in large groups, consider going to the playground on an off-hour, or plan short structured playdates. Many school stressors can be prevented by helpful school accommodations (see chapter 13) that lead to successful completion of academic requirements. Decreased stress and increased success are the bases for a more positive self-image.

Plan Ahead

Planning ahead is essential for success when your child can be forgetful, disorganized, and oppositional. A daily schedule helps in this regard, even if your child needs prompting at each transition. This may mean reviewing the schedule before going to bed and once again in the morning. Having a schedule posted in the kitchen or in the child's room allows your child to check it repeatedly, as necessary. Most important, when there is a glitch in complying with a task, no arguing is necessary. The parent redirects the child to the schedule and that helps him or her to move on.

Proceed Step by Step

A step-by-step approach will help your child stay on track. Along with the big picture, such as planning the next day or week, always tell your child what to anticipate next. For instance, you might say, "After your playdate, it will be time for a bath," or "After the basketball game, we have an appointment with your doctor." This will save both of you a lot of frustration. In the long run, the goal is for your child to be able to follow a reasonable daily schedule without any prompts.

Pace Responses

When you *pace* (slow down) any and all of your responses, it slows down the entire interaction and gives you time to think about the next step. An interesting phenomenon will occur: You will have the opportunity to step back and observe your child and see what is overwhelming and how your child responds. Most importantly, you will be leading your child away from sensory overload, rather than adding to it.

As an essential part of pacing responses, be very careful about reacting to your child's first response. Do not react to an initial irrational or negative response as if it were set in stone. It's a better practice to assume your child has not fully processed the information as it was presented. Calm, patience, and a focused reply on your part will make a difference. When you calmly allow time for your child to figure out what's happening, you will be a role model for all family members.

Comfort Your Child When Necessary

As discussed above, as part of the parent/child team, you may need to help your child calm down more often than other parents. The purpose of comforting is to help with emotional and behavioral stabilization so your child can return to age-appropriate activities. Unfortunately, no amount of planning can cover all of the potential stressors. Even with accommodations specifically tailored for your child, school can be very stressful, especially when your child has a learning disability or social difficulties. At home, when you notice or anticipate stress, comforting helps to decrease emotional overload. The next developmental step will be for your child to tell you he or she needs a break. One long-term goal is for your child to self-modulate; that is, to be able to take a quick break, and then get back to feeling in control.

Problem Solve Together

Problem solving can occur only when you and your child are both calm and detached enough from emotional overload that you can talk about it. Together you can revisit an incident, explore the details, and discuss: what will help if this happens again?

Most parents of children with BD face a dilemma many times a day. You may be confused about whether to comfort and soothe or whether to expect your child to "fend for himself." If you intervene when unnecessary, your child may become dependent on you and will not learn basic self-regulation skills. If you use a meltdown as an opportunity for learning, then problem solving helps you and your child to plan ahead for better outcomes in the future.

Monitor

In the long term, the goal of monitoring is for your child or teen to be able to connect his or her behaviors (complying with the basic tasks) with an outcome. If your child studies for a test, he will get a better grade than if he doesn't study. If your child takes medications, gets regular sleep, keeps to a diet and exercise regime, symptoms will decrease and he or she will feel better. Each visit to the psychiatrist's or therapist's office is an opportunity to monitor the symptoms of BD and see how your child and the parent/child team are coping. Over time, children become used to the questions asked by the doctor and can use the information to enhance their own self-monitoring.

In chapter 11, we present a simple scale that helps young children begin to learn how to self-monitor. Appendix II has a more formal monitoring device that you and your child can use daily, the MoodLog. This helps to monitor the symptoms of BD along with the daily stressors. You will be able to see the effects of treatment and symptoms' fluctuations during maintenance or acute treatment. Eventually, the goal is for your child to take over the job of self-monitoring, know how to respond to daily challenges, and know when to ask for "good help."

DEVELOPING A STRUCTURED DAILY SCHEDULE

When the symptoms of BD are not stabilized, a daily, predictable schedule needs to be developed over time. To begin this process, we help parents to focus on useful, effective interventions, one at a time. If a child is not ready to plan and comply with a full, structured, organized weekly schedule, then we address the most salient aspects of treatment, along with behavioral management that will lead to this end.

The Three Big Tasks to Focus On

To build a daily schedule, intervention and treatment will focus on three tasks:

1. Taking medications on time

2. Getting to sleep on time

3. Getting to school on time

Medication helps to regulate mood, allowing your child to better deal with daily stressors (siblings, homework, getting up, and going to sleep). Getting to school on time helps to organize the day and keeps your child occupied, adequately stimulated, and socially engaged. Going to sleep on time makes it possible for your child to get to school and, again, helps to stabilize mood states. This provides a strong foundation for the work that follows, as it simplifies a very complex situation.

BEHAVIOR MODIFICATION

The use of behavior management is helpful for a simplified, focused approach. Behavior modification is based on reinforcement (both positive and negative), punishment, and extinction. Reinforcement increases a specific behavior: that is, your response will encourage your child's behavior to continue. For instance, "I like how you finished your homework today" encourages efficient completion of homework, sleeping well makes your child feel rested, and winning a game earns a prize (positive reinforcement); disobeying parents can mean losing TV privileges (negative reinforcement).

When your child asks, begs, whines, or threatens (or worse) for something and you give in, that behavior is positively reinforced. The child's negative behavior is inadvertently reinforced by a parent who responds with a reward at an inappropriate time (i.e., the child gets to stay up late or to have ice cream before dinner just by whining).

Extinction, or elimination of a certain behavior, occurs when the behavior does not elicit any reinforcement: thus, the best way to end an unwanted behavior is to ignore it. When a behavior is intermittently reinforced, i.e., sometimes saying yes and sometimes saying no, the behavior is not eliminated, but actually continues, as it gives hope to your child that, with enough persistence, you will change your mind. When your child does not comply with the rules, you can have a built-in consequence, such as no TV time the next day (during your child's free time).

Positive Reinforcement

To change the behavior of a child with BD can be extremely challenging. For your child, a simple task, such as getting to bed or taking meds on time, is often fraught with stress and frustration. Your child's ability to maintain his or her motivation is impaired by mood swings, and often leads to inconsistent behavior and forgetfulness. When you understand how stressful everyday tasks can be for your child, you can positively reinforce attempts to comply, because trying counts. And your child may have to try many times before he or she will be consistently successful at a new behavior. For this reason, it is important to continually monitor, reinforce, and encourage desired behaviors, sometimes at every step of the way, to obtain the same results that many children without BD achieve with little or no effort.

How to Begin

If you are not ready to introduce a full weekly schedule to your child, or your child has difficulty complying, then begin by targeting the "big three": meds, sleep, and school.

You can proceed as follows:

1. **Choose a desired behavior:** Choose taking a medication, getting to sleep on time, or getting to school on time; then let your child know you expect compliance.

2. **Positively reinforce:** Stay calm and focused while you ignore your child's negative responses, and discuss the earned reward (positive reinforcement) and the consequences of non-compliance (the child does not earn a specific privilege).

3. **Monitor:** Monitor behavior and the effectiveness of the plan over time.

4. **Be consistent:** If the plan is unrealistic or ineffective, it can be revised; if it is working, be consistent.

How to Get Your Child to Take Medication

Taking medication is a nonnegotiable task. The prescribing psychiatrist can help give you and your child a sense of how the medication will help him or her. For example, the psychiatrist told Will and his mom, "After taking this medication for a few weeks, you will have fewer tantrums and you'll probably get along better with your parents and your brother."

Step One: Be clear, firm, and calm in insisting medication be taken on time.

Step Two: Convey a sense of confidence that the medication will improve specific symptoms, and use positive reinforcements, as necessary. When a child or teen is resistant to medication treatment, you and the child may discuss a reward (positive reinforcement) desirable enough to the child to overcome his or her oppositional stance. You may be concerned that this is bribery. The difference here is you are focusing on behavior change that will have a positive, life-changing outcome. Moreover, the aim is to eliminate the need for "bribery" and rely on the most natural reward, your approval and the increased sense of well-being your child will experience. When Will refused to begin medication, his parents decided that success depended on paying their ten-year-old son a set amount of money each time he took his medication. He was told beforehand that "earning money for taking medication that helps is only temporary."

Step Three: Together, you and your child can monitor the child's behavioral changes, such as more self-control, control over specific symptoms (insomnia, anxiety, etc.), increased ability to complete schoolwork, and improved self-esteem. After one week, Will's mom saw improvement; after two weeks, Will felt the improvement himself; and after three weeks, Will easily accepted the end of the incentive, just as he had been warned that it would end.

Step Four: Be consistent and make sure your child knows that taking meds on time, daily, is now a part of the everyday routine.

How to Get Your Child to Sleep on Time

Getting your child to sleep on time may be the most challenging task for your family. So many children and adolescents have a disrupted sleep-wake cycle that can exacerbate symptoms.

Step One: Calmly present the exact time for "lights out."

Step Two: Offer an incentive, such as "if the lights are out on time every day this week, you can earn reward x."

Step Three: Monitor and note the behavior change, such as it's easier for your child to make the school bus on time, complete homework, or be less irritable.

Step Four: As your child complies with the program, and turns off the light to go to bed at the proper time for a whole week, he or she earns an additional reward for consistency of the desired behavior (and your gentle praise).

Often sleep regulation can be enhanced by medical intervention, as discussed in chapter 9. However, a word of caution here—entire households may have to be reorganized to make sure a child with BD gets to sleep on time. For many families, from after dinner until bedtime, the focus will be on slowing down activities and quieting the house, such as dimming the lights, closing curtains in the summertime to block out the sunlight, or putting on soothing music.

Getting Your Child to School on Time

Let's say your child takes meds but is extremely slow and cranky in the morning, and is often late to school.

Step One: You clearly and calmly present the expectation that your child will be on the bus every day (or in the car at a specific time, if the parent drives the child to school).

Step Two: This step includes the elimination of nagging and pleading. Most children are capable of getting ready themselves, but lack motivation. The goal is for your child to take over these functions without requiring prompting or supervision. So, you'll need to think about what will motivate your child to get going in the short run. If your child needs a concrete reward to motivate him or her to be on time for the bus, you might consider the following incentives: going to the movies on the weekend, having a playdate, or getting a game or toy.

We suggest that your child should complete the task, such as getting on the bus on time, for at least five days in a row. This gives your child a chance to experience consistent change. If your child is on time for three days and misses the bus on the fourth day, then he or she starts over from day one. No arguing and no fuss, just a reminder that earning the reward depends on five consecutive days of success. Parents can give a positive boost, such as "Maybe next time you can do all five days." When a child has successfully made it to school on time for five days in a row, he or she will have earned the reward.

Step Three: As your child realizes that he or she can make it to the bus on time and does not have to miss school, he or she will feel better about this accomplishment and being rewarded for it.

Step Four: This step is sticking to the plan. One way to help this along is to use a cell phone as a positive reinforcement, especially for your adolescent. Once your teenager earns the cell phone, then he or she gets to use it each day he or she is on time for the ride to school. You have control of the phone and can hand it to your child on the way out. If he or she is late, even by five minutes, then you can calmly and simply say, "Maybe tomorrow." This routine is kept up until morning readiness has become a part of your child's daily routine.

EVERYDAY SANITY: CLEAR LIMIT-SETTING

The goal of all interventions in this chapter is to facilitate a calmer, more organized, and predictable home life. Your job as parent is to set and (positively) reinforce appropriate limits. Having simple routines and clear rules is most helpful to both parents and children. When all the pieces are in place, a structured daily schedule may look something like this chart:

7:00 A.M.: Out of bed; self-care
7:30 A.M.: Dressed and in kitchen for breakfast and meds
8:00 A.M.: On the bus to school
8:30 A.M. – 3:00 P.M.: At school
3:30 A.M.: Bus drops off child at home
3:35 P.M.: Snack, meds, and maybe a break
4:00 P.M.: Homework until dinner and/or psychiatric therapy, or tutoring sessions. No more than one after-school event per day.
6:00 P.M.: Dinner
6:30 P.M.: Free time earned if homework is done
7:30 P.M.: Television, computer, etc., turned off—begin to get ready for bed, meds
8:00 P.M.: Quiet time in bed, with or without parent
8:30 P.M.: Lights out

HOW TO SET A SCHEDULE

To set a schedule, the initial planning is best done among the adults. When a therapist is available, it is helpful for parents and therapist to work together. As parents try to develop the daily schedule, they should go through the following steps:

1. Sit down with pencil and paper and set up a seven-day schedule. Begin with the "musts" in your child's life.

    ■   Start with the hour your child must be on the bus (or in the car) to go to school. Decide how much time your child needs to get ready for school and count backwards. Chapter 9 on sleep disturbances will tell you how many hours your child should sleep daily. For example, if Will has to be on the bus at 8:00 A.M. every morning, and it takes him one hour to get ready, then wake-up time might be at 6:45 A.M., and he must be out of bed by 7:00 A.M. Since he needs ten hours of sleep, parents set lights out at 8:30 P.M., allowing Will some time to fall asleep.

■ Then, add in the times your child must take medication.

■ Add meal times, which, ideally, should be consistent.

2. Then fill in the after-school arrival time, after-school events, and homework time; whatever time is left is for rest.

Setting up a weekly schedule allows for special events on weekends (going to the movies, playdates), but not during the week. Weekend events can also be used as positive reinforcements, something your child must earn. If there is a special TV show or a sports event your child wants to watch and the basics have not been done, you can tape the show or sports event so that it can be viewed during the next earned free time or on the weekend.

How to Present the Schedule to Your Child

Once you have a reasonable schedule set up, then you can present it to your child at a quiet time. Note that this kind of a schedule will be easy for a non-bipolar sibling to comply with, and it will help to normalize daily home life.

When the schedule is presented, there is room for discussion over the rewards (positive reinforcement or earned privileges) or consequences (child does not earn privileges). The earned reward is the motivation to comply with the schedule and it must be something the child values. Also, your child will feel included in the decision-making process, and will feel listened to.

Introduce the full schedule to your child in a quiet atmosphere, staying calm and focused, ignoring any negative responses. Then point out the positive reinforcements, such as earning free time when homework is completed. Stay positive and consistent and keep your focus on the plan. Most children are happy to have a predictable home schedule, even if, initially, they don't like some of the rules. Listen to your child's concerns about meeting expectations. Be practical, as there is always room for a discussion of rewards and small changes to the schedule.

Once basic family rules or a schedule has been set, the parent/ child team can work together to problem solve how to stick to the schedule. For instance, if your child's morning routine is difficult for him or her, you can write out, step by step, what the child is expected to do in order to earn a reward or privilege. These rewards are built into the daily schedule. The consequence of noncompliance is that the child doesn't earn the privilege for that day, but has a clean slate the next day. This approach removes the need for arguments or heated discussions. Either your child sticks to the daily schedule and earns rewards or he or she gets the consequence (usually the loss of a reward).

During the week, parents shouldn't underestimate all children's strong desire for television, computer, telephone, or downtime. Earning downtime with choice, that is, when your child can choose what he or she wants to do, is its own positive reinforcement. The simplicity of this kind of behavior management is that when your child is unable to comply with expectations (and doesn't earn a reward one day), the schedule stays the same, and he or she can try again the next day. Sometimes, however, the child will need encouragement just for trying. For example, your child might get into bed on time, and then be unable to fall asleep. The child's effort to try to get to sleep on time should be reinforced with the reward, regardless of the end result.

Adolescents and Rewards

For an older child, especially those who participate in sports or in after-school activities, this schedule still permits time for homework. Extra computer or TV time is allowed if, and only if, the basics have been done. A later bedtime may be necessary, but make sure it is regular. Weekend sleep schedules cannot be too far off the weekday schedule because it is too difficult for children—especially teens—with BD to reregulate daily sleep patterns. For adolescents who go out with friends on the weekends, set a sensible curfew to make sure the sleep schedule isn't interrupted. If your teen is late one night, he or she will be grounded the next time he or she wants to go out with friends. This way, your teen will have an opportunity to make a choice—stay out late and be grounded or come home on time and go out with friends the next time. Of course, this plan will be effective only if you consistently stick to the conditions set beforehand.

Eliminating Physical Acting-Out

Many of you live with a child who is physically violent toward you and/or other family members. From the beginning of treatment, it is helpful if all members of the treatment team are absolutely firm and clear that no violence (or violation of the personal space of others) will be tolerated. This can be difficult to enforce. If a family is able to establish compliance with medication, a firm bedtime, and getting to school on time, then physical acting-out at home often decreases and the child can comply with these clear guidelines. However, if this is not the case, addressing violent behavior must become the priority. Physical violence is too serious a symptom to ignore. It can lead to the notification of child protection services by those who are legally mandated to report suspected danger in a home. Doctors, nurses, psychotherapists, and school personnel are all mandated reporters.

To eliminate violent behavior, it's helpful for parents to begin with the help of one member of the treatment team: the psychiatrist, psychotherapist, or school counselor. Parents and the professional set the goal of eliminating all the physical acting-out at home, and the plan is then presented to the child with BD. The plan will state that the child will not hit, kick, bite, break property, and so forth for a specified period of time. At the end of that time, the child will receive a reward that he or she wants.

Again, the time period should be at least five or more days for the child to have the experience of being able to inhibit specific behaviors. If, after several earnest attempts (and medical interventions), your child is unable to do this, it may indicate the need for more intensive treatment, a therapeutic school, or hospitalization. Rather than evidence of inadequate parenting, it may mean that your child needs more supervision to comply with a daily, structured schedule. Physical violence must always be brought to the attention of the MD and/or other members of the treatment team.

SYMPTOMS BREAKING THROUGH DURING TREATMENT

One mother, who participated in a parent group, devised a checklist to review whenever she notices that her daughter is having difficulty keeping to the daily schedule, or her behavior seems to be deteriorating. Before responding, this mother tries to figure out what may be causing the symptom (for the purpose of determining what response would be most helpful), and she thinks about the following issues:

1. **Medication:**   Has it been recently changed? Did the child miss a dose? Has the child grown recently?

2. **Medical illness:**   Is there any indication the child has a cold, stomach virus, seasonal or specific allergies, or something else?

3. **Hormonal or other developmental changes:**   Has the child grown? Has he or she developed sexually, or have there been any hormonal changes?

4. **Sleep:**   Has the child's sleep been regular? Has the child had nightmares recently?

5. **School:**   Does the child have an upcoming project or test? Did anything unexpected happen, like a pop quiz? Is the child feeling generally overwhelmed by the academic stressors? Or by the social pressures?

6. **Social life:**   Have there been any changes in the child's social life, such as problems with a best friend? Is the child feeling the stress of not fitting in socially? Did something happen that the child may have misinterpreted?

7. **Seasonal:**   Does this time of the year seem to bring trouble?

8. **Substance use:**   Could the change be explained by substance abuse?

9. **Me:**   Has it been a particularly difficult day for me?

10. **Anything else?**

When your child is showing signs of dysregulation (yet again), it is helpful for you to organize your thinking so that you can rule out many of the specifics noted in the list above. When your child is calm, it is helpful to simply ask, "What's wrong?" If your child reiterates his or her original or other complaints, try asking, "What else is wrong?" With enough time and calm, your child may be able to tell you what the problem is. Then the parent/child team can problem solve together.

FAMILY ISSUES

This chapter began with a description of how a child with BD can disrupt family life. Additional, unwanted burdens arise when relatives and friends do not understand what you are faced with on a daily basis. With little or no support in the immediate or extended family, the pain of isolation can be debilitating. It is an excruciatingly lonely place when you struggle with BD daily without any other adult around to help.

Education about BD is the only way anyone can understand what it means to get through a day with an unstable child. Once you understand the cause of your child's problem behaviors, you can explain it to others. Some family members and friends may rally to help you. However, when relatives and friends are not able to understand or do not want to learn what it is like to be a parent of a child with BD, you may have to let go of the wish that your family members will be supportive "like families should be."

Real support may come from understanding friends and family members, from the new friends you may meet through a support group for parents of children with BD, or from just talking to others. You don't have to do this alone—counseling can help you and all members of your family. Many parents are unable to get out to a parent support group and rely on listservs and support groups on the Internet (see appendix III).

Siblings

Siblings are at a disadvantage in a home with a brother or sister with BD. Parents spend a lot of time and energy dealing with the behaviors of the ill child, and the healthy child may feel abandoned. Siblings of a child with BD are easily confused, hurt, and angered by the way they are treated by the sibling. This has a negative effect on a normal child. You can help your "normal child" by educating him or her about bipolar disorder, letting him or her vent, and talking about the reality of dealing with a brother or sister who is so demanding.

Parenting a non-bipolar sibling should allow that child to have a "normal" childhood, with his or her own friends and interests, as well as problems. Most importantly, all your children need your undivided attention. This may mean that each child has a planned weekly outing with each parent. Your non-bipolar child will then have a time and place to vent as well as to shine—a time when he or she is the center of attention. Books for children, teens, and siblings about BD, as well as information about parenting a "normal" child, are available via Web sites (see appendix III).

11

Irritability: What to Do?

*Sixteen-year-old Max is constantly upset, angry, and irritable—
with his family, but—not with his friends. He is sullen and easily
annoyed by something as minor as his sister asking him to pass
the salt. A few months ago, he punched a hole in the kitchen wall
and left the house cursing so loudly the neighbors called the police.
Most nights, after dinner he goes out to see his friends. His
parents have set a ten o'clock curfew, but he's seldom home before
eleven. When his father reminds him to be home by curfew, he
often says to his dad, "You and your curfew are so stupid. Just
leave me alone." When his father responds with, "That's no way
to talk to your father," Max directs a stream of foul language at
him and storms out of the house, slamming the door behind him.*

*Max has struck his father and beat up his younger
brother on a few occasions; after these incidents he blamed
his parents: "It's all your fault, just leave me alone. Only my
friends understand."*

Children with bipolar disorder (BD) like Max display extreme irritability that can easily turn into anger or even rage when their parents try to set clear limits. When parents are unable to discipline their child, family life can be badly disrupted.

This chapter will help you to understand and respond effectively when you face rages, anger, and irritability. One of the most difficult challenges of childhood bipolar disorder is dealing with irritability. We review the range of irritable reactions you may see in your child, discuss common responses to irritability that actually make things worse, and outline therapeutic principles and helpful responses. We conclude with a simple tool that you and your child can use to prevent and/or shorten these emotional storms.

THE RANGE OF IRRITABILITY

Irritability is one of the most common symptoms of BD in children and adolescents. Is it always a sign of BD? No. Certainly there are many other causes of irritability, but extreme or aggressive irritability like that seen in children with BD is of a special order of intensity. For instance, one adolescent girl describes herself as "flammable." Another says I "feel raw, as if I had no skin."

Irritability occurs in manic, depressive, and mixed phases of BD, so that many parents rarely observe their child free of irritability for any length of time. You may have realized how your child is easily annoyed, frustrated, disappointed, or angered without any provocation or trigger. Many parents have told us that if they had to pick a single adjective to describe their child, it would "irritable."

Your child or teen can be quite cranky, ranging from annoyance to hostility, and from anger all the way to full-blown, out-of-control rages. For this reason, irritability, whether in its mild or more severe expressions, must be dealt with on a daily basis.

Irritable young children are seemingly never satisfied; they are always asking for more. Without something new or exciting to do, or without a parent by her side, four-year-old Janine whines a lot and always seems annoyed. She can shift from playing with her mom to demanding a special toy, and then escalate to screaming and thrashing about, until she gets it.

The desire to prevail (it's "their way or no way") constantly turns into opposing, antagonizing, rebelling against, and fighting with parents, siblings, and/or peers. Many of the patients who experienced the onset of their illness before the age of twelve or thirteen are likely to be the most symptomatic at home but not in school. In teenagers, as a rule, impulsive and aggressive behaviors are more likely to be noticed both at home and in school/social settings.

Other factors also affect the way bipolar disorder begins to cause problems. For example, dysregulated cycles of energy and sleep can cause significant problems in a child's life. Many school-age children with BD are very sluggish and extremely irritable in the morning, work hard at staying in control during the school day, then often have melt-downs as soon as they return home or are alone with a parent. Like nine-year-old Brent, they may fight getting ready and going to school. However, when Brent walks into the school building, he feels okay.

Brent's mother commented on how surprised she had been to see Brent so pleasant and polite during a ride from school when they dropped off a schoolmate. The moment the other child left the car, Brent reverted to his usual cranky, abusive, uncooperative behavior, spitting out a litany of complaints. Usually, a parent, a sibling, or another family member is the target of angry outbursts; sometimes, whoever is around gets the brunt of tremendous abuse and aggression.

Fourteen-year-old Gloria stays in her room most afternoons. Since Gloria was a toddler, her mother has known it is best to leave her alone during the "bewitching hours," usually from 4 to 6 P.M. For years, as soon as Gloria got home and her mom asked about her day, Gloria grumbled and turned her back without answering. If asked to help with dinner, Gloria turns away, stomps across the room, and screams, "I'm busy, why do I always have to help you? Why don't you just leave me alone!"

Although even healthy teens can be quite irritable, when they also have BD as Gloria and Max do, they constantly blame their parents, teachers, and siblings. The combination of poor judgment, the sense of grandiosity ("I know best"), and oppositional behavior ("You are not the boss") puts many adolescents in risky situations. When the impulsivity of BD is added to this mix, the results can range from family discord, social difficulties, and school failure to alcohol and drug abuse, violence, and legal troubles.

Common Responses Worsen the Situation

During a rage, your child is lost in an intense web of emotions without the ability to make sense of those emotions or to control them. This can occur many times a day due to rapid mood shifts, overstimulation, hypersensitivity, or physical triggers like hunger and exhaustion. We've found that typical parenting techniques, which work well for most children, are not helpful for a child with BD, and may actually exacerbate emotional outbursts. For example, when Gloria's parents said she could use her computer to "chat" with her friends only after her homework was completed, Gloria yelled at them, "You can't tell me what to do," then she cursed, ran out of the house, and didn't return home for hours.

Why Typical Parenting Responses Don't Work

Typical parenting techniques, such as explaining your point of view, reasoning with your child about the risks and benefits of certain choices or actions, and warning of consequences (reward/punishment system), all assume that your child has the ability to listen and understand what you are saying at that particular time. When a child with BD is upset, he is *intensely* upset, and often there is no time for warnings. Even the simplest verbal responses from you may add to the child's emotional overload.

Warnings, threats, or any other verbal input often become the external stimulus that allows the progression from mild irritability into a rage. For example, your child may demand that you take him to the store "immediately" to buy something he or she wants. Although your child may be irritable or angry, he or she may still have some degree of self-control. Your immediate response of "No" or "Not now" may be too much for the child and trigger a tantrum before the event is even processed. At that very moment your child loses the capacity to *think* logically. Then, you may have to deal with an intense tantrum that takes an enormous toll on you, your child, and other family members.

For some parents, it is easier to understand how to be helpful if they see a tantrum as an "emotional seizure," with irrational, uncontrollable behavior, from which the child must be protected. It is easier to deal with rages when you remember the child has no control or fault in the intensity of the symptoms. Once a parent is able to see these behaviors or patterns as the expression of BD, dealing with the symptoms becomes less emotionally draining.

Why Parents Are Unable to Be Objective

It is understandable that maintaining emotional balance is difficult for a parent under these circumstances. Many parents have been traumatized by too many tantrums and cannot think clearly when they are confronted again and again by an irritable, angry, or raging child. When a barrage of insults is hurled directly at you, like many overwhelmed parents, you may want reassurance that your child does not actually hate you. Perhaps you just want the scene to end quickly. For some parents, it brings back bad memories of their own childhood, perhaps of an abusive or short-tempered parent. For others, it is evidence that their worst fear has become a reality: they are inadequate or "bad" parents. And, finally, some are exhausted, feel hopeless, and withdraw, thus giving up active parenting and limit-setting.

How to Be Effective

Whenever your child is irritable or loses control, it is all too easy to take his or her behavior personally, rather than seeing it as a symptom of BD. If you remain objective, you are less likely to engage in unhelpful behaviors or responses, such as screaming at or blaming your child, as this will push him or her even further out of control. When in the throes of a rage episode, asking your child to stop hurting you (verbally or physically) is like asking him or her to regain control. Your child may not be able to do so. Would you ask your child to stop coughing or sneezing when he or she has the flu? Would you take his or her cough as a personal insult? Probably not, as it is apparent that the child is unable to control a sneeze or a cough. But when you are dealing with BD, this is not so clear.

Nasty words come out of your child's mouth and certain behaviors appear to be deliberate. It is important to recognize the difference between your child's behavior and the symptoms of the child's illness. Most of the time you will see an overlap, but little by little, you'll be able to tease apart the symptoms from your child's baseline behavior.

If you reset your emotional thermostat and remain calm, along with gaining some objectivity, you can maintain safety, figure out what your options are, and thoughtfully choose a plan of action. When your child returns to a calmer state, he or she might be quite reasonable, agree to the conditions you set, and grasp the consequences, or remember a contract already agreed upon (i.e., the daily schedule).

Before we delineate the basic principles of effective intervention, we will introduce a simple monitoring device that may be helpful to both you and your child.

MONITORING IRRITABILITY WITH THE UPSET SCALE

After an irritable, angry, or rageful episode, you and your child may find that using a simple number scale can be helpful for monitoring the child's irritability.

When you introduce the Upset Scale to your child, it opens the way for a frank and nonjudgmental dialogue and exchange. With the

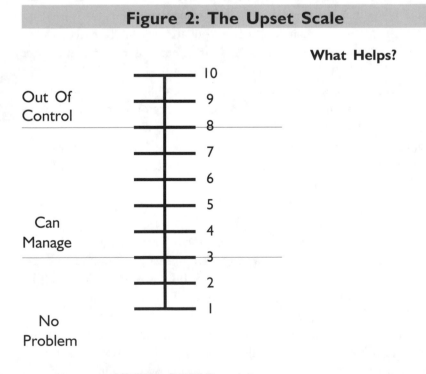

Figure 2: The Upset Scale

UPSET SCALE
© Nancy B. Austin, Psy.D., 2006

Upset Scale, you and your child will have a tool that will help you begin talking about an incident when the child was "out of control." It will also help you to establish a common language and to reach a better understanding of the problem.

For parents who want to use this scale at home, make sure you are calm and able to maintain emotional balance while reviewing what happened. Parents should proceed cautiously through the following steps:

1. Make sure both you and your child are calm, rational, and focused. This will happen only after the effects of the out-of-control event have settled down.

2. In an atmosphere of cooperation, you and your child will identify a recent incident that got out of control, such as "homework time yesterday afternoon."

3. Draw the Upset Scale, and explain that the numbers 1, 2, and 3 mean your child may be a little upset, but it is "no problem"; 8, 9, and 10 mean your child is so upset that "out-of-control" behavior occurs (such as yelling, cursing, kicking, hitting, etc.); and 4, 5, 6, and 7 mean your child has some degree of upset but "can manage" (recognizing that it may take a lot of effort on the child's part to understand this). This midrange has particular significance for a child with BD because the child's distress can escalate so quickly from 1 to 10, without registering in this midrange at all.

4. Ask your child to identify the internal upset feeling in a descriptive way, preferably with a physiological component, such as "the angry, tight feeling in my stomach." To help, you might ask your child, "What does the upset feel like inside your body?" This begins to give the parent/child team a simple way to identify and describe an experience for which they may have few or no words.

5. Let your child identify how upset he or she was by picking a number, such as "When I was yelling and cursing during homework time yesterday, I was a 10."

6. Try to understand together what happened before, during, and after the incident, giving a number to each stage and

identifying the actual trigger that caused your child to go from the "can manage" range to "out of control."

7. Try to identify how long it took to get back in control.

8. Identify "what helps." With your child, write a list as exhaustive as possible of activities or ways to help the child calm down. When the list is complete, you will be able to help your child identify *realistic* interventions that will help at home and in school.

For example, Brent told his mother that he would stay calm if he could go swimming before he does his homework every afternoon. Brent's mother said, "The pool is open only in the summer, but maybe you can think of some other way to let off steam." Together, they decided to hang a heavyweight punching bag in the basement, and Brent could take a "punching-bag break" anytime he wanted during homework time, as long as he came back within ten minutes.

As you and your child use the Upset Scale to reduce the range of irritability in the present, in the future it may also help your child to self-monitor his or her irritability.

The following case story demonstrates how the Upset Scale is used by one parent/child team.

KATIE AND HER MOM USE THE UPSET SCALE

Katie is an eleven-year-old girl recently diagnosed with BD. She was quite relieved to know that there is a name to the disorder that makes her feel so moody and irritable most of the day.

STEP ONE: INTRODUCTION

One Sunday evening, Katie came into the kitchen and began cursing her mom. Mom remembered the Upset Scale, but wisely waited until a quiet moment after school the next day. At that time, Mom said to Katie, "I have an idea about how we can deal with what happened last night when you got so upset." Since both parent and child were calm and Katie was curious, they proceeded. Mom continued, "Here's a simple scale that may help us when you get upset" and she drew the scale, filled in the numbers 1 to 10, and wrote the heading "Upset Scale" at the bottom of the page. She also wrote "What Helps?" on the top-right side of the page.

STEP TWO: IDENTIFYING THE EXPERIENCE

Mom then said, "You know the feeling you get when you're upset, like you were last night? Can you tell me about it?" Katie responded with, "It's like I'm so mad and I don't know why. I have to get up and move around. Sometimes I feel like that at school. It's so hard." Under the heading of "Upset Scale," Katie's mom wrote "Angry, have to move around."

STEP THREE: OBSERVING THE INTENSITY

Mom then added the three categories "No Problem," "Can Manage," "Out of Control" as shown in the figure and asked: "What number were you at last night when you came into the kitchen?" With quite a bit of animation, Katie replied, "I was at a 9." I've been worse, like when I threw the lamp on the floor a long time ago." Mom calmly put an "x" beside 9 on the scale.

STEP FOUR: IDENTIFYING EVENTS BEFORE AND DURING THE UPSET: THE TRIGGERS

When Katie realized she had a social studies test the next day, and also that she hadn't started reading the book for which a report was also due the following day, she became irritable at the 5 level. Mom noted that on the scale by putting an "x" at 5 and she wrote "too much homework" (a trigger). Then Katie said, "Dad came into my room last night and started yelling at me. He always yells at me to do my work." Later, it was discovered that Katie's father had come into her room and asked her, "How's it going? Do you have a lot of work?" and was not actually "yelling" but using his ordinary deep voice and asking "too many questions."

Nevertheless, Mom asked Katie how upset she was when her dad came in and Katie said, "a 7 or 8." That was noted as a 7½ because Katie didn't act-out by yelling back. Next to 7½, Mom put an "x" and

"Dad's questions" (another trigger). Then Mom asked, "Then what happened?" And Katie said, "I ran into the kitchen and saw you were cooking, and you asked, 'What's wrong?' I got so mad because I knew you would yell at me too, just like you do every night." That too was noted on the scale: an "x" next to 9, with the words, "Mom is going to yell."

STEP FIVE: DISCOVERING THE DURATION OF THE SYMPTOMS

Then Mom said, "From the time you came to the kitchen until the time you calmed down, it was about two hours. How did you get back into the 'can manage' range?" Mom learned that Katie went to the den to watch TV where she fell asleep. She woke up, got something to eat, and "That's when I told you about the work I had to do." At that point, Katie was back to a 4 and the change of direction was noted on the scale: an "x" next to the 4, with the words, "After nap, had to deal with homework." Katie and her mom, both calm and rational, now have an outline of what happened in one incident. Now they can work together as a team and plan how to avoid a tantrum the next time.

STEP SIX: WHAT HELPS?

Mom then said, "When you get upset, but you aren't out of control, there are things you can do to help yourself calm down, like watching TV and falling asleep. What else helps?" Mom wrote Katie's responses under "What Helps?" in the upper right-hand corner of the scale. Katie's list included watching TV, sleeping, playing computer games, taking deep breaths, a shower, having a snack, and drawing.

Mom then said, "Try to think of anything else that helps." This left both parent and child thinking about what else might be helpful. A few minutes later, Katie said, "I calm down when I help you cook." Now, Mom and Katie feel hopeful that there are more ways to cope with a tantrum. Mom ended by saying, "The new medicine you are taking will help this. You won't get so angry so fast, and you'll stay in control. This way, you can use some of the things we wrote here to calm down." Katie and her mom found a way to start dealing productively with Katie's irritability.

Using the Upset Scale at Home and School

Once a parent/child team has an easy way to identify the level of distress, they can communicate better. Coming home from school the next day, Katie said to her mother, "I had a terrible day at school today." At that point, Katie was able to easily convey with a number how "terrible" she felt *at the present time*. If she is in the "can manage" range, her mom and she can work together to problem solve the bad day at school. If Katie is too upset, she will be encouraged to follow the "What helps" list to regain control.

Most importantly, each time you discuss an incident with your child, make sure you ask how upset your child was, or is. There are times that you may think your child is more upset than he or she actually is. Also remind your child that "there are things that can help" in that particular situation. This is how you and your child can begin to communicate accurately, think positively, believe that things can actually change for the better, and turn ideas into action.

Many children find that using the scale at school, especially with the teacher, is a helpful way of self-monitoring and communicating whether the child needs a break. This tool will fit nicely into accommodations that can be integrated into a school schedule, as described in chapter 13.

EFFECTIVE RESPONSES TO YOUR IRRITABLE CHILD

Unfortunately, the Upset Scale does not help you when your child is angry, loud, abusive, or physically aggressive. Responding effectively to your irritable child, before he or she is out of control, depends on a good understanding of BD, and accepting that your irritable child is not being "bad" but is dealing with the symptoms of an illness. It is also important that you know (and hopefully will remember) that most symptoms of BD are transient, so that with time and the right approach, as outlined below, the situation will improve. Knowing that you are facing a form of irritability will allow you to:

1. **Observe** what is happening.

    ■ Look at BD and your child as separate (but overlapping) entities.

    ■ Monitor the type, severity, and duration of symptoms.

    ■ Mentally identify triggers and stressors.

2. **Stop** reacting.

    ■ Hold back instinctive, negative responses.

    ■ Calm yourself and reset your emotional thermostat.

    ■ Avoid further escalation.

3   **Provide safety** for your child and all others at home.

    ■ Remove weapons (sharp, pointy objects).

    ■ Restrain if necessary.

4. **Review** your options.

    ■ What has helped in the past?

    ■ What did your treatment team suggest you do? (call someone, use nighttime medication, etc.)

    ■ Do you need outside help? (meds, doctor, police, hospital)

5. **Choose** the most appropriate intervention.

6. **Gently praise success.**

Observe What Is Happening

By using the Upset Scale, you can monitor the degree of irritability you are observing. Make a mental note of the intensity and duration of the irritability. Continue to monitor your child's behavior to see whether your child is going up or down the scale. To begin, shift your focus away from the content of your child's outburst. When your child makes demands, insults, or threatens, first shift your focus to the intensity of the child's mood state. If you are facing a child who is irrational and emotionally unreachable (an 8, 9, or 10 on the scale), then your focus must be to find a way to shift your child to a calmer, more rational state.

In the meantime, silently try to figure out what may have triggered the crisis: Is your child overstimulated, tired, or hungry? Is a sibling's behavior contributing to the tantrum? Can you remove the trigger? For instance, if your child is hungry and you are in a rush to go to a birthday party, it is better to feed the child and be late than to risk the outbursts and social consequences caused by emotional instability. If the trigger is a sibling, separate them, and keep them apart as long as necessary.

Stop Reacting

To remain objective and use your knowledge of BD, you must stay calm. Once you sense that your child's behavior may escalate, hold back any responses that may have a negative impact. If necessary, note how upset you are and remember this rule of behavior modification: Ignoring a behavior is the best way to eliminate it. It often helps to look away, take a few breaths, and pay attention to your own emotional state. While you are taking a few deep breaths, and looking away, think about what you will do next. When you do this, you are deliberately pacing or slowing down the interactions between yourself and your child—with the goal of helping each of you to control your emotions and behaviors.

When you're ready to respond to your child, do so with clarity, brevity, and calm confidence. Many times, distracting your child with an interesting activity, or a change of setting (a walk, or car ride), removing a stressor, or introducing a topic your child likes may be sufficient to shift the child's attention and mood. Whenever possible, use nonverbal signals such as placing your forefinger to your lips to signal silence or lowering the tone of your voice. If you lose the capacity to be calm, take a few deep breaths, and direct yourself to "pretend" to be calm and confident!

Keep Your Child and All Members of the Household Safe

Often, moving away from the trigger helps a child calm down. This is most effective if the parent/child team has discussed and prepared a safe, quiet space that your child is willing to go when out of control. You can also use nonverbal signaling, agreed to beforehand, such as a gentle pointing to the "safe space." If your child cooperates, this gives you time to decide what to do next. (See Review Your Options below.)

Too often, however, a raging child is unwilling to follow the directions of the parent. This does not reflect on your competence as a parent; it shows the intensity of your child's illness at the moment.

If there are other children in the house, direct them to a safe place, even if it is their room. It is helpful for other children to know in advance that they can go to a neighbor or relative, within walking distance, when their brother or sister is severely upset.

When a parent becomes aware that the child is not winding down, then it is wise to call any other adult who might be in the house to come into the room with the child. The same principles apply to any other adult who enters: be calm, quiet, slow, clear, and nonjudgmental. Sometimes, the presence of another adult or the shift in the situation caused by the greeting of the other person is enough to break the "spell," and the child might calm down considerably in a short time.

To prevent violent behavior, if your child does not de-escalate, you may consider gently restraining him or her. Away from any danger, the child is asked to calm down, and is told that "it is all right," reassuring the child that you understand. Sometimes, a gentle restraining turns into a hug, but touching can make things worse if your child is oversensitive to touch. Only you can tell what is the best (and the worst) way to handle your child's rage. Gentle restraining can be an effective way to help your child calm down, if your child is small enough, young enough (under the age of ten), and not oversensitive to touch.

Ask for advice from your child's doctor on how to handle him or her. Unless you are trained in emergency medicine, if matters reach the point that your child has to be restrained frequently, you should let professionals (paramedics, police, nurses) handle these situations (see the next section).

Review Your Options

After following the previously described steps, now is the time to consider what will be effective. Many parents have lived with rages for so long that they have become immune to the seriousness of the effects of rages, and they've never considered crisis intervention. Chapter 14 goes into more detail about the circumstances in which crisis intervention is warranted. For now, consider crisis intervention if your child is in the midst of a violent or destructive rage and you are unable to keep the child and/or other members of the household (including yourself) safe. An emergency call to the local police (or to a mobile psychiatric crisis intervention unit, if your county has one) can be a very effective intervention.

Meanwhile, you must keep calm. When the police arrive, your child may be able to pull himself/herself together when he or she sees an adult with enough authority to "take him away." However, if your child continues to be destructive, or expresses suicidal thoughts or wishes, take this as a signal that the child doesn't have control over his or her thoughts and behavior. The next step is to have your child evaluated at the emergency room (ER) of the closest hospital to determine whether hospitalization is necessary. The police or crisis intervention teams are trained to help with that.

Most irritable or angry responses do not need such a severe intervention. At this point, most of you will want to review or recall what was effective in the past, what suggestions you and your child have talked about, especially if you have agreed upon a "safe space." You might also think about suggestions from other members of your treatment team: psychiatrist, psychotherapist, schoolteacher or counselor, and/or occupational therapist.

If your child is under the care of a psychiatrist or physician, a PRN (per required need, a prearranged emergency dose of medication, when needed) will help your child calm down shortly after ingestion. This medication must be preapproved by the physician and reported to the physician. Proper medical treatment for an accurately diagnosed child on the bipolar spectrum should decrease the number of uncontrollable rages as well as the intensity and duration of the rage episode. Observing and reporting the child's patterns to the psychiatrist will help with making adjustments to the medication.

Choose the Most Appropriate Intervention

Most irritable or angry responses do not need drastic intervention. *What you are aiming for is lowering the degree of irritability, anger, or rage your child exhibits, to a calmer mood state.* When you are ready to respond to your child, say as little as possible and use simple, clear sentences to tell the child what you want. Speak simply, firmly, and quietly, using a simple, nonjudgmental, declarative sentence. Make sure the one (short) sentence you use is the intervention you want. If your child continues to complain, whine, or tries to bargain, or scream, we advise you to repeat the sentence again. The second time, use quieter tones and fewer words.

Here is an example of a confident mother who made a decision and followed through:

> When Eva, age eight, leaves the office in a "cranky" mood, her mother is aware that she is irritable. Eva whines and says she doesn't want to cross the street. She says she is hungry and wants to eat immediately. Eva's mother says nothing, but notes that Eva continues to hold hands while they cross the street. Eva's mom decides Eva's mood is about a 5 on the Upset Scale and that Eva can handle going directly home. After crossing the street, Eva stops, stomps her feet, and screams, "I'm not getting in the car!" After pacing herself, her mom calmly and firmly says, "Eva, it's time to get into the car," *without looking at her daughter.* Eva's mom then pauses, waits, and then quietly says, "The car." Eva's mom has no idea how long it will take but, after a few minutes, while calling her mom "stupid" under her breath, Eva finally gets into the car.

Eva's mom stays (outwardly) relaxed, calm, and quiet, while focusing on getting Eva into the car, she doesn't escalate the situation. Eva realizes that getting into the car is the only way she can get her mom's attention. Eva's mom could feel the reduction in Eva's tension after a few minutes in the car, because Eva's breathing slowed and she started humming. This mother's firm determination was directed toward obtaining the desired result, without causing the escalation of a potentially explosive situation into a full-blown crisis. Direct is not strict, and firm does not have to be harsh.

Gently Praise Success

Many parents are so pleased that they have averted a meltdown that they enthusiastically praise their child. Others are so relieved that praising the child is not even considered. Although it is important to reinforce the child's effort and choice to comply, we do not want to emphasize the child's loss of control or give any reason for further conflict. Irritability can still escalate to anger or rage. A parent's "excited" positive response (too much stimulation) might inadvertently cause an escalation. But quiet positive reinforcement for the effort it takes to calm down will focus on your goal: to de-escalate irritability. In the example above, after Eva stopped humming, her mother said gently, "Glad we're on our way home."

HOW TO ADDRESS "URGENT" REQUESTS

What can you do if your child goes into a demanding mode or pushes for an immediate response from you? As you know, these requests can often come out of nowhere: they have an intense sense of urgency, taking you by surprise and throwing you off balance. Most children with BD can be extremely persistent, repeating the same request over and over; they can be relentless and exhausting in their demands.

If your child is angry, demanding, and on the verge of losing control, don't respond to the content of the "urgent" request. Instead, pay attention to your child's emotional state. *Your job is to focus on reinforcing only rational, in-control responses, calmly and positively.* Thus, if your child runs up to you and makes a demand, wait to respond, and when you do respond, address the child's mood state. Use a soft, slow-paced voice and a simple sentence to tell your child that the most important thing is for him or her to slow down, such as "Find a way to slow down" or "I'll answer when you are calm." If your child persists with urgency, this sentence might be repeated, but be sure that any repetitions of what you say are slower and less frequent than may feel natural to you.

When you do repeat yourself, use fewer words—or better yet, use a prearranged nonverbal signal each time, such as a gentle turn of your wrist and fingers to indicate the need to "lower the volume." Your child will need time to process this new idea when he or she is just recovering from an overstimulated, and chaotic, state.

Remember not to look directly into your child's eyes, as this is more stimulation that can distract your child from processing the request. And do not forget to wait—wait longer than might be comfortable for you—until your child is able to shift to a rational state.

While you are waiting, you will have time to decide whether the child's request is reasonable. If you need to, remind your child it is time to calm down as you tell him or her that this will be discussed at another time, after you and your spouse have given the request some thought.

At that "other time," when your child is calm and receptive, you might ask the child to clarify what the actual request is and why this request is so urgent. If you are willing to go along with the request, you might ask your child to think about another time when the request can be fulfilled (instead of "right now"). Wait to hear your child's response and you two may be able to problem solve together.

For instance, you might agree that "on Saturday, we will go to the store." If you rush out to the store immediately, you are rewarding demanding and impulsive behavior. By delaying gratification, you help your child to plan ahead and increase his or her frustration tolerance. If you are not willing to go along with the demand, then you can give rational reasons for your decision.

By responding this way, you are demonstrating to your child that the most important issue is to de-escalate and calm down (safety); at the same time, you are listening to the request (without antagonizing), you will think about it (pacing), and you will discuss it with the child at a later, specific time, such as in the morning (delay).

If your child is anything like the children we hear about, such simple responses will not be enough. If the child insists and starts getting upset, let the child know you are aware of how important this seems to him or her but that it is not possible to satisfy the demand immediately. Since you have already made the decision to delay talking about the "urgent" request, you need only to repeat the simple idea, such as "Slow down." Eventually, if you stay calm and focused, your child will accept that you have only one response, no matter what the child says. If your child slows down, this may be a time for a gentle, positive comment, such as "Nice calming down."

Remember, if you change your mind and rush to the store because of your child's sense of urgency or arguing, you are (inadvertently) reinforcing behavior you want to extinguish.

HANDLING TRANSITIONS

When your child is angry because you have asked him or her to do something that will require a transition, it's likely that he or she is feeling overloaded. This may not seem to be a big deal to you but it may severely interfere with your child's ability to comply with the simplest transition in the daily schedule. You may notice that, initially, your child ignores your request, and then responds with some degree of anger or irritability.

For example, if you ask your child to turn off the television because it's time to get dressed in the morning or to do homework, or to get ready for bed, your child's first response will likely be to continue what he or she is doing. Or the child might respond (with anger or attitude) and yell, "No!" *This is the moment when you ignore this response, pause, and calmly tell your child what you want him or her to do.* You might say, "It's time to get dressed." And no matter how many screams, objections, or curses result, quietly, calmly, and slowly repeat what he or she must do. Be careful to use only a few words and to say only one message at a time. Be sure that the simple declarative sentence is what you want your child to do.

What your child will hear is only one message and if that message is repeated, there is no way to involve you, the parent, in what we call "butting heads." It helps if what you are asking is part of a prearranged daily schedule, as described in chapter 10. Then you can point to the schedule and say something like, "It's time to get dressed."

ADOLESCENTS

For adolescents, the template is the same. Before responding to an irritable teen, ignore the content of the request. Note the intensity of the outburst and then decide on the intervention. If the teen's tone is irritable, or if there is cursing, ask the teen to calm down. Nothing gets discussed until the teen has calmed down. If the teen is trying to test your patience and is being manipulative, a response such as "I'll respond when you ask in a different way" may be useful. Stay calm, and if your teen is still being inappropriate, try saying, "Try again," until you can honestly respond, "I like how you asked me that." Then slowly respond to your teen's request.

As your parent/child team gains more experience coregulating your child's irritable responses, along with an appropriate medication regime and structured home and school environments, your child will be able to take over more of the self-regulating that has been delayed when bipolar disorder is present from an early age.

A REMINDER

The only constant with BD is change. Even in the worst moments of parenting, the storms always subside. A child will be different later. Parents do miraculous work when they help diminish the length of the storm, keep themselves and others (including the child and siblings) safe, continue setting clear limits at home, and continue the process of stabilization. Parents should not forget to enjoy and internalize the good times. They will return.

12

Psychotherapy

All the therapeutic interventions for bipolar disorder (BD) are woven into the fabric of psychotherapy, becoming integrated and complementary with each other. In this chapter we review basic ideas about psychotherapy, its role and importance in the treatment of children with BD, and how different types of psychotherapy can be useful in the course of treatment.

The importance of flexibility in adapting to the child's age, strengths, and weaknesses; the various stages of illness, as well as familiarity with different techniques, as required by the situation, make the task of providing therapy to a child with BD a truly challenging and complex endeavor. As home, school, and pharmacological interventions become necessary, the therapist often serves as the central communication hub between child, parents, and the whole treatment team.

Psychotherapy for children with BD is crucial to the success of the overall treatment. It complements and facilitates all the other treatments. In this process, the therapist remains consistently on the child's side, providing a safe environment where events can be discussed, understood, and put into perspective. In this environment, fears can be addressed and conflicts can be resolved.

Often the therapist is a psychologist (Ph.D., Psy.D.), a clinical social worker (CSW), or a school counselor who takes a central role in the child's treatment. In some situations, the therapist works with both the child and the parents. Alternatively, the therapist may be actively involved in family education while another professional conducts individual therapy with the child.

The therapist often acts as a case manager, coordinating the different aspects of treatment into a cohesive and comprehensive plan, thus allowing the team members to exchange information and work cooperatively toward common goals. Throughout the treatment program, the therapist maintains involvement with the child and the parents, providing support, information and explanations, as well as reassurance.

Four major factors affect the treatment of a child with BD. They are as follows:

1. The child's age, development, and maturity

2. The stage of illness and phase of treatment

3. The individual's and the illness's characteristics

4. The child's and parents' degree of insight

As the needs of the child change, so does the focus of treatment. For this reason, therapists must be eclectic in their approach, knowledgeable about and comfortable with a variety of techniques, and flexible in order to meet the child's and the family's needs at all the different stages of treatment.

Depending on the child's age, development, and level of relative stability, different types of *play therapy* will be used to facilitate the bonding and communication with the therapist, as well as keeping the child interested and engaged. With young children, play is a natural way to express themselves. Seeing toys, the child might feel more at ease, especially if some of the toys are familiar to him or her. Often children have no words for the symptoms they experience, but they can use play as a way to present their distress in a symbolic way.

For instance, aggressive impulses can be channeled toward toys (animals, dolls, etc.), and elation or euphoria can color the mood of play figures. When children have the capacity to use play symbolically, they can also use play to learn how to solve problems or resolve conflict. Board games, cards, and cooperative building games can also have therapeutic value for children and teens. For a child or teen to sit down, look an adult in the eye, and speak about his or her deepest concerns might feel awkward or embarrassing. It is more likely that while participating in a game or play activity, the child will become more relaxed and engaged.

Different approaches have been used for adults and adolescents with BD, but research on the use of psychotherapy in children with BD is very limited. In most cases, owing to the variety of issues and levels of maturity or stability, an eclectic combination of techniques seems to us to be the most beneficial approach.

GENERAL PRINCIPLES

Some principles are valid for all types of therapeutic interventions. For instance, for children and adolescents with BD, one important issue is that of boundaries. In other words, it is important for the child to have a clear understanding of the role that the therapist is playing in his or her treatment, the rules that parents, therapist, and child agree to follow, including issues of confidentiality between therapist and parents, and the goals of the treatment.

Boundaries

In children with BD, boundaries are an essential part of the treatment. Relationships with parents, siblings, and peers often suffer from the child's inability to understand and/or respect boundaries. One example is physical boundaries, such as one's personal physical space. Children with BD may be unaware of such boundaries, and they may invade others' physical space, becoming overly affectionate, clingy, controlling, or aggressive. They may have difficulties with roles, becoming domineering with younger siblings, trying to impose their view on peers, and arguing with parents. Inappropriate comments may violate a sibling's, peer's, teacher's, or parent's privacy, and have a negative impact on the child's school, social, or family life.

The child with BD can be bossy or demanding, and may interact with parents in a defiant way. Parents may become fearful of antagonizing a rageful child or adolescent. Rules and limit-setting are opposed, with the child manifesting an oppositional attitude in an attempt to impose his or her will on others.

In the course of therapy, this attitude can become apparent around the issue of appointments: for example, the child might show resistance to entering the therapist's office, or enter the office before the correct appointment time or without knocking on the door. Once in the office, the child may refuse to talk, make eye contact, or answer questions. The child may refuse to leave when the appointment has ended. Or he or she might even take an item from the therapist's office and refuse to return it.

During the course of the session, the therapist can use a variety of techniques to foster in the child an appreciation for, and respect of, boundaries, especially physical. For instance, the therapist might ask your child to return to his or her seat when he or she tries to sit on the therapist's lap, or (to show respect toward the child) the therapist may ask permission to keep the child's drawing in the child's folder in the office. An older child might be asked to knock on the door before entering the therapist's office (or a sibling's room), or ask for permission to use a pen or a pad of paper. Positive reinforcement (acknowledging the child's behavior, praising the effort, and reminding the child of the progress made) is used to support the child in his or her struggle to modify their behavior and respect boundaries.

In the verbal exchanges, attention is given to speaking one at a time, waiting for others to finish, not raising the volume of one's voice, and always being respectful to the person being addressed.

Trust

The basis for any relationship, especially a therapeutic one between a child and an adult, is trust. When a child is allowed to feel safe and comfortable with the therapist, a connection is made that will be strengthened through play, open discussions about home, school, or social problems, and a clear understanding of the issues of safety and confidentiality.

It's important for the therapist to explain to the child the difference between privacy and secrecy. When treating a minor (a child under the age of eighteen), most therapists define what information must be disclosed to parents, and what remains confidential. Most children are comfortable with safety issues (self-harm, suicidal ideation, noncompliance with medications) being discussed with parents, as it is the therapist's responsibility to protect the child's well-being.

Other issues—especially those pertaining to sexual development and experimentation, social activities, and experimentation with tobacco, alcohol, and other substances, especially if the child's well-being is not endangered—might be kept confidential, as this allows the development of trust between therapist and the child or adolescent. The therapist can discuss openly with the patient the negative consequences of certain drugs without endorsing the drug, appearing judgmental, or threatening disclosure to the parents, as this would affect the therapeutic alliance and deprive the therapist of accurate information about substance use and its monitoring. Whenever the therapist needs to disclose any information to the parents, the child should be told in advance, and the reason for the disclosure must be discussed with the child.

For instance, a ten-year-old girl was experiencing psychotic symptoms (she heard voices telling her to cut her wrists), but she was afraid she might be punished by her very strict father. After explaining to the child that she had no control over her symptoms, and that she was not going to be blamed or punished, the child was more willing to discuss ways for her parents to help her feel safer. She agreed to have the therapist bring the parents into the session to discuss her symptoms and ways of addressing them.

During the problem-solving portion of the session, her father was very supportive: he offered to stay home from work in case she needed his help and reassurance. The father's willingness to understand and support her allowed the child to feel more secure and loved. She was then more willing to discuss her uncomfortable feelings with the therapist, and she trusted that her privacy would not be violated.

We've found that many children struggling with the symptoms of bipolar disorder are relieved to discuss their concerns with an understanding parent, especially with the support of a therapist.

Support

For a child with BD, besides the trauma of having been diagnosed with BD, additional stress comes from the experience of living with the symptoms of BD and their consequences. For this reason, most children with BD need an ally, an advocate, someone who can understand their distress, and support them through it. Before a child can believe that things can change for the better, the therapist must address the child's sense of failure, guilt, and low self-esteem. Sometimes this will require mediating a conflict with the parents, other times it will require addressing *cognitive distortions* (false beliefs) or helping the child apologize for inappropriate behavior.

Humor

Therapy does not have to be boring, heavy, or serious, at least not all the time. Engaging the child and the parents is important in motivating them to accept the disorder, manage symptoms day to day, and find hope for the future during their long struggle with BD. Shared humor is particularly useful for creating a more relaxed atmosphere, allowing the child and parents to relax and look at the situation in a more hopeful way. Humor is also instrumental in providing a sense of closeness and building a more cooperative relationship between child and parents, and between child and therapist.

Communication

The complex combination of comorbid conditions and special needs that can characterize a child with BD often calls for a diverse treatment team. When the pediatrician, an occupational or speech and language therapist, or a home tutor is involved, their feedback is useful to the whole treatment team. Open, easy communication between all involved in the child's treatment is especially useful for maintaining close supervision of the child's condition. Coordination between disciplines and a shared treatment plan are as important as ongoing communication between parents and treatment team.

Under ideal circumstances, the therapist and the treatment team review progress and treatment goals regularly, sharing observations or changes. However, given the therapist's central role, most team members leave the responsibility of coordinating and harmonizing interventions to the therapist.

Therapists' Characteristics

To be able to help children with BD, a therapist must be flexible and use a wide variety of techniques to provide guidance and support to your child and all family members. Flexibility is also required by the rapidly changing needs of a child becoming more stable as he or she moves from the acute to the stabilization and/or maintenance phase of treatment. As the child grows, the therapist might shift from simple games to more complex play. Therapists also need to be eclectic, able to shift from cognitive and behavioral techniques to more supportive interventions, psycho-education, or insight-oriented work.

The therapist selects and adapts therapeutic interventions to the child's current needs, taking into consideration the child's strengths and weaknesses. This requires familiarity with different treatment approaches, and great tolerance for individual differences in meeting certain goals.

PSYCHOTHERAPY TECHNIQUES

There are a variety of psychotherapy techniques that have proved useful in the treatment of BD. Some of the most commonly used are discussed below.

Psycho-education (Individual and Group)

This treatment emphasizes learning about BD as a necessary step for the patient to play an active role in managing the disorder. The patient and the family are enrolled in a series of individual or group sessions focusing on: (1) symptom recognition; (2) treatment compliance; (3) early identification of a relapse or recurrence; and (4) lifestyle changes. These interventions can successfully reduce the number of relapses and delay their occurrence.

Cognitive and Behavioral Therapy

The use of cognitive and behavioral therapy (CBT) for depression, introduced by Aaron Beck at the University of Pennsylvania in Philadelphia, was based on the benefits of recognizing and correcting cognitive distortions in adults suffering from depression. According to CBT theory, the events we experience elicit feelings, which, in turn, create or are connected to ideas; these ideas lead to maladaptive behaviors or actions. For instance, a child might invite a classmate to visit for a playdate (event). If the invitation isn't accepted, the child might think, "That child doesn't like me" (distorted thought), and "Nobody likes me in my class" (distorted thought), and then, perhaps, the child will refuse to go to school in the morning (action).

The use of these cognitive techniques, in association with behavioral modification techniques, in the treatment of BD has been particularly useful in helping patients to monitor distorted thinking, identify coping strategies, avoid putting into action their distorted thoughts, monitor compliance with treatment, and remove obstacles (or sources of resistance) to compliance. The use of CBT in the treatment of BD has been researched in adults, but its use in youths with BD remains insufficiently studied (Fristad, Gavissi, and Soldano 1998).

The Developmental, Individual-Difference, Relationship-Based Intervention

The developmental, individual-difference, relationship-based intervention (DIR) was developed by Stanley Greenspan, and with Ira Glovinsky (2002), modified for use in children with bipolar disorder. This approach is useful in the treatment of very young children, emphasizing regulation of moods through self-calming, deepening the child's trust with positive interactions within the caregiver/child team, and fostering more mature functioning.

Interpersonal Psychotherapy

Interpersonal psychotherapy (IPT) was introduced by Gerald Klerman and colleagues at Harvard University, and then it was adapted for treatment of BD in the form of interpersonal and social rhythm therapy (IPSRT) by Ellen Frank at the University of Pittsburgh, Pennsylvania (2005). In this approach, the emphasis is on improving daily routines, symptoms' management and communication skills, as well as relapse prevention. In most cases, a combination of various techniques provides the right "mix" of interventions that will be useful to the individual patient or family. The exclusive use of one of these approaches, however, rarely satisfies all of the patient's needs.

Multi-Family Psycho-education Group

The multi-family psycho-education group (MFPG) was organized as a curriculum-based approach for families of children with BD or depression by Mary Fristad and colleagues at Ohio State University in Columbus, Ohio (1998). Utilizing a combination of cognitive-behavioral techniques and psycho-education, this approach provides opportunities for both the child and the parents to learn about the symptoms of mood disorders, as well as to develop ways of coping with symptoms more effectively. Although more time-efficient than working with individual families, this group approach requires that enough children in the same age range, and in similar stages of the disorder, attend sessions for the whole course of treatment.

Family-Focused Treatment

Family-focused treatment (FFT) is another psycho-educational and cognitive-behavioral approach that has been used with adolescents and their families by David Miklowitz and colleagues at the University of Colorado in Denver (2004). The emphasis is on education about the symptoms of BD, improving family communication, and developing problem-solving strategies leading to a better psychosocial adjustment.

Adapting Play Therapy to Bipolar Disorder

Through play, children can become familiar with the depressive and manic symptoms of bipolar disorder. For example, many children in a manic state become aggressive and controlling and may play out their angry, aggressive experience through intensely violent fighting scenarios in which the child's character "always wins." At other times, when depressive symptoms are prominent, the same child will act "bored" or "can't find anything to do," or wants to end the session early to see his parent in the waiting room.

The therapist can help identify the child's changing mood states and connect it to the specific symptoms in the session and to "real life" situations at home and school. This can lead to direct problem solving between child and therapist. Very often, when the therapist and child learn about the symptoms and solve a problem together, they use a few minutes at the end of the session to share the new information with the parent.

AN ECLECTIC APPROACH

As discussed in chapter 7, most cases of childhood-onset BD require a multipronged approach. The child, parents, and other family members need to be educated about the illness and its symptoms, the medications used and their side effects, and the early signs of instability or imminent relapse or recurrence. At the same time, both child and parents need to receive specific, age-appropriate instructions on how to identify and monitor symptoms, or how to manage them more effectively.

As cognitive distortions are identified in the course of individual therapy with the child or the parents, they are addressed using cognitive therapy. Sleep hygiene and interventions are based on psychoeducation and behavioral techniques that must be the focus of both individual therapy with the child and the parents, and in the parent/child therapy.

The sequence of interventions usually includes the following: learning what the illness's symptoms are; recognizing and observing those symptoms in daily occurrences and events; understanding from personal experience the negative consequences of those symptoms; and gaining the benefits of treatment. The first step relies on the use of psycho-education, because often neither the child nor the parents are aware of which symptoms of BD are present. Using cognitive techniques, the child and the parents are gradually trained to make objective, nonjudgmental observation of symptoms and triggers.

Once they have learned how to recognize those symptoms and triggers, children and parents are more aware of the need for alternative or better coping skills. Behavioral techniques, used in the management of sleep and mood disturbances, offer another set of tools in the long struggle to stabilize BD.

Individual Therapy with the Child

One of the challenges of working with children and adolescents with mood disorders is that as their emotions shift, their motivation fluctuates. For these youths, maintaining motivation is crucial, and is one of the most important goals of therapy. For this reason, therapy has to be interesting, interactive, and stimulating.

What does the child need to know and why? As with most medical illnesses, we believe that to effectively manage a chronic illness such as BD, the more information the child has, the better off he or she will be. In other words, in order to manage mood swings one must be able to recognize them. Self-awareness or *insight* is the ability to see oneself objectively, as other do; to see one's mood change in color and intensity, to observe oneself shifting from being in control to being out of control.

In the early phases of treatment, the management of symptoms is often the first priority. However, as BD becomes better controlled, the child can benefit from ongoing self-monitoring and learning ways to manage his or her emotions and social interactions better. Learning new strategies to manage triggers like psychosocial stressors requires stability. During periods of stability, younger children will learn how to ask for your help, and will use age-appropriate behavioral techniques learned in their individual treatment sessions. Older children can develop new ways to manage their emotions and thus minimize the impact of those emotions on their lives.

Managing Moods

The therapist helps the child identify different moods in developmentally appropriate ways. The child learns how to develop an inner sense of certain emotions, and how to recognize the specific features, pleasant or unpleasant, of each mood.

IDENTIFICATION OF THE MOOD STATE

Asking the child where in the body he or she feels rage, joy, or intense frustration (for example: in the head, belly, or chest) or assigning a color to the feeling helps the child to identify and name the emotion (such as "red-hot anger").

LEVEL OF MOOD STATE

As the child becomes better able to identify certain emotions, the *intensity* of the emotion is assigned different levels. This helps the child to recognize being in control versus being out of control, especially after an assessment of the consequences. This assessment is facilitated by the therapist using a nonjudgmental approach. An event from the past week, identified using the MoodLog (see appendix II), can be discussed and better understood with the Upset Scale (see chapter 11).

CONSEQUENCES

Repeated problems arising from "losing it" at home, school, and socially become more and more evident as the child starts to recognize a connection between out-of-control emotions and negative outcomes. Failed playdates, fights, social isolation, and being teased can be the result of impulsive behavior or extreme emotional reactions. These are all powerful motivations for change.

NEGATIVE EMOTIONS

Recognizing negative emotions and inhibiting or holding back their expression helps the child realize that he or she has some control over their behavior. In children with BD, the habit of dwelling on negative emotions and thoughts about themselves and others is not helpful, as it often leads to behavioral acting-out. This is an area where the therapist can help the child develop self-control and find positive qualities in him- or herself and boost the child's self-esteem.

MANAGING TODAY

Managing as best as one can is a success. Many children feel so scrutinized and controlled, or blamed and punished that it is important to acknowledge their struggle, even when the outcome is less than ideal. Children make tremendous efforts to do what is expected of them, but often they feel overwhelmed by the task. For this reason it is helpful to keep a short-term perspective (e.g., "let's get through the next activity") rather than focusing on distant or long-term goals. The therapist can help the child see how well he or she is managing parts of the schedule, or the therapist can break the schedule into segments that the child is able to manage. This approach can be a positive reinforcement in the child's daily struggle to manage shifting moods.

PACING

Most children and teens with BD can recognize their tendency to become too active (overactive) and they need to learn how to slow down or pace themselves and their activities. The therapist plays a large role in modeling this for the child. For instance, responses are delivered slowly, and with a low tone of voice. Slow responses help the child learn how to slow down, rather than constantly accelerating the pace of an interaction. Parents need to be aware of both their child's tendency to speed up verbal exchanges or their own tendency to engage in fast-paced interaction that can easily lead to the child feeling overexcited, overstimulated, and vulnerable to meltdowns.

With younger children, you will be responsible for pacing activities while keeping your child occupied, preventing overinvolvement in too many activities. With older children and adolescents, the therapist will help them learn how to recognize their tendency to take on too much, when they crowd their schedules with sports, social, and extracurricular activities, often interfering with completion of school tasks and normal sleep. Parents will also be involved in a discussion of how to help their child prioritize and choose activities so that their schedule does not become overcrowded. Pacing requires a degree of introspection to be able to see when things are building up to the point that one needs to slow down and reduce the pace.

TRIGGERS

Transitions are obvious triggers to meltdowns and the loss of emotional balance (decompensation) in children with BD. However, this is not necessarily clear to the child. Through careful work and education about the symptoms, the connection between stress, insomnia, and irritability is gradually uncovered. As the child begins to identify triggers (such as sleep deprivation) and reactions (such as being rude to the coach and being kicked off the team), he or she becomes more interested in managing emotions and behaviors.

WHAT HELPS? WHAT DOESN'T HELP

Many children are overstimulated for a variety of reasons, some of which are controllable. The goal is to focus on the trigger that causes the overstimulation and come up with a practical plan that will help.

For example, sleep deprivation can be both the cause (trigger) and the consequence of overstimulation. If the use of caffeine interferes with sleep or causes irritability, the possibility of tapering off is discussed with the child or adolescent, and any resistance is addressed. Late-evening overstimulation with board games, TV, electronic games, computers, phones, or music players often interferes with keeping a regulated schedule as it cuts down on sleep and needs to be monitored, and, sometimes, limited or prohibited.

MONITORING

A diary or chart of the symptoms provides a great opportunity for the child and the therapist to discuss the progress made, the techniques used, and the triggers identified and dealt with. The process of self-discovery allows the child to recognize patterns of cycling and how to best cope with them. This becomes the focus of the maintenance phase because identifying the early symptoms (*prodromes*) of an episode, or its triggers, helps to maintain adequate support and supervision from the treatment team.

Parent/Child Work

The unique role the parent plays in the process of diagnosing BD is further expanded during the course of treatment. The balancing influence that parenting can provide to a child with BD cannot be emphasized enough.

TEAMWORK

The therapist can strengthen the connection and the cooperation between parent and child by showing them how they are dealing with the same symptoms, the same pain, and showing them how they can work together as a team. The importance of open communication for the entire team, with clear goals for all team members, helps to provide a common direction and newfound hope. One of the most useful activities for the parent/child team to engage in is the charting of symptoms. Through this activity, and the use of a common language, parents and child feel closer, united by the common effort to stave off the "enemy" (the symptoms of bipolar disorder). The therapist will introduce the principles of mood charting to the parents and the child separately, and then ask them to collaborate, first by comparing notes and acknowledging differences, and then through common assessments.

IT'S OUR PROBLEM, NOT YOUR FAULT

The understanding that BD is an illness and not someone's fault is perhaps the most important idea affecting the parent/child team. Freed of the "blame game," the team can focus on the day-to-day management of symptoms, compliance, and adaptive changes. As parents and child stop blaming each other, and each takes responsibility in their daily interactions, a new level of understanding is reached.

COMMON GOALS

Dealing with the negative atmosphere of resentment and restoring a climate of affection and cooperation is important to the realization of more complex goals. Eliminating struggles around chores, morning and night routines, schoolwork, and privileges is often perceived by parents and children as the highest priority. Using behavioral techniques that emphasize positive reinforcement, a behavioral point system can be discussed in therapy, implemented at home, and monitored over time. This can be particularly helpful if a similar behavioral point system is also used in school.

PACING

Although the principle of pacing is often introduced separately to the child and his or her parents, it becomes a common goal that helps the parent/child team identify potential sources of difficulty. From sleepovers to birthday parties to travel plans, exams, or homework, the therapist helps the parent/child team recognize how involvement in too many activities may be a potential source of instability and decompensation.

MUTUAL SUPPORT

As the parent/child team starts using effective communication skills to prevent or cope with temper tantrums and other symptoms, a sense of trust, mutual support, and shared satisfaction develops and functions as a motivating factor for all. The benefits of reduced conflict, well-established and clear responsibilities, rewards and consequences, and better understanding of how each person can help in managing the symptoms of BD when they arise reinforce the importance of working as a team to find solutions.

FEEDBACK

In the course of joint therapy sessions, parent(s) and child share observations and assessments of how well or poorly they manage specific situations. Feedback given and received allows the child to feel a part of the team effort, less isolated, and better understood. In a calm atmosphere, therapist and parents can praise the child's efforts, or give advice about better ways to deal with a particular situation when it arises.

ACKNOWLEDGE PROGRESS AND POSITIVE OUTCOMES

Both parents and child need to be reminded of their efforts, their successes, and their progress. Focusing on the benefits of their new approach, the therapist keeps them motivated as they become more hopeful and more willing to go along with the therapist's suggestions. Sometimes, it's useful for the therapist to review with the parent/ child team what changed in their diary or mood chart, as a concrete example of how their efforts are producing good results.

Individual Work: Parent

At different times during the course of your child's treatment, as a parent, your needs will change. Depending on the age of your child and the symptoms of BD, sometimes you will need simple support; at other times you will need help in understanding BD, or encouragement and reassurance. We consider therapy with the parent most helpful in strengthening the parent's role of coregulator of their child's emotions.

PSYCHO-EDUCATION

Help with understanding the different signs and symptoms of the illness and their course over time is essential. Examples from each family's history can be used to help focus the attention on the most prominent features of BD or a comorbid disorder. As new symptoms appear, or recur, parents need the therapist's perspective to better understand what is happening. With the therapist's help, patterns of recurrence or associations of symptoms can be recognized. For instance, the importance of compliance with medication can be emphasized when a delay in administering a medication can result in the child's loss of emotional balance; such information reinforces the parent's commitment to a regular medication regimen.

MODELING

One important source of help for most parents is what they can learn from interacting with the therapist. The therapist is calm and even-tempered, at times taking on a soothing or reassuring role, at other times more firm or direct. When not in agreement, the therapist chooses a nonantagonistic, nonadversarial stance such as "We agree that we disagree." This allows for a useful discussion of different points of view in a cooperative atmosphere. When a therapist shows flexibility, listens carefully to parents, and admits to mistakes, this helps a parent realize that it is okay to make mistakes or to be wrong.

CONSISTENT SUPPORT

Although the therapist's work may be primarily with the child, ongoing contact with the child's parents allows for support and reassurance, as well as feedback on the outcome of shared treatment goals. In the early phases of treatment and in times of crisis, parents often benefit from ongoing encouragement, guidance, reassurance, and support. When the child is stable, parents are reminded of the need for ongoing monitoring, the need to respond appropriately to symptoms and changes, and the importance of compliance with treatment.

PSYCHOTHERAPY FOR CHILDREN WITH BD: SOME CASE HISTORIES

As stated above, the role of the therapist in treating children with BD is essential for successful treatment interventions. The therapist's role is of equal value to both the child and his or her parents, not only because of the therapist's professional expertise but also because there may be times when either the child or the parent(s) will need the unbiased support of the therapist in the event of a conflict erupting between them.

Justine: Early Psychotherapy with an Eight-Year-Old Girl

At eight years of age, Justine (introduced in chapter 3) had huge problems with sleep, separation anxiety, aggression, sensory integration, and emotional regulation. The first three recommendations for her were sleep hygiene, occupational therapy, and individual therapy. Her parents learned about sleep and received instructions and guidance on sleep hygiene; meanwhile Justine began weekly psychotherapy and a course of occupational therapy (OT), with emphasis on sensory integration. At this beginning stage of psychotherapy, the main goal was to help Justine with transitions.

WEEK 1

In the initial session, Justine entered before the correct time and had a temper tantrum when she was asked to wait. When the therapist finally brought mother and daughter into the therapy room, Justine was apologetic and shy, draping herself over her mother. She slowly made eye contact. After ten minutes, she agreed to look at the toys and took the therapist's hand. She was always able to see her mother. And, after playing for a few minutes, she again went back to her mom; this time she briefly sat on her mom's lap and then returned to play. When Justine was reminded that the end of the meeting was approaching, she threw herself across her mother's lap and she refused to stand up when it was time to leave. Oppositional and hostile, Justine became aggressive when leaving the office.

WEEK 2

At the beginning of the next session, Justine was shy but more easily engaged; she went on her own to the toy area and stood in front of a game she was interested in. Justine agreed to play that game but while setting it up, she left the therapist to sit with her mother. She agreed to return to the game only with her mother, but later she allowed her mother to leave. Play was aggressive and rules were ignored.

This time, when Justine was resistant to ending the play on time, the therapist, along with Justine's mother, planned an after-appointment transition: Justine was to have her snack (which her mother had with her) before going home. The therapist had a confident attitude that Justine would be able to do this, and she eventually agreed to have her snack in the waiting room, yet she refused to say good-bye to the therapist.

WEEK 3

In the next session Justine was clearly hypomanic and overactive. She couldn't stop talking, smiling, and giggling, and her mother reported a week of very little sleep. Justine was so hyper she could not settle on any game. She started becoming annoyed and irritable, said she was bored, and became aggressive when she couldn't get her way. Her play was disorganized and chaotic, and her frustration tolerance was very low. When it was time to leave, Justine left easily because she couldn't wait to go to the playground.

WEEK 4

Justine was getting used to the therapy routine and had had five days of regulated sleep. What a difference sleep can make! Justine was warm and affectionate, wanted to play, and left her mother easily. She chattered happily about the pet store she was going to visit before going home. While still in session, Justine decided to play with the toy animals. Her play was still very aggressive, and she did not share or engage in play with the therapist, but she seemed less anxious about leaving, and only asked "How much longer?" twice. This time, Justine and mom left the office with a smile and a polite good-bye.

In the following four weeks, Justine continued to make small but significant progress and started a trial of a mood-stabilizing agent. We fast-forward to week eight.

WEEK 8

After two months of therapy, Justine had been on mood-stabilizing medication for one month. Her sleep was regular and there was no significant separation anxiety. Play was more organized and cooperative. With her therapist, Justine was learning about her different moods, and about staying in control. Justine thought it was her mother's fault when she lost control. Mother and child both commented on the progress made since treatment began, especially in the area of meltdowns: these had become fewer, did not last as long, and were not as severe as before.

WEEK 10

Justine's mother reported there were two incidents in the previous three days: one at home and one at the playground. Justine appeared a bit wired, and she told the therapist about nightmares of an evil doll. When asked about the events (her mother had been bruised by a kick), Justine became very hyper, sang aloud, and refused to play. She was offered a hammer game and banged away with a hammer for some time before she told the therapist: "I don't want to be bad." She left quietly.

WEEK 12

After a small increase of her medication dose, Justine seemed more relaxed. She was comfortable letting go of mom, her play was calm and cooperative, she was able to wait for her turn, and she had not hit her mom in two weeks. Leaving the office was not a problem anymore, but any change of plans still led to a meltdown.

WEEK 16

Justine was working with her therapist on her impulse control. To help with this task, the therapist introduced a new game that required quick reactions and the ability to "stop and do nothing."

WEEK 20

Home life has become organized and predictable and Justine has been working on a star system at home with her mom, and is doing very well. She got her weekly reward (a trip to the zoo) almost every weekend.

WEEK 24

Justine's older sister was sick and had been hospitalized. Justine's grandmother came to stay with her at home and Justine seemed to be okay, but her nightmares started up again. In her fantasy play in the therapist's office, the "doctor" didn't know what to do to help the sick baby. When the doctor also got sick, a cheerful sticker from the therapist's drawer helped the "baby" to feel better. Justine's mom had noticed how clingy Justine was, but she also observed how caring and concerned Justine had been about her sister.

Andrew: Ongoing Psychotherapy with a Young Boy

Andrew, also introduced in chapter 3, had been in treatment for several months and was beginning first grade. At home, things had improved, and he was developing a nice relationship with his therapist whom he had visited weekly after a pause of several weeks during the summer months.

WEEK 30

At this point in his treatment, Andrew was still quite shy, but he accepted playing with the therapist and his mother, as he said it was more fun with the two of them. When things didn't go his way, Andrew still became quite angry but he no longer screamed or lost control as often as he had before his treatment. In play therapy, however, violent confrontations and themes of destruction and over-whelming power were played out repeatedly.

WEEK 32

Two weeks later, his mother reported that Andrew had been poking at and touching his peers and his brother, which was annoying to them and seemed to be a means to get attention. There were several fights at home and one incident in school. His school principal, after a conference with the psychiatrist and the therapist, had agreed to put Andrew on a behavior-modification program that tied into the point system already in place at Andrew's home. During therapy, Andrew initially vented about how this was not fair, but he eventually calmed down and seemed to be able to hear and understand the possible benefits and rewards of learning to control his behavior.

WEEK 36

The system seemed to be working and Andrew was no longer inappropriately touching other kids in school. He had started reading, but even there he became frustrated too easily. In therapy, his ability to maintain control was gently tested. The therapist noticed some pressured speech and restlessness. These symptoms were confirmed by his mother's observations at home and were promptly reported to the psychiatrist.

WEEK 38

Andrew's upcoming birthday had been exciting him for weeks and he couldn't talk about anything else. In all his games with the therapist there was a birthday cake or a surprise present. At school, however, there were fewer complaints.

WEEK 40

After his birthday, Andrew was more cooperative, focused, and pleasant to be around. He was able to play by the rules, didn't complain of boredom, and had no problems waiting his turn. He still had trouble speaking clearly, especially when excited, but he accepted the therapist's feedback and tried to speak more clearly.

WEEK 44

After a vacation during a school break, his mother realized that Andrew was sleeping less. He was up early to go fishing with his dad, and wouldn't take a nap. In therapy, his play reverted to wars and weapons of destruction. Andrew was very restless, as he had been months before, and he seemed to have grown immune to the medication. The therapist encouraged his mother to call the psychiatrist as soon as possible to get his medication adjusted.

WEEK 45

Andrew's blood level showed that the medication's dose was too low. With a slightly higher dose, Andrew was again more cooperative and stable. He asked the therapist, "How can I destroy the bipolar thing forever?" The therapist said that instead of "destroying the bipolar thing," his parents and the team would continue to help him and teach him how to keep the illness from getting in his way. Andrew smiled and the therapist later told his parents, "Andrew is beginning to become a member of his own treatment team."

13

School Decisions

An effective treatment plan requires the school setting to be a learning environment that helps with the stabilization of the symptoms of bipolar disorder (BD). Under ideal circumstances this will go along with a structured, predictable home life. Many children with BD have difficulty at school from a very early age; others do well at school and are symptomatic mostly, or only, at home. As your child gets older, the stress of school and the more complex academic and social demands can trigger and/or exacerbate the symptoms of BD, affecting learning and socialization.

This chapter will assist you in making decisions about school, so that your child will be able to learn in an environment that is interesting, supportive, and consistent with the need for stabilization and good adjustment. We review some basic concepts that can be useful as you and your treatment team determine what your child's needs are and find ways to provide an optimum learning environment for him or her.

WHAT AFFECTS THE CHOICE OF ACCOMMODATIONS?

The choice of school accommodations depends on individual needs and circumstances. When making decisions about school, we carefully consider the following factors:

- The stage of the illness

- The effect of BD on school functioning

- Comorbid psychiatric disorders

- School-related stress

Stage of Illness

During the *acute phase* (see chapter 7), a child may not be able to get to school on a daily basis, unless in a hospital setting. Some parents have described their child as experiencing "a mind freeze" after an acute episode of BD. During a *mind freeze*, concentration and the ability to focus are significantly impaired and medical stabilization is the primary concern.

The *stabilization phase* may last up to eighteen months or even longer. This time is needed for a child to recover emotional balance, show normal behavior, and start recovering the learning skills that may have been affected by the onset of BD. At the beginning of this phase, your child may be at home full-time or attend school part-time.

Many school districts will provide homeschooling, such as a tutor at home for up to two hours per day. Other children may attend a partial-hospital program (during the day). Parents, children, and school staff should be prepared for some unevenness during the stabilization phase. The emphasis, however, continues to be on slowly recovering and adjusting to home and school life. The accommodations necessary during the stabilization stage will change as your child regains his or her emotional, cognitive, and social capacities.

When a child is in the *maintenance phase*, parents often find that he or she is still too easily overwhelmed or anxious to attend school in a traditional educational setting. Accommodations and/or a special school setting may be necessary to sustain gains.

The Effect of BD on School Functioning

The symptoms of BD, as described in chapter 3, include many shifts of mood, energy, motivation, and concentration that affect the child's ability to learn. When depressed, a child's mind may slow down; he or she may show a lack of interest and have poor memory and a poor ability to concentrate, along with low motivation and self-esteem. When manic or hypomanic, a child's mind is overactive with racing or crowded thoughts, and along with grandiosity, the child is subject to distractibility, overconfidence, and physical restlessness. Until these symptoms are treated, most children will struggle in school.

In chapter 6 we explored the effects of BD on learning, including the impact on memory, attention, fine and/or gross motor functioning, and processing (auditory, verbal, and so forth). Higher order processes of problem solving and executive functioning (including planning ahead, organizing, and following through on tasks), as well as difficulties in mathematics, may be affected, even when a child is in the maintenance phase.

The intensity of your child's emotional reaction to academic challenges adds an additional burden. Neuropsychologist Steven Mattis (2006), based in New York, pointed out in a personal communication that the "characteristic catastrophic reaction of children with mood disorders impairs their ability to compensate for what might be a minor deficiency. Intense and uneven emotional reactivity affects normal adaptation and exacerbates even minor learning problems in children diagnosed with bipolar disorder."

How is it possible that a child can show little or no signs of bipolar disorder in school, but be so out of control at home? Over the years, school staff and personnel have begun to understand that educating a child with BD offers the same challenges that parents experience every day at home. However, many school personnel are not aware that a child's most regulated part of the day often occurs during school hours. Frequently, the school reports the child with BD is doing "just fine," and some educators may not believe the parents' reports of home difficulties.

As discussed in chapter 7, the daily activity or circadian rhythm of children with BD is abnormal. This is particularly true for elementary school-age children (ages five to eleven), and their daily cycle is often as follows:

- They are slow to get started in the morning (depressive symptoms), which can cause tardiness and/or lethargy during the first few school periods.

- Highest functioning occurs in the middle of the day, coinciding with school hours.

- After-school activation (manic symptoms of restlessness, racing thoughts, distractibility) interferes with homework and sleep.

Comorbid Psychiatric Disorders

As reviewed in chapter 6, several disorders may co-occur or are a result of BD. Drug and alcohol abuse, anxiety, eating disorders, behavioral disorders, and suicidal or violent behaviors must be addressed in order to stabilize BD. A tendency to be impulsive, a compulsion to seek danger, excitement, attention, and, ultimately, control are all common with these conditions. As a result, educational accommodations will be more restrictive for the purpose of treating both BD and comorbid psychiatric conditions.

Before being diagnosed with BD, many children have already received special services. Some have specific learning disabilities; others have difficulties with speech and language, sensory integration, and/or sensory-motor coordination (including poor handwriting). As noted in chapter 6, co-occurring diagnoses might need to be addressed separately. School accommodations will benefit most children with BD regardless of the school setting, or whether your child's ability to learn is impaired by BD or by another co-occurring disorder.

School-Related Stress

Many parents report that their child is fine during summer months and vacation time, but as soon as school begins, the child becomes tense and worried about completing schoolwork. Other parents are most concerned by their child's poor social skills. Some kids with BD are bullies, some are class clowns, some can't participate in organized activities due to anxiety, and others just don't know how to make friends. As we have discussed in previous chapters, academic and social issues can be the stressors or triggers that lead to activation of the symptoms of depression and/or mania.

HOMEWORK

This particular facet of school life is often a focal point of stress that causes irritability, anger, and rage in children with BD. The after-school period is frequently characterized by an increase (activation) of symptoms, including hyperactivity and distractibility, that make homework difficult for the child. Because reducing stress and conflict is vital to stabilization, it is of paramount importance for parents to find a way to deal effectively with homework.

SOCIAL COMPETENCE

The range of social competence in children with BD is as wide as is the intensity of their other symptoms. However, many children are motivated to stay in their local school because of friends, and/or they enjoy participating in group sports. Many other children with BD have not had the experience of strong friendships, and may be too awkward, anxious, or perfectionistic to participate in group activities, such as sports.

When the disorder is most active, social interactions are often impaired. If the child is unstable (withdrawn, paranoid, or grandiose), he or she may be ridiculed by classmates or may misinterpret others' facial expressions (including teachers and peers) as proof that they are out to get him or her. Social skills are important developmental tasks that are too often derailed by BD: this factor should always be considered in school accommodations.

The stress caused by school and social demands must be countered by school accommodations. Helping your child develop effective coping strategies is always a priority. A plan for educational accommodations must include interventions to reduce stress and develop coping strategies to help your child deal with academic and social issues.

SCHOOL ACCOMMODATIONS: BASIC PRINCIPLES

The following steps are necessary to facilitate school accommodations:

- Become familiar with federal and state education laws.

- Contact your local school district's Department of Special Education.

- Complete the evaluation to determine your child's eligibility for accommodations.

- Attend the meeting to determine eligibility for special services.

- Know what to ask for in the individual education plan.

- Attend all subsequent meetings with your child's school team and find out how to report any concerns you or your child might have.

Education Laws

The most recent federal law, PL 108-466, called the Individuals with Disabilities Education Improvement Act of 2004, often referred to as IDEA 2004, uses the same definition of learning disability quoted in chapter 6 under Learning Disabilities. It excludes hearing, vision, or motor deficits, mental retardation (IQ 69 or lower), traumatic brain injury, emotional disturbance, or other health impairments (OHI) affecting learning.

IDEA 2004 has the "child find" requirement, which is meant to increase the identification of underserved children. It also makes provisions for early intervention services for infants and toddlers, preschoolers (ages three to five), school-age children (ages six to eighteen), and post-high schoolers (ages eighteen to twenty-one). There are recommendations for transition planning from infant to preschool, from preschool to school-age, and from high-school to post-high school services.

Most of the provisions of IDEA 2004 went into effect in July 2005. Local school districts must comply with state and federal legislation.

For this reason, special education services can be different across state or school district lines. Although each state has a different name for the committee that evaluates special education needs, we will refer to this committee as the Committee on Special Education (CSE), as it is known in New York State, throughout this chapter. The information relevant to your child can be obtained from your school district's special education office, or from your state's Department of Education's Web site.

Help with Education Laws

Parents can contact a parent advocacy group, specifically for information about special education, in the county they live in, by using a phone directory or by contacting the school district, a local mental health organization, or a local bipolar parent support group. At little or no cost, parent advocacy groups may provide you with educational and legal assistance to obtain special accommodations for your child.

Paying for a good educational lawyer (one who specializes in educational issues) may be worth the investment. An attorney, experienced with educational issues in your state, can help you obtain the best educational accommodations available under the current legislation. Parents can make inquiries to find an attorney familiar with BD and educational accommodations available in their state by asking a local parent support group or the child's therapist or psychiatrist.

Recent changes in the federal law favor the school district, putting the burden on the parents to demonstrate the need for special education services. Parents should involve doctors, therapists, neuropsychologists, lawyers, and child advocates early in the process. It is better to have the support of an attorney or a parent advocate early on than to lose years of necessary services. In many cases, when a parent and mental health professional agree on the best way to educate a child with BD, there is often a legal means to obtain full or partial funding for it.

Help with the Educational Options

Many parents are not sure what options are available for their child. An experienced educational consultant with a strong background in special needs can advise parents through the process of school placement. The Web site of a national not-for-profit clearinghouse for independent educational consultants can help you find a reputable expert (see appendix III). An educational consultant will assist you in finding an appropriate current placement, and will facilitate the transition to the next placement as your child grows.

Based on information obtained from you, your child, the treatment team, and recommended evaluations, an educational consultant will review the options available to you, and will work with you to figure out how to choose the best option for your child. If a private school is involved, the consultant will help you determine whether the school district might pick up some or all of the cost.

Clearinghouses for schools accommodating children with special needs can be found on the Internet (see appendix III). Your state education department's Web site also provides a list of state-approved private schools.

Referral for Special Education

To begin the process, it is necessary to obtain a referral to the committee that evaluates special education needs, such as the CSE (Committee on Special Education). This referral must be in written form and the CSE will respond in writing to the request (from you or the school) for special services' evaluations. If the letter is from the school, it must outline the reasons for the referral. If you write the letter of referral, it is helpful to attach a letter from a psychiatrist, psychotherapist, or primary care physician justifying your request. The school district must complete an evaluation and hold a formal special education meeting within sixty school days from the date of the request. Parents should be careful to keep all this material organized, including copies of all correspondence.

Evaluation for Special Education

Eligibility for special education services and the specific services to be provided are determined by the school district through an evaluation process. This process includes a social history, generally obtained in a parent interview by a social worker; a classroom observation by a teacher or psychologist; a written educational evaluation by a special education teacher; and written evaluations by speech and language and occupational therapists, if requested by you or the referring professional.

Since 2005, not all assessments for special education include an IQ test or "projectives" (tests to evaluate current emotional functioning). This is unfortunate, because the newest and most widely used IQ test, the Wechsler Intelligence Scales for Children, fourth edition (WISC-IV), has subscales that are helpful in assessing executive and processing skills, as discussed in chapter 6. Sometimes, if you request it, the psychologist from your school district will administer the WISC-IV and "projectives." This will help differentiate whether your child's school problems are due to BD, learning disabilities, or both, making the recommendations to the CSE more helpful to your child.

NEUROPSYCHOLOGICAL EVALUATION

We strongly recommend all children with bipolar disorder be assessed at least once by a neuropsychologist to determine special education needs. Currently, with a written request by a physician, some school districts will provide (and pay for) a neuropsychological evaluation (see chapter 5). All too often, however, parents may have to pay for a private neuropsychological evaluation, which can cost upwards of thousands of dollars. Note that some medical insurance companies will partially reimburse parents for this extensive evaluation under specific circumstances.

To begin the evaluation, you will meet with the neuropsychologist and explain why you want the consultation. The neuropsychologist will listen to your concerns and gather a developmental and medical history, and an account of home and school functioning. Extensive background information about your child will guide the testing. The tester will also help you to prepare your child for a series of assessment sessions and sometimes will observe the child in the classroom.

Neuropsychological assessment includes an IQ test (such as the WISC-IV) and a test of current academic skills, including many aspects of reading, writing, and arithmetic (such as the Woodcock-Johnson Test of Cognitive Abilities). Based on the child's history and the outcome of these tests, the next set of tests will address the underlying *processing* difficulties that may be interfering with your child's brain functioning. Some of the specific areas that should be addressed are language functioning, sensory-motor issues (including fine and gross motor functioning), tactile or touch functioning, attention, concentration, short- and long-term memory, and retrieval of learned information.

Assessment of executive functioning can be done by a series of specific tests determined by the neuropsychologist, or by a specific test of executive functioning such as the Delis-Kaplan test. As stated above, "projectives" are tests that assess current emotional functioning, including the degree of emotional control a child has. These tests include the Rorschach, the Thematic Apperception Test, the Sentence Completion Test, drawings, and others. Because of ongoing neuro-cognitive and emotional development, a neuropsychological evaluation of a preschooler will be somewhat different (and shorter) than one for a school-age child or an adolescent.

LEARNING FROM THE ASSESSMENT

After all the testing has been completed, you will have a feedback session with the tester in which you will learn the degree to which your child's learning, emotional, and/or behavioral issues affect his or her ability to function at home, at school, and with peers. You will also learn to what extent BD interferes with your child's ability to control responses and to utilize his or her natural abilities. The written report with recommendations will provide recommendations for appropriate special education accommodations. A list of specific recommendations may include referrals to a speech and language specialist, an occupational therapist who specializes in sensory integration, a host of specific school accommodations, and a variety of ways to improve home life.

Disclosure of BD

Some parents are concerned about disclosing that their child has received a formal diagnosis of BD, while others are open with the CSE. A letter from your child's psychiatrist and/or psychotherapist with specific recommendations for school accommodations is often helpful, especially if the psychiatrist spells out that the child with BD (or a mood disorder) may have "catastrophic reactions" that interfere with learning, even when the learning problems are relatively minor.

Attendance at the Special Education Meeting

Education law says you must receive written notification at least five school days before a formal special education meeting is held. The meeting is attended by the CSE chairperson, who runs the meeting, a psychologist, and a parent representative (the parent of a child receiving special education in your school district). These three are the voting members of the CSE, but it is also common for the current teacher and others who have participated in the evaluation to attend. You have the right to attend and to bring whomever you choose to the meeting with you, including a friend, the neuropsychologist who evaluated your child, your child's psychotherapist or psychiatrist, a parent advocate, or an educational consultant.

Most education lawyers do not attend the initial meeting, but they will consult with you beforehand to help you list your requested accommodations prior to the meeting. In the event of disagreement (see below), the attorney will become an active participant in the process of getting your child appropriate services under the current education laws.

Most school districts appreciate knowing in advance who will be attending. Also, if notified in advance, many districts will provide a speakerphone, so a busy psychiatrist or therapist can participate by phone. In addition, you may ask to record the meeting, which is especially useful should you decide the accommodations are not adequate. We encourage parents who are working with an educational attorney to arrange private phone access to the attorney during the meeting time, should questions arise; a quick consultation (outside of the formal meeting) may also be helpful.

Eligibility for Classification

Most meetings begin with introductions of everyone present and a review of all the relevant information. That means your concerns and observations should be part of this meeting. There will be a review of all written reports that have been submitted. Based on the results of the written reports and discussion at the special education meeting, your child's eligibility for a special education classification is decided. In many cases, the process is cooperative and the decision is made by consensus, rather than by a strict vote.

Special Education Services and Classification

If your child is eligible for special education services under IDEA 2004, he or she will be classified in any one of the following categories: autism; deafness and/or blindness; emotionally disturbed (ED); hearing impaired; learning disabled (LD); mental retardation; multiple disabilities; orthopedic impairment; other health impaired (OHI); speech and language; traumatic brain injury; and/or visual impairment.

The definition of "emotionally disturbed" specifically includes depression and schizophrenia. The definition of the classification called "other health impaired" includes difficulties with alertness in the educational environment due to "chronic or acute health problems," and names such conditions as ADD, ADHD, asthma, diabetes, and other specific medical conditions. Where bipolar disorder might be categorized has not yet been specified.

The decision about which classification is right for your child may depend on the particular kind of placement you are aiming for. Each special needs program, whether it be within the local school district or in a private school, will admit a child only with specific special education classification(s). If you have an educational advocate, consultant, or attorney, he or she will advise which classification will help you to reach your educational goals, based on the results of the written evaluations.

WHAT IS A "504?"

If the special education team that assesses your child determines that he or she is not eligible for a special education classification as outlined above, they have the option of providing services within the school under what is called a "504 plan." Section 504 of a different federal law allows a school district to provide educational accommodations within the current school setting for children with "disabilities," without a formal individual education plan (IEP).

There can be a wide range of services offered and if it is sufficient for your child with BD, he or she will remain in the "least restrictive environment" (i.e., a mainstream classroom setting as much as possible), which is what current federal legislation mandates. If a 504 is appropriate, the special education team dismisses the original request for special education services and reconvenes the meeting (often right then and there), outlines the 504 accommodations, and appoints a team leader to coordinate these services.

Developing an Individual Education Program

An IEP clearly spells out accommodations to meet the stated educational goals, which will be provided and paid for by the school district for the purpose of educating your child. As a result of the assessment by your school district for special education services, if the committee is in agreement, an individual education program will be developed.

If there is a disagreement about the services offered, this is when an educational attorney will be most helpful. A parent can request mediation; and if this is still not satisfactory, an impartial hearing is held within the school district, which may be appealed to your state educational agency; or you may bring a civil suit to a state or district court within ninety days of the appeal of the impartial hearing. Legal fees for a hearing or court suit may be reimbursed under some circumstances; however, if a suit against a school district is deemed "frivolous" by a court, the parents may be liable for the legal fees of the school district.

Finding a good match for your child's needs is challenging. If the public school cannot make adequate accommodations, you may be able to choose from a list of schools that the state agrees to pay for, as long as it is acceptable to both the parents and the school district. These schools may provide small classes, remediation for learning disabilities, and/or a therapeutic environment in a day school or residential program. In the sections below we will go over the range of possibilities of what to ask for in an IEP. Just remember that if it is not written in the IEP, a district does not have to provide the service.

Built into the special education laws are meetings with parents throughout the school year. Be sure that when the school district holds these meetings, you attend each and every one. Also be sure that you have adequate contact with the designated case manager, as well as with your child's teachers, whenever you have any questions about the program or your child's performance.

What to Ask For

In this section, we will go through the basic accommodations that will help address the emotional and educational needs of a child with BD. Even when services are provided for specific learning disabilities (such as reading, math, spelling, writing), for speech and language therapy and/or for occupational therapy, specific services related to BD should also be part of your IEP.

Below, we focus on accommodations for BD, going from the least to the most restrictive accommodations:

- Support within the public school classroom

- Special programs within the public school setting

- Private day schools

- Residential schools

Accommodations Within the Public School

The following is a partial list of accommodations within a "regular" school setting that can be helpful during the period when your child is unstable:

1. **Allow child to take a break when he or she is beginning to feel overwhelmed.** This helps the child to monitor how stressed (or upset) he or she is, and allows the child to take responsibility for his or her behavior in school. The break may be used to go to the bathroom, water fountain, school psychologist, or nurse's office. Some classrooms are set up with a separate desk for a child who needs to take a break. There, he or she can calm down (by reading, drawing, or other agreed-upon activities). The goal is always for the child to reregulate his or her mood and to return to learning in the classroom as soon as possible.

2. **Individual prompting and support in the classroom.** Because so many children with BD find it difficult to start or complete a task, a student may require teacher prompting and support to organize, refocus, and complete daily assignments. If the job is too demanding for a mainstream teacher, some children may benefit from a full- or part-time aide in the classroom. A "core-inclusion" program, popular in many districts, has a special education teacher in the classroom with the mainstream teacher. The special education teacher supports a small number of children within the classroom, and the child reinforces gains in a resource room, generally for one period per day.

If your child receives a "resource room" recommendation (a period with a few other special needs children and a special education teacher to focus on the individual requirements of each child), it is often useful to have it at the end of the day, in order to review the daily work and to organize the homework assignments. It is also useful for your child to meet with the special education teacher (even briefly) at the beginning of a school day to check whether assignments have been completed. This takes a lot of the responsibility for homework from the parents and gives it to a teacher/ child team.

3. **Limit the number of classes in the upper grades.** Many children can't keep up with a full schedule. It can be helpful to take only two or three major subjects and make up the missed classes in summer school, or to extend graduation by a semester or two. Once parents get used to the idea that school is not a time-limited race but training that can take place at the child's pace, everyone in the family can breathe easier.

4. **Individual and/or group counseling.** This counseling will address academic, emotional, behavioral, and social issues within the school setting. In therapeutic schools, counseling may extend to home life.

5. **Opportunities for extra time and a quiet place for taking tests.** This is helpful for anxious children whose ability to process information is compromised.

6. **Completion of as much homework as possible during the school day.** This can be done in extra study periods, an after-school program (if available), and/or a modified homework schedule.

Many more educational accommodations are available, along with model IEPs; they are referred to in appendix III.

SPECIAL CLASSES WITHIN THE PUBLIC SCHOOL SETTING

Some school districts organize their own innovative programs for academically and/or emotionally fragile children. Be sure to ask about programs for special needs children in your area and neighboring districts. Some of these programs are in a separate location, away from the local public schools; others operate within the school's structure, allowing special education students to interact with mainstream students.

"Therapeutic" classes are small, with a high teacher-to-student ratio, and the students work with special education teachers, teacher-aides, and school psychologists. Each child has individual and group therapy, as well as a detailed individualized academic program. Some students are encouraged to "step-out" from a more restrictive school environment (small self-contained classes) into "regular" classes. This is done gradually, and with great support. The special education students may have lunch, gym, recess, and special classes (such as art, music, and technology) with the rest of the school, if the child is ready.

When stable enough, students may join a mainstream class in a subject they are competent in and feel confident. The teacher and psychologist are available for support in a separate homeroom/classroom. Throughout this program, the therapeutic component is helpful for children and teens to work on accepting their illness, and find the motivation and learning techniques to overcome their unique academic, emotional, and social difficulties. This program helps children figure out "what helps" and to find the incentive to follow through, with the eventual goal of being mainstreamed.

Some school districts have small, supportive, structured classes for children with learning disabilities who do not have behavior problems in school. When your child has a co-occurring specific learning disability, or ongoing processing or executive skills difficulty, one of these small classes may provide quiet support when your child is in the maintenance phase, especially if there is an experienced and skillful head teacher. Sometimes, the school will provide ongoing individual and/or group therapy, but if the school program doesn't have a therapeutic component, you may want to supplement your child's medical needs with psychotherapy outside the school.

As with all special education programs, many children (and parents) are reluctant to participate because of the stigma of being seen as "special ed." When the program addresses the social, emotional, and academic needs of a child with BD, everybody benefits. The stigma can motivate the child to work hard to return to the mainstream classes or school.

Private Schools

If the public school cannot make adequate accommodations, then a parent may be able to pick from a list of schools that the state agrees to pay for, if the IEP conditions coincide with the admission requirements of the private school. There will be a formal admissions process in which both the private school and the parents will participate. These schools may provide a therapeutic environment for children with psychiatric illness and/or substance abuse, along with small classes to facilitate learning. Some private schools that focus on learning disabilities may have small, supportive classes and can accommodate a child with BD.

However, some of the private schools on the state list may not be suitable for the uneven performance that is characteristic of a child with BD. Thus, it is very important to visit a prospective school to see if it is right for your child. Some parents send their children to a private school that is not on the state-approved list. With an IEP, under certain circumstances, a school district will pay for all or some of the services provided. Parents should get advice from an educational attorney before proceeding in this direction. Almost all private schools for special needs children have Web sites. A clearinghouse for these programs is listed in appendix III.

Therapeutic Boarding Schools

Many parents of children with BD are reluctant to send their children to be educated away from home. A residential treatment center (RTC) generally provides more intense behavioral and psychiatric supervision than a therapeutic (or therapeutically oriented) boarding school. If either is recommended by the school district as the most appropriate learning environment for your child, the district is obligated to pay for the school. In this section, we discuss both of these options and call them "therapeutic boarding schools."

Therapeutic boarding schools are most often recommended for adolescents who are caught in a web of oppositional behavior with their parents. If an adolescent is unable or unwilling to attend school, to take meds, and/or get to sleep on time, and prides him- or herself on being defiant to parents, he or she may be a candidate for a therapeutic boarding school. If a child engages in risk-taking behaviors (running away, sexual promiscuity, eating disorders, drug use, alcohol use, or illegal activities), the parent may not be able to provide a safe environment.

When asked how a parent knows that going to a therapeutic boarding school is the correct decision, one mother said, "When I could no longer imagine he could become a successful, independent adult, I knew he needed to be in residential treatment." At this point, parents may feel intensely sad and disappointed that they cannot provide enough support at home for their child. Many parents find this experience more difficult than the actual diagnosis of BD. Contact with one's own therapist or with other parents of children with BD helps.

Once the decision to look for a therapeutic boarding facility is made, parents must decide which schools to interview. Ideally the treatment team (and especially an educational consultant, if you have one) can help in finding an appropriate school. When you and your child finally visit the school(s), it needs to be done with an open mind. One important factor for parents of a child with BD to look for is whether there is adequate psychiatric coverage at the therapeutic boarding school.

There are times when a child is not eligible to be hospitalized (see chapter 14) and not stable enough for even the most structured residential therapeutic school. Some parents find that a short-term placement (up to ninety days) at a wilderness program is an effective intervention, in preparation for attending a therapeutic boarding school. When it is appropriate, an educational consultant can help you find a safe, effective wilderness program. Since this is exclusively a therapeutic program (without an academic component), most school districts will not fund a wilderness program; however, some insurance companies may provide partial funding.

A well-run wilderness program helps teens, often with co-occurring diagnoses (such as BD along with substance abuse or an eating disorder) begin to accept that he or she actually has a problem. In an effective wilderness program, the atmosphere is completely therapeutic and each child is carefully monitored. The wilderness treatment team will include a psychotherapist, a psychiatrist, and medical coverage. Many programs can also provide a neuropsychological evaluation.

In a wilderness setting (useful because there is no place to run away from), your child will participate in group therapy with other teens and receive individual therapy, as well as take part in activities and chores structured to provide for his or her basic needs. Your child will begin to learn about the need to cooperate with others, and the effect his or her behavior has on others (perspective-taking). Most importantly, your teen will gain the knowledge that he or she has a choice with each and every behavior. The family component is very strongly integrated into a good wilderness program, so that upon "graduation" you will find an improved relationship with your child and a smoother transition into a therapeutic boarding school.

TRANSITION BACK HOME

A situation often fraught with problems occurs when a child or teen has completed eighteen months to two years at a therapeutic boarding facility, and may be ready to return home to complete high school. A discharge plan should include contingencies for all concerns. In conjunction with the local school board, an IEP can outline what happens if the teen doesn't attend school regularly and/or begins to fall behind. In chapter 14 on crisis intervention, we will explore even more restrictive environments for children and teens who are acutely ill, unwilling, or unable to participate in the educational programs outlined in this chapter.

14

Crisis Management

In this chapter, we will address some special topics related to safety issues and violence that often call for crisis intervention. These interventions are aimed at preventing harm. Sometimes this requires help from professionals, often in hospitals or other supervised therapeutic settings.

SELF-HARM

Among children with bipolar disorder (BD), aggressive tendencies and behaviors are frequent, have an early age of onset, and are associated with poor impulse control. When deliberate aggression is self-directed, we speak of self-harm. Self-harm can occur at any age, in the course of depression, a mixed state or dysphoric mania. Self-harm occurs on a spectrum of severity, from hitting oneself for making a mistake (or any other disappointment) to scratching, cutting, burning, or biting. Sometimes head-banging or punching a wall can be used to cause self-harm and self-inflicted pain, causing fractures and other severe lesions.

These symptoms can cause severe disability and often lead to serious consequences, including hospitalization. Significant harm can result from these behaviors, even though they are usually not associated with a desire to die or to commit suicide. Actually, most children and adolescents report a calming effect after engaging in these behaviors, almost a sense of relief from inner tension. Physical pain seems to provide a focus away from painful feelings or thoughts.

All too often, these behaviors are dismissed as "attention-seeking," or worse, they are ignored or ridiculed by the family. These acts of self-harm are more common in girls, but are not rare in boys. Seemingly harmless behaviors like lip-biting or picking at scabs can be so pervasive and resistant to behavioral modification that it becomes a reason for psychiatric evaluation and a major source of disability. These behaviors are commonly attributed to borderline personality disorder. However, the validity of the diagnosis of borderline personality disorder in patients with a positive family history for BD and a good response to mood stabilizers has been questioned.

Suicide

In the United States in the year 2001, suicide was the third leading cause of death in adolescents and young adults, ages fifteen to twenty-four, and the fifth leading cause of death in children and young adolescents, ages five to fourteen (Anderson and Smith 2003). Compared to the general population, patients with mood disorders, especially BD, have higher rates of suicidal ideation and attempts, as well as completed suicides.

Since the risk for suicidal behavior seems to be greater in the first few years of illness, it is not surprising that suicide attempts are very common in early-onset BD. Other risk factors include frequent depressive recurrences; past suicidal behavior; a history of antidepressant-induced mania; comorbid alcohol abuse; recent discontinuation of lithium treatment; and/or a familial history of suicidal behavior.

VIOLENCE

Aggression has a developmental evolution, often peaking at two to three years of age. After, the child can use language more easily to get his or her needs met, problem-solving strategies are developed, and socialization (such as nursery school or peer interaction) fosters learning how to inhibit aggressive behaviors. High rates of aggression in toddlers are associated with aggression later in life. Language-delayed children, who have difficulty getting their needs met, have higher rates of both depression and aggression.

Difficulty with inhibiting aggression is common in children and adolescents with BD. This often becomes the reason for difficulties at home, school, or both. Lack of self-control in children with mood disorders causes acts of impulsive aggression. These are frequent precipitants to inpatient (hospital) treatment.

PSYCHIATRIC HOSPITALIZATION

The decision to hospitalize a child is often dreaded by parents and children alike. Even clinicians may be uncomfortable suggesting such a drastic intervention, and they do not discuss this option until there is a crisis or an emergency situation. This is not a useful approach as it fosters fear of the hospital in both parents and children, reinforces the stigma attached to this intervention, and, ultimately, interferes with the process of decision making based on medical necessity.

Hospitalization is one of the many therapeutic interventions available to parents and mental health professionals. Therapeutic interventions can be seen on a continuum, from less restrictive (outpatient treatment) to more restrictive, depending on the amount of supervision required, a hospital being the highest level of care and supervision.

Parents must recognize when it might be necessary to hospitalize their child, how to convey the information to the psychiatrist, how to choose an appropriate facility, where to call for help in an emergency, and how to maximize the benefits of hospitalization. Informed parents may have explored available alternatives, and, if they decide inpatient treatment is necessary, they may know how to present the idea to their child.

In most cases the hospitalization is voluntary, that is, the parent or legal guardian agrees to have the child hospitalized for treatment. Sometimes, especially after court-mandated treatment, the treatment is not voluntary. Familiarity with your parental rights as the child's legal guardian will help in making decisions about treatment while the child is in the hospital.

Most families cannot afford to pay out-of-pocket for inpatient treatment (hospitalization in medical jargon), and rely on insurance coverage. This adds another layer of complexity, as the insurance company must: (1) recognize that hospitalization is necessary; (2) approve the treatment; and (3) approve of the facility (hospital) selected by the treatment team and family. Some health care management organizations will pay only if the hospital is on their approved list, and most insurance companies will attempt to dictate the duration (and sometimes the type) of recommended treatment.

Most insurance companies will try to avoid a hospitalization to limit costs, and sometimes try to avoid a medically indicated and necessary course of inpatient treatment. Most parents cannot, or do not want to, incur the cost of admitting a child without insurance authorization. If an insurance company is not willing to pay for the hospital stay, a medical appeal is both available and required to overturn their decision. Often, if insurance is a problem, the social work staff at the hospital can help you.

When to Call for Hospitalization

Parents dealing with potential threats to the child's safety (or that of other family members) must always err on the side of caution. This is a case where one is better safe than sorry. Let a professional assess the situation and give you his or her recommendations. The assessment of the potential for violence is difficult even for professionals, and an intervention should be more readily invoked if there are vulnerable targets at home, including infants, toddlers, or younger siblings.

You can always decide whether or not to go along with the recommendation, unless your child is considered a danger to self or others. In that case, if you do not agree to have the child hospitalized, the licensed professional can admit the child for a period of observation without your consent. As we have emphasized throughout this book, a collaborative relationship with the treatment team will help you trust the recommendation of the treating MD; and in the case of a potential hospitalization, if you understand the need for it, you will be less reluctant to take this step.

Also, consider the danger of those out-of-control behaviors. If a child hits, kicks, or throws objects at a parent or at someone else while driving, stop the car immediately. If the child is unable to calm down, the police must be called and the child will be escorted to the nearest emergency room by a police officer. Out-of-control children need to see and hear that their parent is able to protect them and the rest of the family.

In other situations at home, if a parent does call the police, either the child will be able to calm down, realizing that his or her parent can and will protect the family, or the child will not be able to control him- or herself. In the latter case, reassurance and a simple, calm explanation that more supervision is necessary—more than can be provided at home—will help with the transfer to an emergency room or to a psychiatric hospital.

Parents must trust their judgment and instincts. Some parents are better than others at reading the signs of a decline in functioning that requires more intensive treatment. It's important that parents and professionals avoid using the hospital as a threat. A hospital stay is not a punishment, but a way of improving the child's health, thus protecting the child and the rest of the family from the dangers of the illness; it's also a hopeful step toward faster or more complete stabilization.

In general, one of two criteria must be fulfilled to obtain insurance approval for the hospital stay: the child must be considered either an immediate danger to him- or herself, or to others.

Danger to Self

"Danger to self" implies a current and present danger that the child will harm him- or herself without the supervision provided by the hospital and its staff. This means that if a child is not currently planning or expressing the intent to hurt or kill him- or herself (even if he or she is actively thinking of ways to commit suicide), the authorization might be denied. Previous suicide attempts, a family history of suicide, alcohol/substance abuse or dependence, and access to lethal means are not considered sufficient to justify inpatient treatment, even though these are well-known clinical predictors of suicide and serious self-harm.

Parents should always take very seriously any reference (even in passing) to death, self-harm, suicide, or a wish that one had not been born. Any morbid thought of this nature should be evaluated immediately by a qualified mental health professional, usually a psychiatrist or an emergency room physician. A mobile crisis unit may also be helpful. As a preventive measure, make sure there are no weapons or knives accessible at home and be watchful of your child until he or she is evaluated.

Danger to Others

"Danger to others" can be difficult for parents to determine. Parents and siblings of a child with BD are so used to explosive, threatening, or violent behavior that their ability to assess danger objectively may be impaired. The fact that a child might calm down quickly and act appropriately for a while (especially after a severe episode) may give an erroneous impression that things have improved or that the situation is under control. If the situation is not under control, parents need to consider the following:

- Is the violent behavior predictable (i.e., always in response to some provocation) or is it impulsive and unprovoked?

- Has there been any threat or warning of impending violence?

- What is the destructive potential? (Consider the difference between a two-hundred-pound, athletic, sixteen-year-old boy versus a fifty-pound first-grade girl.)

- Does the child use weapons to hurt (such as silverware, pointy or sharp objects, or fire)?

- Does the child have free access to weapons such as knives or guns?

- Have there been past instances of violent or destructive behaviors?

- Does the child lose complete control of his or her actions and act as if in a trance?

- Is there a target for the violence, such as a vulnerable sibling, peer, or parent?

- Is there substance abuse or lack of compliance with prescribed medication?

HOW TO PREPARE FOR HOSPITALIZATION

If a psychiatric hospital stay is indicated, it is much better if both parent and child are prepared in advance. If a child is unstable and there is a high potential for inpatient treatment, we immediately present the idea to parents and child that, should things get out of control, an assessment at the local emergency room might be necessary. We tell the child that if the illness takes control, their parents will ask for help either from the police or the hospital. The focus is always on safety, rather than blame for out-of-control behavior. In a crisis, the most efficient way to keep everybody safe is to call the police, and we make sure to tell this to both parent and child.

Before calling the police for help, parents can visit the local police department and meet with personnel to discuss the home situation. During that discussion they should ask what will happen if the police are called and where they will bring an "out-of-control" child. Generally, it is to the nearest psychiatric emergency room to be medically evaluated.

Alternatively, parents can bring a child directly to the nearest emergency room, or to a hospital of their choice. Call in advance and find out the process to go through, but understand that the clinicians in the emergency room (ER) are trained to help restrain a child if need be. It is often best to go to an ER in a hospital that has inpatient child psychiatric services to avoid wasting precious time and resources with transfers from one facility to another and the attendant, unavoidable delays. In an ideal situation, the treating MD will have attending privileges at a local hospital (so the MD can continue to treat your child while he or she is in the hospital), as continuity is both more efficient and less traumatic for the child and the family.

Some areas have a "mobile crisis unit" (which can be found in the local phone book) specifically for psychiatric emergencies. The crisis team, consisting of at least a psychiatrist and a social worker, will come to your home. If the child is unstable, we encourage parents to contact the crisis intervention team before any trouble arises to let them know about the situation, provide some history, and explain the current diagnosis and treatment. This way, the parent is assured that, if the team is called to the home, they will understand the issues. Hopefully, this will reduce the trauma and expedite a necessary hospitalization.

Parents can also call or go on the Internet to investigate beforehand any local inpatient psychiatric unit for children and adolescents. When clear about the need for hospitalization, a parent or the child's psychiatrist or psychotherapist can call to arrange for an *elective admission* (as opposed to an emergency one). Sometimes, a planned hospitalization for the purpose of medication changes may be the quickest and safest way to address a problem. This option, however, is becoming less and less common in the present managed-care environment.

First Hospitalization

It is only natural that both you and your child will be frightened and confused during the first hospitalization. Hospitals have their own way of working and, generally, parents learn the system by going through the hospital's admission procedures. Parents must trust that their child will be treated well and protected from other children in the facility. But do ask questions.

Initially, the nurses are often the most helpful members of the treatment team. Your child or teen will be assigned a treatment team including a psychiatrist and a case manager (who may be a psychologist or a social worker) who will handle the psychotherapeutic component of the hospitalization. There are educators, nurses, recreation and supervisory staff, and nursing aides who are involved in the child's care. Usually, the case manager is the contact person for the family, and will be helpful within the context of family therapy and planning for the child's discharge.

WHAT TO EXPECT

Before leaving for the hospital, prepare a bag with clothing, toilet articles, and medication for two days to hand over to the admitting nurse. Pictures of family members and familiar items associated with comfort, such as blankets, stuffed toys, games, and so forth, may help your child with the separation from the family.

After arrival at the hospital, whether the wait is short or long, eventually a psychiatrist will interview you and your child. The psychiatrist will want to know your child's history and that will include information about the following:

- Past psychiatric history, including past hospitalizations and treatments

- Current medications and symptoms (to assess if it is necessary to admit your child to the hospital)

- Precipitants (or triggers) leading to the hospitalization (e.g., changes in medication)

During the admitting process, if your child needs to be restrained, allow the hospital personnel to handle it, as they are trained. If your child cries, begs, or bargains to be taken home, or screams, "You are the worst parent ever!" and vows that he or she "will never forgive you," be prepared to say good-bye quietly and calmly. You might say something like, "We can get the help we need here," and that will help your child make the transition into the hospital. This might seem like the darkest moment of your life, but it is probably the best and most hopeful alternative at this time. The hope is that, as a team, you and your child will leave the hospital with better tools for dealing with the symptoms of BD.

Coordinating Care

If your child is admitted on Friday, Saturday, Sunday, or a national holiday, the hospital treatment team will not be fully staffed, and this time will be used for observation of the child. Whenever your child is admitted, it is essential for the hospital staff to contact the outside treating MD and psychotherapist, if there is one. If you insist on this at the time of admission, then you will be asked to sign consent forms.

Don't sign blank forms upon admittance. It is worth the wait to make sure the hospital team has the correct names, addresses, and phone numbers of all treating personnel. In addition, if your child is under eighteen years of age, insist that all medication changes, including decreasing, stopping, or starting medication, and emergency sedation, be discussed with and approved by you. If you've learned which meds might be helpful, then you can more readily participate in a meaningful conversation with the hospital MDs. If you feel your opinion "doesn't count" with the hospital MD, then insist on a consultation between the treating inpatient and outpatient MDs.

In the hospital, your child's day will be a full one. There are meals, therapy groups, individual appointments, and family meetings. Many hospitals have a school on site, and most have a behavior modification program (point system) for your child to earn privileges.

How to Get the Most Out of a Hospital Stay

Safety and medical stabilization are the main goals of hospitalization. However, parents have a chance to focus on the most "out-of-control" behaviors. It makes sense to ask the family therapist at the hospital to focus on eliminating all physical acting-out. This means that with the help of a therapist, when the urge to hurt others arises, parents and child learn to work together to keep the child in control and to find more adaptive responses. If the parent/child team finds a way to eliminate one undesirable behavior, then as a team, they can work on changing other behaviors, one at a time!

Before leaving the hospital, an appointment to review the hospital stay and future treatment recommendations should be scheduled with the hospital's treating MD and the psychotherapist. If a child needs a change in educational placement, such as transfer to a therapeutic day program or a residential school setting, then this recommendation must be clearly stated in the discharge summary, prepared by the case manager.

If some school accommodations or a change of school is necessary (because of BD and its effect on school functioning), this will help the school district understand the child's needs and will facilitate the placement. If more intensive outpatient care is recommended, such as frequent (weekly) psychiatric or psychotherapy appointments, this should also be stated in the discharge summary, as this may help with medical insurance. Make sure all outpatient treating doctors and psychotherapists get a copy of the discharge summary.

TRANSITION FROM THE HOSPITAL

Most likely, your child will be relieved to come home, and there will be a honeymoon period upon family reunion. We recommend a calm return home, without gifts or excitement. Use this time to positively reinforce the gains from the hospital, keep a structured schedule (see chapter 10), and do not change the sleep schedule. Be careful not to try a new behavioral regime as soon as the child returns home. The hospital staff should help you adapt the schedule your child was following in the hospital to home life. No special foods, staying up late, overstimulating visits from relatives, or long playdates.

Some hospitals have a partial-day program for children. The child goes back to the hospital grounds for the school day for a limited time; generally, no longer than a month. Your school district must approve funding for the educational component and your insurance should cover the rest. This provides a gradual transition from inpatient to outpatient care, and the extension of group and individual therapy, along with a school program, provides support and supervision for your child.

If your child is to be transferred to a therapeutic boarding school, a return home might be necessary. It may take several months to complete the school placement; during this time, home tutoring and outpatient treatment may be all that is available.

Epilogue

To conclude our book, we step aside and listen to Sondra, who is a teacher in the same school as her daughter, Anna, who is in the fourth grade and has been diagnosed with bipolar disorder (BD) and treated for two years. Sondra tells us that:

Although Anna is bright and friendly, school presents many challenges for her: classes with a substitute teacher, being picked for the "wrong" team, or a classmate teasing her all require a great deal of extra effort for her to deal with them in an appropriate way. During a manic or depressive period, brought on by outgrowing her medication or a seasonal change, these small "glitches" in her day pose a tremendous problem.

The same girl who can normally transition to math now sits and cries; explaining that her head is already racing, she can't possibly think of numbers right now. Her handwriting gets increasingly more difficult to read; she leaves out words, punctuation, and sometimes misses the entire point of the assignment. Her spelling deteriorates and becomes completely phonetic; organization in essays (which she is very strong in) completely dissolves.

Anna changes from a child who looks forward to learning new things to one who is overwhelmed by the task of reading a simple short story.

At times like this I worry about her progress, because recalling simple multiplication frustrates her to the point of tears and anger. Then, as suddenly as it hit, with the passing of the winter, or an adjustment to the medication, Anna is herself again. Her work is complete, organized, and done well. She happily enjoys the challenges of math and can recall her facts for multiplication. Simple transitions in her day are no longer greeted with complete resistance, but are once again embraced as an interesting part of her day.

The instability at school is reflected at home and in social situations. When Anna is not stable, she will push her younger sister out of the way just to be the first one at the table. She will shove past my husband and me just to show her disapproval of bedtime, and she will stiffen when we try to hug her. One moment she will be happily playing a board game; the next she is throwing the pieces in tears because she did not roll what she expected. Everything about her says to stay away.

But when Anna is well, she is the first one to give hugs to her family and friends. She has been known to ask if you need a gentle "bear hug" if you look sad or upset at school. She is also an ardent rule follower, often reminding others that games are just for fun.

While going through these periods of instability with Anna, I had begun to worry. I understood the impact BD had on her emotionally and the difficulties it causes socially. But, after witnessing its effects on her academically, I must express my utter amazement that some of the information she tries to recall is truly not accessible to her during these manic/depressive periods. She is not being lazy or uncooperative. It is as if there is a "disconnect" in her thoughts, and she is unable to build the bridge to access them.

Anna will forget to do chores such as feed the dogs, which she usually does automatically after dinner. When questioned, she will burst into tears saying we are unfair! She will make plans with her sister to play an incredible game of imagination with tents, and when we get home from school she will ignore her sister and retreat to the computer, leaving her sister with hurt feelings. A similar occurrence happens at recess with friends becoming upset and angry because Anna will simply become "bored" and walk away from the game, seeming to forget she was ever playing with them. This "disconnect" runs through every aspect of her life.

For these reasons, communication between parents and all professionals working with my daughter is of paramount importance. As a teacher, I see that after parents educate themselves about BD, they must educate their child's teachers so the teachers can replace their own frustration with compassion. Without knowledge of what our children are going through, we are all left with the impression they are obstinate, defiant, and careless in their schoolwork, on the playground, at home, and with friends. These difficulties lead to poor relationships and, ultimately, to a lack of self-esteem. When we share all the difficult aspects of BD—emotional, social, and academic—we give teachers and others who work with our kids the tools they need to help our children do well in school, adjust at home, make meaningful friendships, and to feel good about their accomplishments.

Appendix I

CRITERIA FOR MAJOR DEPRESSIVE EPISODE

A. Five (or more) of the following symptoms have been present during the same 2-week period and represent a change from previous functioning; at least one of the symptoms is either (1) depressed mood or (2) loss of interest or pleasure.

Note: Do not include symptoms that are clearly due to a general medical condition, or mood-incongruent delusions or hallucinations.

(1) depressed mood most of the day, nearly every day, as indicated by either subjective report (e.g., feels sad or empty) or observation made by others (e.g., appears tearful). **Note:** In children and adolescents, can be irritable mood.

(2) markedly diminished interest or pleasure in all, or almost all, activities most of the day, nearly every day (as indicated by either subjective account or observation made by others)

(3) significant weight loss when not dieting or weight gain (e.g., a change of more than 5% of body weight in a month), or decrease or increase in appetite nearly every day. **Note:** In children, consider failure to make expected weight gains.

(4) insomnia or hypersomnia nearly every day

(5) psychomotor agitation or retardation nearly every day (observable by others, not merely subjective feelings of restlessness or being slowed down)

(6) fatigue or loss of energy nearly every day

(7) feelings of worthlessness or excessive or inappropriate guilt (which may be delusional) nearly every day (not merely self-reproach or guilt about being sick)

(8) diminished ability to think or concentrate, or indecisiveness, nearly every day (either by subjective account or as observed by others)

(9) recurrent thoughts of death (not just fear of dying), recurrent suicidal ideation without a specific plan, or a suicide attempt or a specific plan for committing suicide

B. The symptoms do not meet criteria for a Mixed Episode.

C. The symptoms cause clinically significant distress or impairment in social, occupational, or other important areas of functioning.

D. The symptoms are not due to the direct physiological effects of a substance (e.g., a drug of abuse, a medication) or a general medical condition (e.g., hypothyroidism).

E. The symptoms are not better accounted for by Bereavement, i.e., after the loss of a loved one, the symptoms persist for longer than 2 months or are characterized by marked functional impairment, morbid preoccupation with worthlessness, suicidal ideation, psychotic symptoms, or psychomotor retardation.

CRITERIA FOR MANIC EPISODE

A. A distinct period of abnormally and persistently elevated, expansive, or irritable mood, lasting at least 1 week (or any duration if hospitalization is necessary).

B. During the period of mood disturbance, three (or more) of the following symptoms have persisted (four if the mood is only irritable) and have been present to a significant degree:

(1) inflated self-esteem or grandiosity

(2) decreased need for sleep (e.g., feels rested after only 3 hours of sleep)

(3) more talkative than usual or pressure to keep talking

(4) flight of ideas or subjective experience that thoughts are racing

(5) distractibility (i.e., attention too easily drawn to unimportant or irrelevant external stimuli)

(6) increase in goal-directed activity (either socially, at work or school, or sexually) or psychomotor agitation

(7) excessive involvement in pleasurable activities that have a high potential for painful consequences (e.g., engaging in unrestrained buying sprees, sexual indiscretions, or foolish business investments)

C. The symptoms do not meet criteria for a Mixed Episode.

D. The mood disturbance is sufficiently severe to cause marked impairment in occupational functioning or in usual social activities or relationships with others, or to necessitate hospitalization to prevent harm to self or others, or there are psychotic features.

E. The symptoms are not due to the direct physiological effects of a substance (e.g., a drug of abuse, a medication, or other treatment) or a general medical condition (e.g., hyperthyroidism).

Note: Manic-like episodes that are clearly caused by somatic antidepressant treatment (e.g., medication, electroconvulsive therapy, light therapy) should not count toward a diagnosis of Bipolar I Disorder.

MIXED EPISODE

EPISODE FEATURES

A Mixed Episode is characterized by a period of time (lasting at least 1 week) in which the criteria are met both for a Manic Episode and for a Major Depressive Episode nearly every day (Criterion A). The individual experiences rapidly alternating moods (sadness, irritability, euphoria) accompanied by symptoms of a Manic Episode and a

Major Depressive Episode. The symptom presentation frequently includes agitation, insomnia, appetite dysregulation, psychotic features, and suicidal thinking. The disturbance must be sufficiently severe to cause marked impairment in social or occupational functioning or to require hospitalization, or it is characterized by excessive activity, impulsive behavior, poor judgment, and denial of problems. Attention-Deficit/Hyperactivity Disorder is distinguished from a Hypomanic Episode by its characteristic early onset (i.e., before age 7 years), chronic rather than episodic course, lack of relatively clear onsets and offsets, and the absence of abnormally expansive or elevated mood.

A Hypomanic Episode must be distinguished from *euthymia*, particularly in individuals who have been chronically depressed and are unaccustomed to the experience of a nondepressed mood state.

CRITERIA FOR HYPOMANIC EPISODE

A. A distinct period of persistently elevated, expansive, or irritable mood, lasting throughout at least 4 days, that is clearly different from the usual nondepressed mood.

B. During the period of mood disturbance, three (or more) of the following symptoms have persisted (four if the mood is only irritable) and have been present to a significant degree:

   (1) inflated self-esteem or grandiosity

   (2) decreased need for sleep (e.g., feels rested after only 3 hours of sleep)

   (3) more talkative than usual or pressure to keep talking

   (4) flight of ideas or subjective experience that thoughts are racing

   (5) distractibility (i.e., attention too easily drawn to unimportant or irrelevant external stimuli)

   (6) increase in goal-directed activity (either socially, at work or school, or sexually) or psychomotor agitation

   (7) excessive involvement in pleasurable activities that have a high potential for painful consequences (e.g., the person engages in unrestrained buying sprees, sexual indiscretions, or foolish business investments)

C. The episode is associated with an unequivocal change in functioning that is uncharacteristic of the person when not symptomatic.

D. The disturbance in mood and the change in functioning are observable by others.

E. The episode is not severe enough to cause marked impairment in social or occupational functioning, or to necessitate hospitalization, and there are no psychotic features.

F. The symptoms are not due to the direct physiological effects of a substance (e.g., a drug of abuse, a medication, or other treatment) or a general medical condition (e.g., hyperthyroidism).

Note: Hypomanic-like episodes that are clearly caused by somatic antidepressant treatment (e.g., medication, electroconvulsive therapy, light therapy) should not count toward a diagnosis of Bipolar II Disorder.

DIAGNOSTIC CRITERIA FOR CYCLOTHYMIC DISORDER (301.13)

A. For at least 2 years, the presence of numerous periods with hypomanic symptoms and numerous periods with depressive symptoms that do not meet criteria for a Major Depressive Episode. Note: In children and adolescents, the duration must be at least 1 year.

B. During the above 2-year period (1 year in children and adolescents), the person has not been without the symptoms in Criterion A for more than 2 months at a time.

C. No Major Depressive Episode, Manic Episode, or Mixed Episode has been present during the first 2 years of the disturbance.

Note: After the initial 2 years (1 year in children and adolescents) of Cyclothymic Disorder, there may be superimposed Manic or Mixed Episodes (in which case both Bipolar I Disorder and Cyclothymic Disorder may be diagnosed) or Major Depressive Episodes (in which case both Bipolar II Disorder and Cyclothymic Disorder may be diagnosed).

D. The symptoms in Criterion A are not better accounted for by Schizoaffective Disorder and are not superimposed on Schizophrenia,

Schizophreniform Disorder, Delusional Disorder, or Psychotic Disorder Not Otherwise Specified.

E.   The symptoms are not due to the direct physiological effects of a substance (e.g., a drug of abuse, a medication) or a general medical condition (e.g., hyperthyroidism).

F.   The symptoms cause clinically significant distress or impairment in social, occupational, or other important areas of functioning.

DIAGNOSTIC CRITERIA FOR BIPOLAR II DISORDER 296.89

This information is reprinted with permission from the *Diagnostic and Statistical Manual of Mental Disorders-IV* (American Psychiatric Association 2000).

A.   Presence (or history) of one or more Major Depressive Episodes.

B.   Presence (or history) of at least one Hypomanic Episode.

C.   There has never been a Manic Episode or a Mixed Episode.

D.   The mood symptoms in Criteria A and B are not better accounted for by Schizoaffective Disorder and are not superimposed on Schizophrenia, Schizophreniform Disorder, Delusional Disorder, or Psychotic Disorder Not Otherwise Specified.

E.   The symptoms cause clinically significant distress or impairment in social, occupational, or other important areas of functioning.

Specify current or most recent episode:

Hypomanic: if currently (or most recently) in a Hypomanic Episode

Depressed: if currently (or most recently) in a Major Depressive Episode

BIPOLAR DISORDER NOT OTHERWISE SPECIFIED (296.80)

The Bipolar Disorder Not Otherwise Specified category includes disorders with bipolar features that do not meet criteria for any specific Bipolar Disorder. Examples include

1. Very rapid alternation (over days) between manic symptoms and depressive symptoms that meet symptom threshold criteria but not minimal duration criteria for Manic, Hypomanic, or Major Depressive Episodes

2. Recurrent Hypomanic Episodes without intercurrent depressive symptoms

3. A Manic or Mixed Episode superimposed on Delusional Disorder, residual Schizophrenia, or Psychotic Disorder Not Otherwise Specified

Appendix II

The MoodLog helps you record important information about the symptoms of bipolar disorder (BD) and its treatment over time. It is a journal, a diary that reminds you to observe details that would otherwise be lost or forgotten. To do this, follow these simple instructions:

- On the top line, write the child's name, date of birth (DOB), the doctor's name, and the month and year.

- Enter today's date in the column on the left.

There are five groups of variables to monitor: Medication, Mood, Sleep, Energy/Ideation, and Events/Diet.

- **Medication:** Enter the name and dose of the medication (total daily dose, e.g., 5 mg twice daily = 10 mg). Repeat this for as many medications as your child is taking.

- **Mood:** Rate both the severity and impairment associated with anxiety and irritability using the 0 to 3 scale (0 = no symptoms, 1 = mild, 2 = moderate and 3 = severe, i.e., severity 2, impairment 3 would be entered as 2/3). The next step is to rate the severity, duration, and impairment of depressive and manic symptoms on the appropriate scale from 0 to 3. Normal mood is marked in the middle column.

- **Sleep:** The number of hours asleep (including naps) is recorded, along with any difficulty falling or staying asleep, or waking up early. Sleep events such as nightmares, night terrors, bedwetting, and sleepwalking are also recorded.

- **Energy and activity levels (hyperactivity, lack of energy):** These are rated in the fourth column under Energy/Ideation. Cognitive processes, ideation (thoughts), speech, aggression (verbal or physical) and suicidal/homicidal ideation are also rated here.

- **Event/Diet:** In the last column, record any event that might have taken place during the course of the day, e.g., loss, illness, sleep deprivation, family discord, stressful events or trauma, substance use, medication changes, interpersonal conflict, and school deadlines. A weekly body weight should also be included here.

MoodLog™

DATE	MEDICATION						MOOD SYMPTOMS								SLEEP			ENERGY/IDEATION	EVENTS/DIET
Enter the day of the month	med 1	med 2	med 3	med 4	med 5	med 6	Symptoms' Severity and Impairment: 0=none; 1=mild; 2=moderate; 3=severe	Rate duration as: 0=never; 1=sometimes; 2=often; 3=very often or always							Rate previous night's sleep			Rate Presence, Duration, Severity (if present)	Mark events

Medication row units: mg | mg | mg | mg | mg | mg

Mood Symptoms detail:

- Irritable, Angry
- Anxiety, Fears, Worries, Panic
- Depression — Severity / Duration / Impairment
- OK — Normal mood
- Euphoria, Dysphoria — Severity / Duration / Impairment

Sleep detail:

- Total sleep hours, including naps
- Problems: 1=Falling asleep, 2=Staying asleep, 3=Wake up early
- 1=Nightmares, 2=Night terrors, 3=Bedwetting, 4=Sleepwalking

Energy/Ideation detail: Hyperactivity, restlessness, or lack of energy, tiredness; racing, crowded thoughts; overtalkative, loud, pressured, argumentative; aggression (verbal, physical; to self, others, or to property); suicidal/homicidal ideation or plans

Events/Diet detail: Record: events, type and severity of emotional reaction (i.e., illness/loss; blood levels taken/results; alcohol, drug, caffeine use; Omega-3 FFA, vitamins, etc.; jet lag; menstruation; sleep deprivation; traumatic events)

Appendix III

WEB SITES AND OTHER RESOURCES

Web Sites

CABF: Child and Adolescent Bipolar Foundation. A parent-generated Web site with online support groups, professional journal articles, educational information—including a model individual education program (IEP)—chat rooms, a bookshop, and links to other resources. This is an excellent place to begin. http://www.bpkids.org

IECA: Independent Educational Consultants Association. Web site of a national not-for-profit clearinghouse for independent educational consultants that supplies names of experienced professionals, including many who specialize in special needs, listed by state. http://www.educationalconsulting.org

ISBD: International Society for Bipolar Disorders. A professional organization with international conferences, a membership-only Web site, and a monthly journal, *Bipolar Disorders: An International Journal of Psychiatry & Neurosciences*. http://www.ISBD.org

JBRF: Juvenile Bipolar Research Foundation. A foundation dedicated to juvenile bipolar research. It has a professionally moderated listserv for physicians, a listserv for psychotherapists treating children with BD, and an excellent education forum in which parents and professionals can participate. http://www.jbrf.org

J. PRESTON, PSY.D.: Web site of Dr. Preston includes the *Quick Reference Medication Chart, 2006 Update*, available for free download by clicking on "Books" and scrolling to the end. This online reference is well-suited for nonprescribing professionals and parents. http://www.psyd-fx.com

J. SAFER, PH.D.: Web site of Dr. Jeanne Safer, author of *The Normal One: Life with a Difficult or Damaged Sibling* (Delta, 2003), offers specific recommendations regarding parenting "normal" siblings of a mentally ill child. http://www.thenormalone.com

MOODCENTER: The Lucio Bini Mood Disorders Center Web site is a source for information about the center, education about BD, including journal articles, and Lucio Bini Mood Disorders center research projects, in which families can participate and inquire about services. http://www.moodcenter.org

NAPSEC: National Association of Private Special Education Centers. This organization offers a free referral service, listed by state, for parents and professionals who are looking for an appropriate placement for their child or client. http://www.napsec.org/referral.html

NCLD: National Center for Learning Disabilities. This center offers practical, up-to-date resources and information about learning disabilities, including information on the most recent federal education law, Individuals with Disabilities Education Improvement Act of 2004 (IDEA 2004). http://www.ld.org

NIMH: National Institute of Mental Health Web site. This Web site provides a source for learning about ongoing research in BD in children and adults. Online newsletter archives are available. http://www.bipolarnews.org

THE BIPOLAR CHILD. The Web site of Demitri and Janice Papolos, authors of *The Bipolar Child* (Broadway Books, 1999), includes detailed up-to-date newsletters, a model IEP, and other useful information. http://www.bipolarchild.com

TRISTATE PARENT SUPPORT GROUPS. Contact information about monthly parent support groups in the New York, New Jersey, Connecticut region. There are articles and notes of interest to parents of children with BD. http://www.tristatesupport.org

Other Helpful Resources for Parents

Anderson, M., J. B. Kubisak, R. Field, and S. Vogelstein. 2003. *Understanding and Educating Children and Adolescents with Bipolar Disorder: A Guide for Educators.* Northfield, IL: The Josselyn Center.

Goldberg-Arnold, J. S., and M. Fristad. 2003. Psychotherapy for children with bipolar disorder. In *Bipolar Disorder in Childhood and Early Adolescence.* Edited by B. Geller and M. P. DelBello, 272-294. New York: Guilford Press.

Greenberger, D., and C. A. Padesky. 1995. *Mind Over Mood: Change How You Feel by Changing the Way You Think.* New York: Guilford Press.

Smith, K. A., and K. R. Grouze. 2004. *The Sensory Sensitive Child: Practical Solutions for Out-of-Bounds Behavior.* New York: HarperCollins Publishers, Inc.

Stern, M. G. 2002. *Child-Friendly Therapy: Biopsychosocial Innovations for Children and Families.* New York: W. W. Norton & Company.

Williamson, G. G., and M. E. Anzalone. 2001. *Sensory Integration and Self-Regulation in Infants and Toddlers: Helping Very Young Children Interact with Their Environment.* Washington, DC: Zero to Three: National Center for Infants, Toddlers and Families.

References

Ainsworth, M. D. S., M. Blehar, E. Waters, and S. Wall. 1978. *Strange-Situation Behavior of One Year Olds: Its Relation to Mother-infant Interaction in the First Year and to Qualitative Differences in the Infant-Mother Attachment Relationship.* Hillsdale, NJ: Erlbaum.

Akiskal, H. S., and G. Mallya. 1987. Criteria for the "soft" bipolar spectrum: Treatment and implications. *Psychopharmacology Bulletin* 23:68-73.

American Psychiatric Association. 2000. *Diagnostic and Statistical Manual of Mental Disorders.* 4th ed. Text revision. Washington, DC: American Psychiatric Association.

Anderson, R. N., and B. L. Smith. 2003. Deaths: Leading causes for 2001. *National Vital Statistics Report* 52:1-86.

Badner, J. A. 2003. The genetics of bipolar disorder. In *Bipolar Disorder in Childhood and Early Adolescence.* Edited by B. Geller and M. P. Delbello. New York: Guilford Press.

Bowlby, J. 1940. The influence of early environment in the development of neurosis and neurotic character. *International Journal of Psycho Analysis* 21:1-25.

————. 1944. Forty-four juvenile thieves: Their characters and home lives. *International Journal of Psycho-Analysis* 25:19-52.

————. 1951. Maternal care and mental health. *World Health Organization Monograph* (Serial no. 2):53.

Carlson, G. A., and J. H. Kashani. 1988. Manic symptoms in a non-referred adolescent population. *Journal of Affective Disorders* 15:219-226.

Carlson, G. A., J. Loney, H. Salisbury, J. R. Kramer, and C. Arthur. 2000. Stimulant treatment in young boys with symptoms suggesting childhood mania: A report from a longitudinal study. *Journal of Adolescent Psychopharmacology* 10:175-184.

DelBello, M. P., R. A. Kowatch, C. M. Adler, K. E. Stanford, J. A. Welge, D. H. Barzman, et al. 2006. A double-blind randomized pilot study comparing quetiapine and divalproex for adolescent mania. *Journal of the American Academy of Child and Adolescent Psychiatry* 45:305-313.

Faedda, G. L., and M. H. Teicher. 2005. Objective measures of activity and attention in the differential diagnosis of childhood psychiatric disorders. *Essential Psychopharmacology* 6:239-248.

Faedda, G. L., R. J. Baldessarini, I. P. Glovinsky, and N. B. Austin. 2004a. Pediatric bipolar disorder: Phenomenology and course of illness. *Bipolar Disorders* 6:305-313.

————. 2004b. Treatment-emergent mania in pediatric bipolar disorder: A retrospective case review. *Journal of Affective Disorders* 82:149-158.

Faedda, G. L. 2004. Childhood onset bipolar disorder: Pharmacological treatment overview. *Journal of Developmental and Learning Disorders* 8:37-64.

Faedda, G. L., R. J. Baldessarini, T. Suppes, L. Tondo, I. Becker, and D. S. Lipschitz. 1995. Pediatric-onset bipolar disorder: A neglected clinical and public health problem. *Harvard Review of Psychiatry* 3:171-195.

Frank, E. 2005. *Treating Bipolar Disorder: A Clinician's Guide to Interpersonal and Social Rhythm Therapy.* New York: Guilford Press.

Fristad, M. A., S. M. Gavissi, and K. W. Soldano. 1998. Multi-family psychoeducation groups for childhood mood disorders: A program description and preliminary efficacy data. *Contemporary Family Therapy* 20:385-402.

Geller, B., K. Sun, B. Zimmerman, J. Luby, J. Frazier, and M. Williams. 1995. Complex and rapid-cycling bipolar children and adolescents: A preliminary study. *Journal of Affective Disorders* 34:259-268.

Greenhill, L. L., S. Pliska, and M. K. Dulcan. 2002. Practice parameter for the use of stimulant medications in the treatment of children, adolescents, and adults. *Journal of the American Academy of Children and Adolescent Psychiatry* 41:S26-S49.

Greenspan, S., and I. P. Glovinsky. 2002. *Bipolar Patterns in Children. New Perspectives on Developmental Pathways and a Comprehensive Approach to Prevention and Treatment.* Bethesda, MD: The Interdisciplinary Counsel on Development and Learning Disorders.

Lewinsohn, P. M., D. N. Klein, and J. R. Seeley. 1995. Bipolar disorders in a community sample of older adolescents: Prevalence, phenomenology, comorbidity, and course. *Journal of the American Academy of Child and Adolescent Psychiatry* 34:454-463.

Lish, J. D., S. Dime-Meenan, P. C. Whybrow, R. A. Price, and R. M. Hirschfeld. 1994. The National Depressive and Manic-Depressive Association (DMDA) survey of bipolar members. *Journal of Affective Disorders* 31:281-294.

Mattis, S. 2006. Personal communication.

McClellan, J., and J. Werry. 1997. Practice parameters for the assessment and treatment of children and adolescents with bipolar disorder. *Journal of the American Academy of Child and Adolescent Psychiatry* 36:157-176.

Miklowitz, D. J., and M. J. Goldstein. 1997. *Bipolar Disorder: A Family-Focused Treatment Approach.* New York: Guilford Press.

Micklowitz, D. E., D. George, E. Axelson, B. Kim, C. Birmaher, C. Schneck, et al. 2004. Family-focused treatment for adolescents with bipolar disorder. *Journal of Affective Disorders* 82:1001, S113-S128.

Papolos, D., and J. Papolos. 1999. *The Bipolar Child: The Definitive and Reassuring Guide to Childhood's Most Misunderstood Disorder*. New York: Broadway Books.

Shaffer, D., P. Fisher, M. K. Dulcan, M. Davies, J. Piacentini, M. E. Schwab-Stone, et al. 1996. The NIMH Diagnostic Interview Schedule for Children, Version 2.3 (DISC-2.3): Description, acceptability, prevalence rates, and performance in the MECA Study. Methods for the Epidemiology of Child and Adolescent Mental Disorders Study. *Journal of the American Academy of Child and Adolescent Psychiatry* 35(7):865-877.

Gianni L. Faedda, MD, is a psychiatrist and psychopharmacologist with an extensive background in research and treatment of manic-depressive illness. Dr. Faedda trained at the Lucio Bini Center in Cagliari and Rome, then at Harvard's McLean Hospital. In 1991 he completed a Fellowship in Psychopharmacology at Albert Einstein College of Medicine. From 1992 to 1995, he served as the Director of Research in the Division of Child and Adolescent Psychiatry at Albert Einstein College of Medicine. In 1992 he founded and still directs the Lucio Bini Mood Disorders Center of New York.

Dr. Faedda has published several influential articles on the onset, phenomenology and course of bipolar disorder (BD); the effect of seasonal, pharmacological and environmental factors on BD; and the clinical features of BD in children and adolescents. Subsequently, Dr. Faedda developed a unique approach to the diagnosis and treatment of children, adolescents, and adults with MDI. He conducts independent research and collaborative projects with centers in the U.S. and Italy, and has been pioneering the use of Activity Monitoring and other objective measures in the differential diagnosis of BD. Dr. Faedda was a member of the Scientific Advisory Board for the Child and Adolescent Bipolar Foundation and has recently joined the Scientific Advisory Board of the Juvenile Bipolar Research Foundation (JBRF), and co-moderates their professional listserv for physicians.

Nancy B. Austin, Psy.D., a graduate of the Ferkauf Graduate School of Psychology School/Child Program at Yeshiva University, has been a child psychologist in New York since 1988. She is also a psychoanalyst, with training from the Westchester Center for Psychoanalysis and Psychotherapy (WCSPP). Austin is currently the associate director of the Lucio Bini Mood Disorders Center of New York, which specializes in research, consultation, diagnosis, and treatment of mood and anxiety disorders in children, adolescents, adults, and their families.

Austin also maintains a private practice, specializing in children and adolescents diagnosed with bipolar disorder and their families. Her teaching and supervisory positions in New York State include the Lucio Bini Mood Disorders Center; New York Presbyterian Hospital, Psychology Internship Program; Ferkauf Graduate School of Psychology, Yeshiva University; Manhattanville College; the Child and Adolescent Program of WCSPP; and The Center for Preventive Psychiatry. She is currently a moderator for the therapists' listserv for the JBRF. Austin's clinical work and research on the IQ pattern of bipolar children has been presented at conferences and cited in several books on the subject.

more titles for children with special needs
from new**harbinger**publications

The Gift of ADHD

$14.95 • Item Code: 3899

Helping Your Child Overcome an Eating Disorder

$16.95 • Item Code: 3104

Helping Your Depressed Child

$14.95 • Item Code: 3228

Helping Your Child with Selective Mutism

$14.95 • Item Code: 416X

Helping a Child with Nonverbal Learning Disorder or Asperger's Syndrome

$14.95 • Item Code: 2779

Helping Your Child Overcome Separation Anxiety or School Refusal

$14.95 • Item Code: 4313

Helping Your Anxious Child

$14.95 • Item Code: 1918

When Your Child Is Cutting

$15.95 • Item Code: 4372

Helping Your Child with Autism Spectrum Disorder

$17.95 • Item Code: 3848

Helping Your Child with OCD

$19.95 • Item Code: 3325

 available from new**harbinger**publications
and fine booksellers everywhere

To order, call toll free **1-800-748-6273** or visit our online bookstore at **www.newharbinger.com**
(V, MC, AMEX • prices subject to change without notice)